Ice Bound

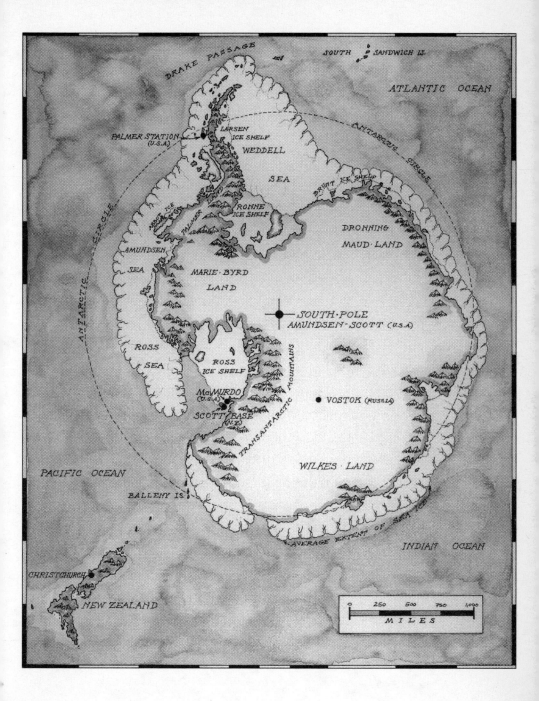

DRAKE PASSAGE

SOUTH • SANDWICH IS.

ATLANTIC OCEAN

ANTARCTIC CIRCLE

PALMER STATION
(U.S.A.)

LARSEN
ICE SHELF

WEDDELL

SEA

RONNE
ICE SHELF

BRUNT ICE SHELF

DRONNING
MAUD • LAND

AMUNDSEN

SEA

MARIE • BYRD
LAND

SOUTH • POLE
AMUNDSEN-SCOTT (U.S.A.)

ANTARCTIC CIRCLE

ROSS
SEA

ROSS
ICE SHELF

McMURDO
(U.S.A.)

SCOTT BASE
(N.Z.)

VOSTOK (RUSSIA)

TRANSANTARCTIC • MOUNTAINS

WILKES • LAND

PACIFIC OCEAN

BALLENY IS.

AVERAGE EXTENT OF SEA ICE

INDIAN OCEAN

CHRISTCHURCH

NEW ZEALAND

0   250   500   750   1,000

MILES

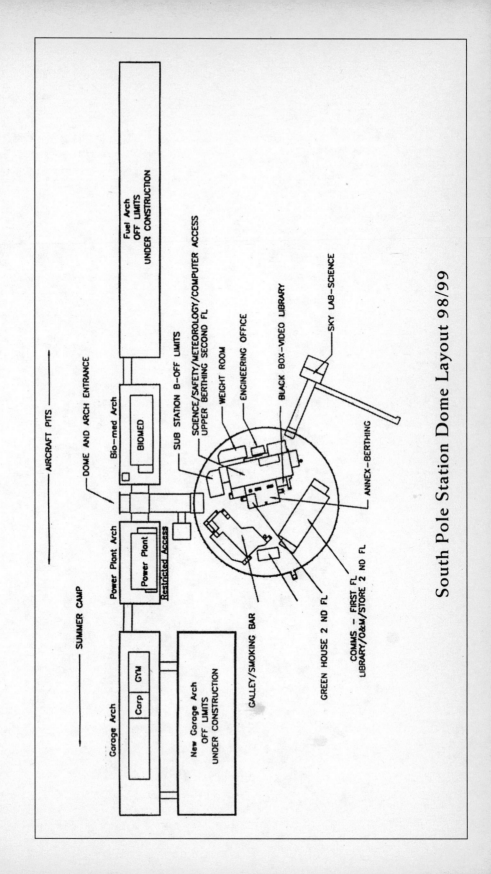

South Pole Station Dome Layout 98/99

ICE BOUND

*One Woman's Incredible
Battle for Survival
at the South Pole*

JERRI NIELSEN

with Maryanne Vollers

EBURY PRESS
LONDON

The author and publisher wish to thank the following for permission to reprint copyright material:

Scribner, a Division of Simon & Schuster, for permission to reprint the poems "An Irish Airman Foresees His Death" and "For Anne Gregory" by W.B. Yeats from *The Collected Poems of W.B. Yeats, Revised Second Edition* edited by Richard J. Finneran (New York: Scribner, 1996); Veronica A. Shoffstall for permission to reprint "After a While" by Veronica A. Shoffstall ©1971; Wallflower Music (Admin. by Copyright Management) for permission to reprint material from "Flowers on the Wall" by the Statler Brothers © 1965 Wallflower Music; Universal-Northern Music Co., a division of Universal Studios, Inc. (ASCAP) for permission to reprint "Wild Women Don't Have the Blues", by Ida Cox © 1924 Copyright renewed International Copyright Secured All Rights Reserved.

Every effort has been made to trace copyright holders, and the publishers will be happy to correct mistakes or omissions in future editions.

3 5 7 9 10 8 6 4

First published in 2001 by Talk Miramax Books,
an imprint of Hyperion, New York.
This edition published in 2001 by Ebury Press,
Random House, 20 Vauxhall Bridge Road,
London SW1V 2SA
www.randomhouse.co.uk

Random House Australia (Pty) Limited
20 Alfred Street, Milsons Point, Sydney,
New South Wales 2061, Australia

Random House New Zealand Limited
18 Poland Road, Glenfield,
Auckland 10, New Zealand

Random House South Africa (Pty) Limited
Endulini, 5A Jubilee Road,
Parktown 2193, South Africa

The Random House Group Limited Reg. No. 954009

Papers used by Ebury are natural, recyclable products made from wood grown in sustainable forests.

Printed and bound by Mackays of Chatham, Chatham, Kent

A CIP catalogue record for this book is available from the British Library

ISBN 0-09-185623-X

To the brave men and women who risked
their lives to save me.

And for the many, behind the scenes,
who worked and prayed and supported.

To those who stayed with me during the dark days.

Here is my heart.

ACKNOWLEDGMENTS

I would like to thank Maryanne Vollers who helped me to tell my story. It is a vulnerable thing to open one's journals, personal letters and soul to a stranger; and an honor that the result would be to gain such a remarkable friend.

I would also like to thank Big John Penney who shared personal correspondence and diaries to provide a special prospective, and who worked as my assistant and sounding board to help me to remember.

Thanks are due to the following: to Lisa Beal, Tom Carlson, Charlie Kaminski, Floyd Washington, Tim Briggs and Dar Gibson for providing technical details; to Polie friends who gave me permission to speak of their medical problems—I consider that permission to be a great personal gift to me—because to describe a physician's life without detailing how these concerns impacted me would be hollow; to Kathy Miller, M.D. for everything; to Lance Armstrong for sharing his struggle; to Joe Armstrong, Hilary Bass, Melanie Bowden, Tina Brown, Jonathan Burnham, Farley Chase, Susan Mercandetti, Kristin Powers, Carol Shookhoff, Kathy Schneider, and Margaret Wolf at Talk Miramax Books for excellent editorial and publication assistance; to Robert Barnett, Kathleen Ryan, Devereux Chatillon, and Jim King for expert legal advice; to Joel Michalski, Chris Rock, and John Penney for photos; to my friends and family in the world who shared their hearts and private letters for the book; to the United States government, National Science Foundation, Antarctic Support Associates for deciding to save me, and to the Air National Guard and US Air Force for rescuing me.

My deepest gratitude belongs to my family: To my brother, Eric Cahill and his wife Dee Dee, who acting as my business managers, made this project easier for me to accomplish while ill; to Phil and Lorine Cahill, my parents, for unwavering support; and to my brother, Scott Cahill, for his dreams when I had lost my own.

Every one of the events described in this book actually took place, and in almost all cases I have rendered them exactly as they happened. In a few instances I have altered names and descriptions of people and places to protect the privacy of my patients, and those who preferred not to be identified in this book. Some of the emails reprinted here have been lightly edited and shortened for the sake of clarity. I have done my best to recount this extraordinary adventure as openly and honestly as possible. To my continuing sense of wonder and awe, all of it is true.

I cannot rest from travel; I will drink

Life to the lees. All times I have enjoyed

Greatly, have suffered greatly, both with those

That loved me, and alone; on shore, and when

Through scudding drifts the rainy Hyades

Vext the dim sea. I am become a name;

For always roaming with a hungry heart . . .

—From "Ulysses"
Alfred, Lord Tennyson

Who's Who of the Amundsen-Scott
Winterover Crew, 1999

There were forty-one people, including Dr. Jerri Nielsen, who wintered at the Amundsen-Scott South Pole Station in 1999. What follows is an abridged list of the crew, as some participants do not appear in the book, and others prefer not to be named.

Donna Aldrich: Cook

Bob Allard ("Boston Bob"): Electrician Foreman

Dennis Aukerman ("Dennis the Plumber"): Plumber

Bai Xinhua: Nuclear Physicist (AMANDA project)

Lisa Beal: Senior Computer Technician

Wendy Beeler: Cook

Yubecca Bragg: Materials Person

Tim Briggs ("Tool Man Tim"): Construction Coordinator

Thomas Carlson ("Comms Tom"): Communications Technician/Electrical Engineer

Andy Clarke: Science Technician for National Oceanographic and Atmospheric Administration (NOAA)

John Davis ("Middle John"): Maintenance Technician for Center for Astrophysical Research in Antarctica (CARA)

James Evans ("Pic"): Heavy Equipment Operator/Hazardous Materials

Walter Fischel ("Welder Walt"): Ironworker

Larry Fordyce: Carpenter

Loree Galpin: Meteorologist

Dar Gibson ("Weatherboy"): Meteorologist

Greg Griffin ("Giant Greg"): Astronomer, CARA (VIPER telescope)

Roger Hooker: Electrician

William Johnson: Carpenter

Charles Kaminski ("Choo Choo Charlie"): Astronomer, CARA
 (Spirex telescope)

Paul Kindl ("Pakman"): Electrician

Ken Lobe: Maintenance Specialist

Liza Lobe: Inventory Control Specialist

Mike Masterman ("Master Mike"): Winter Site Manager;
 Radio Electronics Engineer

Joel Michalski: NOAA officer (physicist)

George (Thom) Miller ("Power Plant Thom"): Power Plant
 Mechanic

Reza Mosaddeque: Science Technician

Roopesh Ojha ("Roo"): Astronomer, CARA (AST/RO radio
 telescope)

John Penney ("Big"): Heavy Equipment Mechanic

Heidi Schernthanner: Heavy Equipment Operator

Kirk Spelman ("Captain Kirk"): Senior Materials Person

Nick Starinski ("Nuclear Nick"): Nuclear Physicist (AMANDA
 project)

Floyd Washington: Maintenance Specialist

CONTENTS

Prelude

Amundsen-Scott South Pole Station, October 16, 1999. Today I take my last snowmobile ride in Antarctica—from the ice-crusted dome where I have lived for eleven months, to the edge of an airfield plowed out of the drifting snow. Normally I could walk the distance in a few minutes, but I am too weak. My best friend, Big John Penney, drives me up the mountain of snow we call Heart Attack Hill to the edge of the flight line. We are bundled in our red parkas and polar boots, extreme-cold-weather gear that weighs nearly twenty pounds. I'm wrapped in so many layers of fleece and down that I can barely move. My hair was long and blond when I arrived at the Pole, but now my head is completely bald, and coddled like an egg in a soft wool hat beneath my hood. I wear goggles and a neck gaiter up to my eyes to keep my skin from freezing. It is nearly sixty degrees below zero.

Big John helps me off the machine and we stand together for a moment, staring into a solid wall of blowing snow. The winds are steady at twenty knots, causing a total whiteout over the station. Incredibly, we can hear the droning engines of a Hercules cargo plane, muffled by the weather but getting louder by the second. It is the first plane to attempt a landing at the South Pole in eight months.

"He'll never make it," says Big John. "He'll have to circle and turn back."

I can't decide if I am frightened or relieved. I am sick and quite possibly dying. There is no doubt that I have to leave here to get treatment for the cancer growing in my breast. I am the only doctor among forty-one scientists and support staff at this U.S. research station, and I've been worrying about what would happen if I became too frail to care for my patients. Dozens, perhaps hundreds, of people have worked for weeks to organize this extraordinary rescue flight. I feel grateful, and humbled and, at the same time, overwhelmed with grief.

In reporting my predicament, some journalists have described the South Pole as "hell on earth." Others refer to my time here as "an ordeal." They would be surprised to know how beautiful Antarctica has seemed to me, with its waves of ice in a hundred shades of blue and white, its black winter sky, its ecstatic wheel of stars. They would never understand how the lights of the Dome welcomed me from a distance, or how often I danced and sang and laughed here with my friends.

And how I was not afraid.

Here, in this lonely outpost surrounded by the staggering emptiness of the polar plateau, in a world stripped of useless noise and comforts, I found the most perfect home I have ever known. I do not want to leave.

But now as the sound of the engines grows to a roar and shifts in pitch, I strain to take a last look around. I am hoping for an opening in the storm, as much for me as for the pilot. I want to see the ice plain one more time, and lose myself in its empty horizon. But the notion passes, like waking from a dream, and within moments begins to seem unreal.

Ice Bound

CHAPTER I

The Geographic Cure

I f this story is to begin anywhere, it should begin in the night. I have always been a night person. When the sun goes down, my spirits rise. I'm more alert, quicker, more in tune with the rhythms of the world. There are many nights to choose from, but one comes to mind now, in the emergency room at a hospital in Cleveland, Ohio, two months before I went to the Ice:

For me, each shift started before I reached the hospital gates. I drove into the city like a soldier preparing for battle, chugging coffee and listening to rock tapes to shake my brain awake and get my blood pumping. Dangerous Minds. Queen. "We will, we will *rock* you!" As I passed the ambulances and police cruisers parked at the back entrance, I felt an enormous energy and dread. The automatic doors slid open with a sucking sound, and I was pulled into the ER like a swimmer in a riptide.

Oh dear God, let everything go right tonight. I navigated my way through anxious families huddled in the hallway, past the rows of injured people immobilized on backboards, the sick on stretchers, some crying out for help. By now, I was on. *It's show time!* I had to be composed, acutely aware, and ready to think on my feet, no matter how little sleep I'd had the day before, what had happened at home before leaving for work, how I felt.

As I walked into the nurses' station, I arrived in the safe zone of emergency medical technicians, nurses, x-ray techs, and lab techs. My physician partners looked stressed and hurried as they usually did at this time of night, prime time for emergency medicine.

"Nielsen, really good to see you!" said Max, a friend and fellow ER doc as he raced toward a trauma room. "Grab some charts, we just took a big hit."

No time to get a cup of coffee or converse, there were eight charts in the rack, representing patients ready to be seen. An emergency room in a big American city is a crucible of human suffering and desperate behavior. Everybody and everything rolls in off the streets at one time or another, and anything can happen. The walk-in case might have the flu or viral meningitis, the man on the stretcher might have a bruised shoulder or a bullet in the heart. Many of our late-night visitors were gang members and crack addicts. I never knew what to expect when I pulled back the curtain: Once, when I was pregnant, a man pulled a knife while I cut off his leather jacket with trauma scissors. I was only saved by a savvy ER nurse, a former medic with two tours in Vietnam. He saw the knife coming toward my ribs and threw me out of the way into a wall before I knew what was happening.

I should say here that I am only five foot three, but nobody has ever thought of me as small. It was a lesson I always taught my female interns: Doctors are not short. Doctors have no gender. Doctors are in control—or at least you have to seem that way as a patient's world spins into chaos. Through it all you have to wear a face that shows no judgment, no revulsion—only empathy and calm. After a while it becomes second nature.

This night, the first few cases were routine. I talked with them, examined them, and "dispositioned" them, deciding if they went to intensive care, critical care, surgery, or home. The stroke victim would go to the ICU, the child with abdominal pain was sent directly to surgery for an appendectomy, the man with a fractured ankle was splinted and then released home in the care of an orthopedist. There were multiple heart attacks, overdoses, and a cancer patient with acute pneumonia. A woman walked into the waiting room with two black eyes and a gash on her forehead that clearly needed stitches. She told the triage nurse that she had "fallen down." After treating her wounds, I referred her to a domestic violence counselor.

Before long, I had twenty cases in my head—in "orbit," as we say. It was what I was trained to do, and I settled into the night's tempo. Still, it seemed there was never enough time to spend with patients. The object of a commercial ER is to move people through as quickly as possible, "to meet and street" them without compromising care. Sometimes we all felt like hamsters spinning in our wheels.

At 2 a.m. we got a call on the radio that a gunshot wound was coming in by ambulance. I made my way to the EMTs' break room and downed three packs of crackers and a cup of black coffee. I was pulling on my gown, mask, foot protectors, and goggles when a second call came over the box:

"Three minutes out. Twenty-three-year-old male, gunshot wound to the head."

The other members of the trauma team left their workstations and descended on the empty cart in our biggest room. Everyone had a job to do and everyone knew how to do it and how to function together as a team. This was what I loved about emergency medicine, how everyone worked so well in unison. Nurses laid out sterile packs and hung IV bags. The trauma clock was set. Heat lamps were turned on above our heads.

I rushed to the ambulance entrance. This gave me precious minutes to get information as the patient was being wheeled in. "What do you have?" I asked the paramedic.

"Twenty-three-year-old male, self-inflicted GSW to the head, left frontal, twenty minutes down. Vitals: pulse one fifty, BP ninety over fifty, resp twenty-two, intubated." I glanced at the patient and at the cardiac monitor on the stretcher. His heart was racing. The rundown was repeated to the trauma team as we transferred the patient to our bed. The bullet had entered his left temple at close range; the wound was ringed with black specks of gunpowder and it was pumping blood. We stopped the external bleeding with pressure and a few sutures. He was hyperventilated on a respirator to decrease intracranial pressure. We could find no other injuries but we left the cervical collar on until his spine could be x-rayed. He was quickly stabilized and sent to CAT scan with the neurosurgeon. Now it was time to talk to his family.

This was always the hardest part. I preferred to have the family at the bedside, if they wished, during serious cases like this. Not knowing and forever wondering if something else could be done is so much worse for a loving family than being present while decisions were being made. They would know how the team fought for the life, how well we did our job, how hopeless or hopeful the situation was. But in this case, the family arrived too late to be with me in the trauma room.

The look on your face and the way you walk in prepares them for the news. As I sat down and introduced myself, I kept the look of disbelief that I felt, to see a young man in his prime try to take his own life. I often say that you can't be a good ER doc until you've had a stare-down with the devil and lost. The job puts you in the position of sharing people's darkest hours, their greatest fears and terrible shames.

"It's bad," I said, letting it sink in, allowing them see it in my eyes. "He is still alive but I don't know if he will survive, and if he does, how the rest of his life will be." Pause. "Do you want to see him now?"

Just then a nurse walked in and whispered, "Doc, you'd better come to Room Four, stat." I nodded and stood up. I told the family I was needed to attend another emergency, but assured them that the neurosurgeon would do everything she could and would be able to answer their questions. They could speak to me again if they wanted. But I knew the man would go to surgery and I would never know his story, probably never know his fate.

The charts were piling up again at the nurses' station, and the show still had to go on.

The sun was coming up over the farms and rolling fields of eastern Ohio as I drove home from the hospital. Home—what a concept. I was forty-six years old and living in my parents' house, sleeping in a bedroom decorated with the ruffled curtains and daisy wallpaper of my teenage years. I parked the Volvo in the gravel drive and breathed deeply to banish the lingering smell of blood and disinfectant from my lungs. The autumn air was already touched with winter. The leaves in the canopy of maples and beech trees over the driveway were just starting to turn.

This was not the place where I grew up—that was a ranch house in the country a few miles away. This was the house made of the dreams and quirks of the Cahill family in its boisterous prime. My father, Phil, was a master builder. He had taught my two younger brothers, Scott and Eric, his trade while constructing this house. We had built the house, stone by stone, deep in a rugged forest, with big picture windows on all sides. Every cupboard, each tile, the doorways, the rocks in the massive fireplace, all had been placed there by a close relative. The paneling in the hall came from a barn that I had helped to tear down. The slate roof was scavenged from an old farmhouse. I remember sitting tied to the roof of the three-story gothic building, ripping off slate and sending it down in a box to the girl whom Eric would one day marry. My mother, Lorine, had started college when I was twelve and became a psychologist. She decorated the house with found objects and treasures bought at flea markets and estate sales.

We have always been a close-knit clan, and the house was our monument to ourselves, a shrine to loyalty and love and good hard work. I will always think of it as my mother's house, as her spirit pervades it, but it has my father's soul in its strong foundation and solid frame. It was the obvious refuge for me when everything else in my life fell apart.

This morning, as always, my mother had carefully stacked my mail on the kitchen table. As I made myself some tea I absently fanned through the pile of bills and journals and then started to read. The back pages of *The Annals of Emergency Medicine* usually carried ads for job openings in the medical field, and that was where I was looking when some display type caught my eye: POLAR MEDICINE. PHYSICIANS NEEDED FOR U.S. ANTARCTIC PROGRAM.

The job called for a full year of work at one of the three American bases in Antarctica. Half of the time would be spent in the isolation and darkness of the austral winter. I felt a prickling sensation up and down my skin, like the kind of physical excitement a child feels at the sight of a bicycle under the Christmas tree. I read the words over and over again, and my pounding heart told me this was what I had been looking for without knowing it.

I believe in geographic cures—they allow you to throw all your cards in the air and see where they land, then pick them back up and deal them again. I was ready for a new deal. I had stayed in a terrible, suffocating marriage for twenty-three years and lost everything by the time I saw that losing was inevitable. In the end, I lost my self-respect, almost lost hope. Like an animal in a leghold trap, I gnawed away at parts of myself to escape. I survived, got a divorce, but I lost my three children in the process. And that is something that still seems impossible to me.

You would think that as an ER doctor I would recognize the signs of abuse in my own marriage, but I am here to tell you that I did not. I could take a woman's history in the examination room, run through the clinical checklist, explain to her that emotional and psychological abuse are another form of battery, and understand, on a rational and detached level, that it can happen to anyone. But like so many women, I couldn't see it happening to me. It is difficult to explain, and painful to talk about the raw, private matters within a family. But since I have chosen to tell you about my journey to the South Pole, and the community of friends and strangers who rescued me, I need to tell you something about my life and why I made the choices that brought me there.

* * *

I grew up believing anything is possible if you just work hard enough to get it. I remember most of my childhood as sun-splashed and magical, full of friends and freedom and adventures. I was given the name Jerri Lin Cahill, but from the time I was learning to talk, I was known as Duffy, or Duff, for short. It had something to do with the first sounds I made: *duff-duff, duff-ree.* The nickname caught on. It was Irish, sporty, lively, and it suited me well.

My brother Scott was two years younger than I, and Eric was born four years later. Scott and I sat in the hospital parking lot on that cold February night with our aunt Mona and saw the aurora borealis in the Ohio sky for the first time. When Mr. Baby came home (that's what we called him then, and still do) he was placed in my bedroom and I moved into Scott's room. Dad had built matching beds for us. As soon as we were roommates, Scott and I started to imagine things together. We were pirates on the high seas. There were alligators under the beds and witches in the closets. He would chase after them with a baseball bat, screaming, "Get out of there, you dirty thieves!" Forty years later, he would spin wonderful fantasies for me when I was trapped at the South Pole, to help give me the strength to survive.

As a child I spent a lot of time looking after the boys, or trying to, but it never slowed me down. We lived at the end of a dirt road, surrounded by dairy farms, next door to a family with seven kids. We ran in a pack all summer long, making our own fun. We would play in bogs full of wild roses and in abandoned farms, where we made up elaborate games. We built huts in the forest and dug deep holes and tunnels to hide in. We waded barefoot in the swamps, catching snapping turtles and making dams.

As my brothers got older life became more dangerous. They liked to blow things up. One day Scott made a rocket and attached it to his bike. All the neighborhood kids watched as the first boy from Salem, Ohio, launched himself into space. We never worried about how he would come down. Of course, all we got to see was his pants on fire. Another time, I was upstairs and heard a terrible boom. I ran to the basement to find Scott with his arms outstretched and his eyes closed. He said, "Just pick the glass out of me." He had taken a sledgehammer to an old TV tube to see if it would explode or implode.

Even as a baby, Eric was always climbing to the top of trees and getting stuck. I would spend hours trying to get him down safely. After many unsuccessful attempts, I'd call for Mom, who would simply demand that he come down, and down he would come.

Scott never stopped trying to reach the stars, while Eric grew into the strong, rational one in the family. Eric became an engineer with great lifelong friends and a stable, loving marriage to Diana—nicknamed Dee Dee—whom he had met at age fourteen. While I was in Antarctica, Eric wrote me detailed, reasonable instructions to help me keep things in perspective. Scott lived life with the throttle wide open. He married and divorced several times, gained and lost as many fortunes over the years, and never looked back. I would think, "I have two brothers; one is a rock and one is the wind."

I was a good student and a natural athlete, with phenomenal balance and strength. I spent much of my girlhood upside down. At age five, I asked for gymnastics lessons. There are scratchy home movies of me as a child, tumbling in the front yard and standing on my hands and falling again and again until I got it right. Gymnastics taught me to push myself to my limits, and how to train my body to act reflexively, without thought. I would practice acrobatics for hours after school, and then read my homework standing on my hands against the wall. Eventually I could depend on my body to do anything. I could hang by one hand from a railroad trestle and not be afraid, because I knew I could pull myself up. This impressed the boys in my life. In fact Bill, my high school boyfriend, once told me he liked me so much because I was "the only girl who would jump into the river from the railroad bridge"!

Bill had an MG Midget convertible. We spent so many evenings riding around in that car listening to sixties music with the wind in our hair. It felt like we were flying in an open airplane. I loved to go fast, whether it was upside down and backwards, off a balance beam, or riding my bike endlessly to nowhere. It was on my bike or on a trampoline that I dreamed, and where I first decided to go to exotic places like Africa and Antarctica when I grew up. I was disappointed that the world had become so civilized, and I was determined to find the frontier, even if it meant going to the moon.

I owe my curiosity about the world to my mother, who was a most unusual role model, a woman ahead of her time. She had—and still has—a brilliant mind, and she always wanted to be a doctor, not really an option for middle-class girls in the1940s. She settled for nursing school instead. She was only eighteen when she met my father and fell in love. I was born a year after they were married. My mother dropped out of school to raise the children, but she was never a typical house-wife. She fascinated us all. She would talk about science and nature instead of telling us fairy tales. We discussed everything: politics, religion, history. She would talk while I helped her clean the house or chop vegetables. She'd hand me a stack of laundry to fold and say, "Let's talk about justice." She wrote poetry and read poems to us and had poets come to our home.

Once Mom went to college, things got even more interesting. She would often bring home people from different countries for us to meet. I remember a Sikh who removed his turban to show us his long black hair. She would take us into the warehouse district of Cleveland to visit a Buddhist temple on Buddha's birthday. Above all she was a scientist, and also a real character, one who loved life and wanted to experience it. She encouraged us to do the same.

My mother's heritage is German Swiss, and a strong Teutonic streak runs though her. While she embraced life, she also saw it as a duty. Heavy lines were drawn between right and wrong. She taught us a harsh code to live by: One never shows weakness to colleagues who need you to be strong. A strong person must take care of the weak. "Death before dishonor" was one of her maxims. She would rather see us die than live as cowards, not have served our people, not have done our duty. We were raised to charge the hill, never to look back except to pick up our fallen comrades and save them before taking the bullet, gladly, ourselves.

There were many other aphorisms in my mother's arsenal of beliefs: "When you are the hammer, strike; when you are the anvil, bear" was a favorite. Another, which I have laminated and always keep with me in a little sack with my daily medical equipment says: "To whom much is given, much is expected."

Dad, on the other hand, saw his life as gravy. Phil Cahill had been born poor and lived through the Depression, so all that he accomplished was a pleasant surprise. He was of Irish and English descent, and he understood the magic of the Irish—or pretended to. When he found a parking spot right in front of the restaurant where we had a reservation, he would say it was the charm of "the little people." He was a very lucky man because he thought himself, during a very hard life, to be very fortunate. Of course he made that good fortune with a lifetime of labor. Like my mother, he believed that you measured a person by how hard he worked.

Mom always claimed that Dad was the risk-taker in the family, but we called him "Look-Out Cahill" behind his back—because he was always warning us to be careful. His caution was earned by experience. Dad had always been in a risky business, first as a carpenter, then as the owner of a construction company. As a young man in demolition, buildings had literally fallen around him. He always made us think about our escape routes. In unfamiliar buildings he would ask, "How will you get out?" This served me well in a hotel fire years later. I was pregnant, in a leg cast, and carrying a two-year-old, yet I was the second person out of the darkened building because on the way in I had instinctively counted the doors to the exit stairway.

Once I tried to take my father to what I thought was a nice restaurant, but he wouldn't eat there, insisting that the structure could collapse at any moment. We ate across the street. A few months later, I called Mom to tell her that the restaurant had collapsed in the night, and she should tell Dad that he had been right. She said, "Please, don't encourage him."

I always thought my mother had a wonderful, wicked sense of humor. Even though we didn't have the money for such things, she once bought an octopus at the supermarket because she had never seen one available before and wanted her children to experience it. We each took it to school in turn in a glass jar. Then, to get the full use of it, she put the octopus in my dad's bathwater. Mom always drew him a bath to warm him up after he'd worked outside on cold winter days. This time she added bubble bath. We all waited outside the bathroom door in gleeful anticipation. When we heard Dad yell, we ran giggling down the hallway. He was half-amused and half-irritated, and it seemed that the octopus joke had run its course. The next morning, however, when Dad went to use the bathroom, we heard him shout, "Lorine!" The octopus was in the toilet. After that, we certainly couldn't eat the octopus, so we dissected it. (Mom was always bringing us things to dissect, like cows' eyes and hearts from the butcher.)

A career in medicine seemed a natural choice for me. I think I was always a healer. I was the sort of child who nursed wounded birds and frogs I found in the woods. The other kids always ran to me when they were afraid or hurt. I couldn't stand to see another child in pain, or left out, or humiliated, because I felt their suffering with them. Some call it empathy or hypersensitivity, but I believe I was born with thinner membranes than most people, and a heightened awareness. This has been a blessing and a curse. As a doctor, I can quickly absorb a tremendous amount of information, both physical and emotional, from a patient. But as a child, I felt too much: I was too alert, too sensitive to changes in my environment, easily startled by loud noises and upset by anger or grief.

Like my father, Look-Out Cahill, I often found myself imagining worst-case scenarios. My emotions ran close to the surface. Sometimes I sat in class, unable to stop the tears running down my face while I waited to be called for a spelling bee. (I am still a terrible speller.) I would see a speeding car and forecast the crash in all its horrific details. I couldn't stand the sight of blood and would run in terror if I found a dead animal, hit by a car, on the side of the road.

These anxieties were a serious inconvenience for someone in a family that valued strength and disdained weakness, not to mention a mother who brought home cattle parts to dissect. I coped by learning to control my perceptions, and consequently, my emotions. Just as I had trained my body to reflexively perform gymnastic routines, I trained my mind to deflect disturbing thoughts and images. I practiced imagining that things were the opposite of what they seemed: "The sky is not gloomy because it is dark," I would think. "It just seems dark. It is really full of light, it is beautiful, and everything is okay." I would test myself constantly, forcing myself to confront my fears, and learned not to be afraid.

I began saving lives at a young age. I can't remember how many people I have fished out of the water. Scott and I were twelve and ten when I did my first rescue. Everyone in the family was a strong swimmer, and we lived in the water all summer long. One day a young boy had swum too far out into a lake. When we saw that he was in trouble we raced out to help him. He nearly drowned us when we tried to pull him to shore. We had not yet taken lifeguard lessons, so we made up our own plan. I would go underwater and hold him up by the body so he couldn't fight, while Scott surfaced and shouted for help. Then Scott went under and held the boy's face above water while I shouted for help. When the official lifeguard finally noticed us, we got in trouble for interfering, but I know we saved that child's life. I was hooked.

I was a cheerleader in high school, a track star, and a scholar. I spent my senior year abroad, as an exchange student in Sweden. Suffice it to say that being a seventeen-year-old girl sprung from Ohio into the Europe of 1969 was a mind-bending experience. Like many kids my age, I was also drawn to the civil rights and human rights movements, and I was determined to change the world.

One of my great friends in Sweden was another American exchange student. We were such opposites. Jeannie couldn't understand my politics, and I couldn't understand her seemingly trivial concerns. Once we were to travel around Norway over the Easter holidays in a small RV, and she spent hours fretting over how to hide four Easter baskets in such a tiny space. I said, "Jeannie, I don't know why you're worried about something so inane."

"Jerri," she said, "that's the difference between you and me. You worry about things you can't affect, like the Vietnam War. And I worry about how I'm gonna hide these baskets in an RV for two weeks." Those few words changed my way of looking at life. She was right. She could bring happiness to four people by surprising them with Easter baskets, while I worried about things I couldn't change. After that, I decided to live my life doing things that could positively affect people on a daily basis, giving something of myself to one person at a time. Sometimes, the world turned on a small gesture or an act of kindness.

Instead of marching for civil rights, I realized I could make a difference by treating everyone with respect and dignity. I remember, as a young ER doc, meeting some street people, whom I had cared for earlier that night, outside the emergency room doors. I offered them coffee and then sat on the sidewalk with them during my break. They offered me a cigarette and I took it. The intern whom I was training at the time came outside looking for me. When he saw me smoking, he was horrified. Later, he confronted me: "I didn't know you smoked."

"I don't," I explained. "But it was all that they had to give me, so I took it."

Years later, when he had become a family doctor, he wrote me that what I had told him that night had changed his life and the way that he practiced medicine forever. He told me he learned to listen to people, and give them what they needed, not just what he thought they needed. So four Easter baskets, hidden in 1969, continue to make a difference to this day.

After returning from Sweden I entered Ohio University, in Athens, Ohio, and signed up for pre-med classes. I wanted to be swallowed up in the enormous campus and the sprawling town where I could feel anonymous and unobserved. Even though I seemed to be a well-adjusted teenager, I never really felt that I fit in anywhere. After coming back from Europe, the rules and expectations of American society seemed so arbitrary and contrived to me. Appearance was more important than substance. The feminist movement was in its infancy, and men still exerted an archaic control over women. I didn't want anyone to control me, or tell me which career choices or living arrangements were appropriate for a young woman.

The movie *Cabaret* came out while I was in Europe, and Sally Bowles had become my personal icon. When people talk about past lives, I always feel I could have been a cabaret singer in Berlin between the wars. The literature and music of that era always enthralled me. I admired how Sally Bowles didn't care what anyone thought of her. And I have been attracted to the dark side of human experience ever since I was a child, when I learned to manage my emotions. The process can become habitual, as the thrill of conquering demons pulls you closer to the things that you fear. I know that's what drew me to emergency medicine. It was a way for me to encounter the dangerous, seamy aspects of life and still stay within the law and inside its safety net.

I wanted to know the people who were struggling, who had fallen by the wayside. I wanted to see human behavior as it really was, without the distortions of civilization and its refinements. And I soon got my chance.

When I was twenty-three, I had just entered medical school and had all the physical confidence of an athlete. I still believed that good fortune was not a gift, it was something that you worked for. And then, in one moment, everything changed forever.

I remember driving my Volkswagen Beetle through a terrible rainstorm, on my way to my first clinical experience at the hospital. I was sitting at a red light when I was hit from behind by a speeding Porsche. These were the days before shoulder harnesses and headrests. I felt my neck snap back like a cracking whip. The rear end of my Beetle was crushed, but I jumped out of the car without thinking, wearing my white lab coat. The driver of the Porsche was an ophthalmologist, and he felt terrible about hitting a med student. I didn't think I was badly hurt and refused to go to the hospital. After the police left, he took me back to my dorm. In a few hours my neck tightened up and I couldn't get out of bed. It turned out I had ruptured four discs, and although it wasn't discovered for years, they were compressing my spinal cord. This was before MRIs were available, and x-rays kept missing the problem.

I was almost incapacitated. My sense of balance disappeared, and I suddenly became clumsy. I could no longer dance or do anything that I used to do. But luckily, because I was in such good shape at the time of the accident, I was able to compensate for these deficits and finish my education through sheer will power. (I suffered great pain for thirteen years until a neurologist I was working with recognized the problem from the way I held my neck. An operation corrected the spinal cord compression.)

The accident that debilitated my body humbled me at a very important time, right when I began medical training. I learned that a person could lose everything in an instant. It made me realize that all these people who were sick or hurt weren't that way because they hadn't tried hard or willed themselves to be better. It was that they'd had bad luck.

I know the experience made me a much more compassionate physician, because I was in the same position as many patients with undiagnosed conditions. I dropped things, I had terrible pains shooting down my arm, I developed urinary problems. I knew I wasn't making up these conditions, yet my doctors couldn't find anything wrong, and some of them implied that I was imagining symptoms. The doctors' assumptions changed my whole way of looking at people and their complaints. Just because I couldn't help them didn't mean they didn't need help. As one of my professors told me, there is no such thing as a crazy patient, just a dumb doctor.

My injuries taught me that when I could no longer rely on my body to give me an edge, I had to use my mind. But first I had to give up the idea of myself as an athlete: Mourn it, bury it, put it away. All humans have to learn to move on after unbearable loss, and we all do this in different ways, at different times. As a physician, you have to try to teach people how to bury and mourn what they have lost, but then find something in what they still have. I did it once, when I lost

my health. But who would think I would have to do it again, when I
lost my children?

At age twenty-three—practically a spinster according to my mother—
I married a fellow medical student for a number of bad reasons that
seemed logical at the time. I was injured and tired of dating. We had
known each other for three months when he proposed, and I thought
that no one would want to marry an aging, disabled woman doctor. This
med student seemed smart, zealous, and oddly charming. His impul-
siveness, at that time, excited me. The first time I met his parents, he
announced that we were engaged. This was news to me. But before long,
he swept me up in his plans for our marriage. I mistook his enthusiasm
for love. Later I would learn that was how he responded to everything
new, at first. He showered me with attention and affection. He could
make anyone feel like the only worthwhile person on earth when he set
his mind to it. He was full of schemes and grand ideas, and he led me to
believe that we would be doctors and partners together in an adventure
overseas, in poor countries where medical care was needed. This was, of
course, just what I wanted to hear. I thought it meant that he really cared
about helping the sick, and that he cared, most of all, about me.

My professors, my parents, and my brothers never liked him, and
that should have been a warning to me. He started to change soon
after the wedding ceremony. It began with small, cutting comments
and minor demands. He would laugh when I dropped things. He told
me I was awkward and ugly, an "overachiever" with little natural tal-
ent. He made all the decisions in our marriage, from what we had for
dinner to where we lived. He exaggerated and twisted everything, so I
lost track of what was real and true. If I corrected him or disagreed
with him he flew into a rage that wouldn't stop until he got his way. It
wasn't worth fighting over the small things, but soon there was nothing he didn't control. I abdicated everything, gradually but completely. People who had known me before the marriage couldn't
believe how meek I had become.

My ex-husband kept me isolated. He hated my family and rarely allowed me to visit them. If I didn't believe the lies he made up about my family (that I had supposedly been abused as a child, or when he falsely accused certain family members of being alcoholic) he would say that I had "suppressed memories." He drove off my old friends, and behaved so jealously toward any new people I met at work that I stopped making new friends. If I refused to drop someone, he screamed and pushed until I gave in, or he would sabotage the relationship behind my back. Often, I wouldn't know why someone no longer called, but if he or she confronted me, the whole awful scenario would unfold: He'd have lied about me to find a way to separate us.

He convinced me that I was the source of all the problems in our marriage. If I could just change my behavior, learn how to do things right, then I wouldn't be so unhappy and everything would be perfect. Sometimes, when he sensed I had taken enough abuse and was ready to leave him—in fact I ran away several times—he would suddenly transform back into the warm, exciting man I had married. It never lasted long. Still, I clung to the hope that I could change him, and I felt it was my duty to try to make the marriage work.

We waited to have children until we had finished our medical training. Julia was born when I was twenty-nine. Ben came two years later, and then Alex two years after that. I loved being a mother and adored my children. I switched from emergency medicine to family practice so that I could be home more when the children were small. We went everywhere together, to zoos and parks, hiking and swimming. We lived in the country where we kept dogs and goats and geese, and where the children could spend their summers barefoot, as my brothers and I had done before them. I used to put them all in a wagon and pull them along the forested trails around our house.

When I think of those times I see a van full of my kids and their friends, and I hear high-pitched laughter and shouts and singing. My ex-husband's face and voice are not in these memories, because he was almost never there, too preoccupied with his business plans and investment schemes. When we were all together, the tension was awful. He criticized me constantly, and if I defied him he would retaliate in terrible ways.

Once, when we were driving along a two-lane road with the children in the back seat, I told him that I wanted to see our checkbook. There was no money in the joint account and I wanted to know where it had gone. My husband pulled into the oncoming lane and stepped on the gas. I swear he would have kept going if I hadn't given in and told him I didn't need to see the checkbook. He drove into oncoming traffic another time with my parents in the car, I suppose just to show them that he could kill us all if he wanted to. He and the children laughed when I cried for him to stop.

Another time, he strangled the family dog right in front of me and our daughter, to teach us a lesson. He later told my mother how he'd watched the look of disbelief on the dog's face as he squeezed its throat. Then he shot it to finish it off.

After years of this treatment, I forgot how to fight him. It wasn't worth the battle for each inch of ground. But always, as soon as his behavior became unbearable, he would ease off the pressure. It was such a relief it felt like a gift.

Looking back, I now believe that this was a textbook case of domestic abuse. The obsessive jealousy and control, the isolation, the constant berating and threats of violence: all of it was characteristic of emotional and psychological battery. Not all domestic violence involves physical beatings: he never left a visible wound, and I always managed to rationalize his behavior. Abusers usually apologize for their attacks, and the period that follows is called the "honeymoon" phase, in which the victim is rewarded with renewed affection for staying in the relationship. Psychologists call this pattern "intermittent reinforcement" and it is a very difficult cycle to break in a marriage, especially when you are brought up to believe that there is no way out of a bad situation except to try harder.

If someone with my profile walked into the ER I would have spotted her immediately, but I could not see her in the mirror. Others noticed, however. Once, when I slipped away for an afternoon to visit a friend, I was surprised to find a domestic violence counselor waiting with her. It was a planned intervention to try to talk me into leaving my husband. At first I insisted there was no problem, I could handle it. I had actually convinced myself that things would be all right, just as I had done as a child, training myself to change my perceptions. But after the counselor showed me a survey on domestic violence that seemed to me to be describing my marriage, everything started to make sense to me. It was like coming out of a spell. But like smoking, gambling, or other destructive habits, an abusive marriage is a form of addiction, and it can take many tries to break the cycle.

I first tried to run away with the children after my ex-husband started physically hurting the boys. Julia was always his favorite, and he treated her as his confidante. But he was usually cruel to our young sons, ignoring them or telling them they were stupid. Then one day I caught him slamming both boys—who were in grade school—into the living-room walls, complaining that I had let them run "out of control." I knew we had to get out. I waited until he left the house for a medical conference, then I packed up the van and drove the children across Ohio to my mother's place. A judge granted me a restraining order to keep him away from us.

The separation lasted a month. I looked for a new job and found a school for the kids. Then my husband sent mournful, apologetic letters to each of us, begging for another chance. He sent twelve dozen roses to the house. I made the mistake of agreeing to meet him, just to talk. Afraid of a trap, I insisted we meet at an airport, where there were plenty of people and security officers if his anger got out of control. To my surprise, the man who greeted me looked like the man I had fallen in love with. There was tenderness in his eyes, not the rage that I was accustomed to. When he hugged me I felt tenderness, instead of the stiff, perfunctory embraces I'd known for years. He told me he had changed and realized how much he loved me. He would never, ever hurt the children again. I fell for it and agreed to come back to him.

At his insistence, I retracted the restraining order. Now, I tried even harder to be the perfect wife; after all, didn't he now realize how much I meant to him? The "honeymoon" did not last long. While he no longer hit the boys, he was cold to them and brutally critical of everything they did. If I challenged his judgment or contradicted him, he took it out on the kids, knowing how much that hurt me. Soon the cycle started all over again, the jealousy, the anger, the obsessive control, and the fear. I felt trapped.

Finally I found a way to escape him once and for all. I had to do something he couldn't forgive, so that he wouldn't try to win me back again. I had a brief affair, out of town, with a man who treated me with kindness and respect, something I hadn't felt in years. At last, my husband agreed to a divorce.

When I finally left for good, I asked the children to live with me in another town. Ben and Alex agreed, but Julia wanted to finish her senior year in high school. My ex-husband was amazingly amenable to the proposal, but suggested, to make the transition easier for everyone, that I remain at home while we worked out the details of the divorce and I found work. That was another mistake. While I was working and trying to build a new life for my kids, he became the attentive father they had always wanted. Suddenly he was warm to the boys and involved in their lives. When it was time to go, the boys changed their minds. They said they wanted to stay together in their school, and live with Dad.

Before the divorce, once the children were old enough to handle it, I had gone back to emergency medicine. I took a succession of ER jobs at progressively larger hospitals, building my career and skills. Now I had a new job waiting for me back near my old hometown, a four-hour drive away. I had arranged to live with the boys at my mother's house, to save enough to soon get our own place. I was blindsided by the sudden change in plans.

My first impulse was to fight for custody in court. I consulted my lawyer, who told me to avoid a messy legal battle that would only alienate the kids. He advised me to grant custody to my ex-husband, accept weekend visits, and wait for the children to change their minds on their own. You can't force teenagers to do anything, he said. I reluctantly agreed. I moved back to my mother's house and left my children with their father. It was safer for them this way. I knew from experience that any time I defied their father, the children paid the price. I was afraid if I fought too hard to get them back he would make us all suffer in the end. They had suffered enough.

Over the next few months, my weekly visits with the kids grew shorter and stranger. Repeatedly, after driving all morning to pick them up, I would arrive at the house to be told they would be available for only a few hours, not the weekend I had planned. Sometimes they wouldn't be there at all. Again my lawyer advised me not to fight, to just give it time. But time was working in favor of my ex-husband.

Just as he had done to me, it seemed that he was now isolating the children in his own narrow world. He intercepted my messages and gifts to them. My parents were not allowed to visit them or speak to them at all. I was permitted to telephone them only if he was listening in. When he didn't like the conversation, he would get on the phone, tell me that was enough, and hang up. Now that I had broken free, he was using the children as bait to lure me back into his control. Once they insisted that I come into the house for a "family meeting" where he berated and belittled me. He encouraged the kids to criticize me, and clapped and laughed when they did. He had apparently convinced them that I was the villain for "breaking up the family." One of my sons told me that I had prevented him from getting close to his father before the breakup. I couldn't believe it. I was hearing my ex-husband's words coming out of my children's mouths. Finally, I had to put a stop to these destructive encounters, for the children's sake as well as mine. I didn't want them to wake up one day and realize how cruel they had been to their mother. They were not to blame. It was better for me to simply withdraw than allow them to be used.

After a year had passed, I was seeing my children only on rare, brief occasions, and when I did, they seemed increasingly remote and stiff, like strangers to me. My work was all I had left by now. I had recently started a new job as an ER physician at a major university teaching hospital in Cleveland. It was the job I had always thought I wanted, but it was not enough to fill the void in my heart where my children had been. Life had taken on a sameness, with diminishing returns for the effort expended. I loved the work but hated hospital politics and the assembly-line mentality of commercial medicine. I was back where I started, living with my parents, with no future in sight. My dreams had frozen. I wondered: Is this what it was to become old?

Then I saw the ad for the job in Antarctica, a place I had always wanted to see. Why not? I faxed my CV to the Denver offices of Antarctic Support Associates or ASA, the company contracted to staff and supply the U.S. government's research facilities there. A few days later, Norman Wolfe, the medical recruiter, called and offered to fly me to Colorado for an interview. There was just one opening left—for the doctor at the South Pole—and they needed to fill it immediately. I was on a plane to Denver two days later.

CHAPTER 2

Through the
Looking Glass

The Antarctic Support Associates offices were housed in a cluster of boxy, mirror-finished buildings in a landscaped industrial park in Englewood, Colorado, a suburb of Denver. For the past ten years ASA had held the government contract to support U.S. scientific bases, camps, and vessels in Antarctica for the National Science Foundation (NSF). Although the civilian-run NSF has held overall authority for U.S. operations in Antarctica since 1971, and the U.S. government has gradually been reducing its military presence on the continent, ASA was filled with ex-military types. As I would soon learn, many of the company's management traditions were carried over from the days when all logistics, supplies, and construction for the U.S. Antarctic Program were handled by the U.S. armed forces.

Norman Wolfe met me in his office, where I was introduced to Mike Masterman, a young man with short, sandy-colored hair who would be the South Pole station manager next winter. He was an electronics engineer who had worked at the National Radio Astronomy Observatory in West Virginia, designing telescope systems. We chatted for a while, just to get a feel for each other. I was comfortable with both of them and very interested in the job.

They gave me a rundown of facts about Antarctica, most of them so bleak that they came across as a warning: Antarctica, I was informed, was "the highest, driest, coldest, windiest, and emptiest place on earth." The continent was one and a half times the size of the United States, and 97 percent of it was covered with ice. Nobody owned Antarctica; it was administered by an international treaty. The United States, however, had a large scientific presence on the continent. It maintained two scientific research vessels, the *Nathaniel B. Palmer* and the *Laurence M. Gould,* for marine and atmospheric studies, and three land-based stations at McMurdo, on the western coast, Palmer, on an island off the Antarctic Peninsula, and the South Pole, where I would be assigned. Temperatures at the Pole could slip to below minus 100 degrees F. For eight and a half months each year, between February and October, the Pole was totally unreachable, since it was too cold to land an aircraft. Half of that time would be spent in darkness.

It was during this interview that I first heard the word *winter* used as a verb. One does not spend the winter in Antarctica, one "winters" or "winters-over." If I took this job, I would "winterover" at the South Pole, as the only doctor among forty-one scientists and support staffers. There would be a certain amount of data collection and paper-work, but not that many patients. I was shown a set of statistics from previous years: On average, the South Pole doctor saw only three patients a week during the winter.

It would be challenging and cold, very cold, and I would be taking a huge cut in pay. But the upside was that it would be a hell of an adventure, with plenty of time to read and study, explore and reflect. I needed that time. I had been on an out-of-control roller coaster for so long: going to work, coming home and going to sleep, only to go to work again with little time for anything else. I no longer knew who I was. With a year's sabbatical from the routine, I could put my life into perspective again. But would I lose my medical skills and derail my career if I left emergency medicine for a year? And what about my children? Would spending a year at the South Pole improve or hurt my chances to get them back? I had some hard thinking to do before I could accept the job.

I talked it over with my parents and my two brothers, around my mother's kitchen table. Most major family decisions were made at that table. It was where good and bad news was given, where we celebrated our victories, honored holidays, and mourned our dead. It was where the women cut and colored each other's hair, the place where splinters were removed, where the girls giggled and told stories late at night, where we beat each other at poker. It was where I cried about my children to my sisters-in-law, Dee Dee and Lisa, who listened, many times, to what they already knew as if it was the first time, until I was too tired to keep crying. There was always a pot of tea on the table.

For this occasion, Scott and Lisa flew in their single-engine Cherokee from Richmond, Virginia. Scott had gone through many stages in his life, as a sailor and a pilot and an all-purpose rogue. Now he was following in Dad's footsteps, running a construction company that took only the most difficult jobs that nobody else would risk tackling, such as repairing damaged dams and bridges in diving equipment. Eric worked as a high-level engineer for BFGoodrich Aerospace in Troy, Ohio. He and Dee Dee, his girls, Laura and Kathleen, and Dee Dee's grandmother, Guggy, made the five-hour drive in their minivan. When everyone had settled in, we all gathered around the table to discuss my latest idea.

My mother, typically, was excited. She thought I needed an adventure at this time in my life. She believed that when things were really in the dumps, you were better off not going down the same path repeatedly, trying to make small adjustments. You needed a total paradigm shift, a new hypothesis, in order to make discoveries. And, speaking as a psychologist, she felt that if my kids saw me strong and in a new life, they might have the courage to come back to me. She believed that children instinctively ally themselves with the more powerful parent. It all added up, and Mom was very clear: "You'd be nuts not to go, Duff."

"Duffy! This is the chance of a lifetime!" Scott said, not even having to think about it first. "I would do anything to go to the South Pole."

"Do you think they need engineers?" asked Eric. He said he, too, would go if he had the chance, and didn't have the responsibilities of a family.

Dad was not so sure. "It's mighty cold there, Duff," he said. "What would you do there for a year? It sounds sort of miserable."

This was to be expected from Dad. We listened quietly as he spelled out his fears.

"You know, Duffy, there is no way out of there," he said. "If your friends get sick or die, it will only be you to take care of them. It's a big responsibility. And if you get sick, there will be no doctor to take care of you. What if you get appendicitis, or even cancer? You can save everyone else, but could you save yourself? Would you have the courage to operate on yourself, to save your own life?"

"Of course she would!" said both brothers simultaneously. Dad just shook his head. His face was a war zone of pride and love and resignation. "You can change your mind, Duffy dear," said Dad, offering me one last exit route. "You know, you don't have to do this." But by then we all knew that I must.

Mom, as usual, had the last word. "You've always been a survivor, Duffy, and you survive well," she said. "Get on with life, have the best one that you can imagine. A life is not just measured in years."

In the end, they all concurred: It was time that I changed course. The unspoken subtext to all their arguments was also obvious to me: I needed to put an ocean or two between my ex-husband and myself. Otherwise, I might fall back under his spell, or even return to the marriage, just to be with my kids again.

My children were the only ones who could have changed my mind. When I called to talk it over with them, my daughter would not even come to the phone. I told my boys that I had an opportunity to go to the South Pole, but that I would not go if there was any chance for us to be together again, for weekend visits, not just the occasional meal once a month or whenever I was allowed to see them in the presence of their father. They told me no, it wouldn't happen.

I knew that it was not my children's decision to hurt me. I had been unable to defy my ex-husband when I was living with him, and I was an adult. How could I expect any more of them? My children were the most important thing in my life and always would be. But I knew I couldn't let him use them to keep punishing me, even if it meant not seeing them for a long, long time.

I realize that not every woman would choose the same path. I lie awake at night wondering how things might have been different if I had tried another strategy, hired a new lawyer, fought in court until there was blood in the aisles. But I still might have lost the children, and in fighting for them, I would have destroyed what little peace remained in their childhood.

All I can tell you is that I broke my heart trying to change things, and when I saw that my efforts were useless, I decided to try a new direction. I had jumped into a life raft to save myself and in doing so, to save them. No one wanted to get in with me. I would have to move on and go it alone for a while. I would make another life, a wonderful life, if possible. By becoming stronger, perhaps I could give my children the strength to follow me. I would always keep the lines between us open if I could, and let them know that the life raft would return for any refugees at any time.

I called Norman Wolfe to tell him I would take the job.

It was now late October, and there was little time to prepare for my journey. I was quickly called back to Denver for a complete physical with a battery of lab tests, an EKG, a cardiac stress test, and a mammogram. Everything was fine. Nothing was left to chance. Dental x-rays showed a dead tooth, and a root canal was done on the spot, since there was no dentist at the South Pole. In fact any dental emergencies that came up during the winter would have to be handled by the doctor: me.

So after performing the root canal, the dentist kept me in his office until late that night, giving me five hours of remedial dental training. I was thankful that my extensive surgical background made me reasonably comfortable working with small instruments in the mouth. But I couldn't help thinking that it takes four years to make a dentist. I could only hope that there wouldn't be many serious dental problems at the Pole.

The next day I was scheduled for psych screening. All people wintering in the Antarctic must pass extensive psychological testing—said to be similar to choosing candidates for nuclear submarines. The ASA recruiters were looking for people who were stable, easy to get along with, and intuitive: Living in extreme conditions requires a flexible intelligence, where the ability to quickly absorb and react to new situations is a valuable asset. They wanted to weed out people with personality disorders, chronic complainers, the chronically depressed, substance abusers, and who knows what else. After multiple written tests, I had a personal interview with a psychologist.

Once I got to Antarctica, almost everyone I met joked about the screening process. One story going around described an ASA manager with a good deal of experience on the Ice who was interviewing candidates to winter at Pole.

"Do you drink?" she asked.

"No."

"Do you smoke?"

"No."

"You will."

On my second visit to the ASA offices I was introduced to employees who had clocked months of Ice time. It was peculiar. Every one of them seemed to take a step back when they learned I would be the doctor wintering at the Pole. There was a deference, even awe in the way they looked at me, and for the first time I started thinking *Holy shit! What am I getting into?*

* * *

There was much to do back in Ohio. I had less than a month to prepare for and take my emergency medicine boards, part of the continuous cycle of education and certification a doctor needs to rise in her field. I also had to set up a power of attorney to handle my finances, clear up my unfinished business affairs, and pack. How do you pack for a year at the South Pole when you really don't know what that means? I was allowed three suitcases, three orange duffel bags (which would be issued to me later by ASA, stuffed with seventy pounds of special cold weather gear), and a carry-on. Included had to be all my clothing, soap, toothpaste and toiletries for a year, books, bedding, my stethoscope, and the one nonessential item I just couldn't leave: a small Celtic harp.

A lovely woman whom I visited daily, as her family doctor, at the end of her life, had once told me how to pack for a trip. "Pack what you think you will need," she said. "Then a week later take out half your clothing and put in twice as much money." I thought of her before every trip thereafter. Her words had become my packing motto, but clearly, they would not work for the South Pole.

I was staring, overwhelmed, at the piles of my possessions stacked around my room when Mike Masterman called. Mike would be the winter site manager at the South Pole station and was visiting friends nearby, in West Virginia. He wanted to stop and see me and meet my family before departing for the Ice.

"Things get pretty spooky when you're getting ready to leave for the South Pole for a year," he explained. I had noticed. He offered to help me with anything I needed to know, and I jumped at the chance to get together.

Both my parents were thrilled and relieved to finally meet someone who had lived at the South Pole. My mother prepared one of her famous huge dinners for him. As we wolfed down steaks, Mike answered all of our questions and put most of our fears to rest. Only thirty years old, he had crammed a lot of experience into his life. He was a firefighter and instructor, an experienced SCUBA diver, and certified cave rescuer. He had already wintered at the Pole as a scientist in

1995. Now he was returning as the winter site manager, the civilian equivalent of a ship's captain.

As he talked, I kept seeing the station as the Starship *Enterprise,* Mike as Captain Kirk, and me as Bones. I managed to keep that vision to myself while he patiently explained to my father that every berth in the South Pole has an emergency escape door in case of fire.

After dinner, Mike looked over my packing list. "You won't need ten bottles of deodorant, Jerri," he laughed. "You won't even need one. We all stop using it when winter hits. No one will smell you through all those clothes, and no one cares anyway."

He scrutinized the rest of my alleged necessities: "You don't need razors, no one shaves. Six bottles of shampoo is way too much when you only shower twice a week. You will need a couple of cameras, they all go bad. Have yours fitted with low-temperature grease. And take film; we can develop it in the darkroom.

"Do you like western novels? If so you can read mine. Otherwise, better take more to read. Don't take things that need batteries, they don't last in the extreme cold. Contact lenses? They freeze onto your corneas. Glasses? They fog so badly that you can't see anyway. Perfume? Come on, it's illegal on the continent, just another contaminant. Clothing? You really don't need much. Wear the same thing for a year and then throw it away when you're done. Music? Now that's important. You will get very tired of the same music. . . ."

After Mike Masterman headed off for the Ice, I began an email correspondence with Will Silva, the South Pole doctor over the past winter. He was still at the station, waiting for me to relieve him. Will had useful information about what sort of computers and medical equipment I would find at the Pole. He told me to bring good sunblock, and even though he said he wore Teva sandals in Biomed—the tiny hospital center—he said that some Polies preferred the sheepskin slip-on boots you can buy in New Zealand, on the way to Antarctica. For indoor clothes he gave me the email addresses of some of the women he knew at Pole. My female correspondents said that a few "frivolous things" went a long way at Pole. They told me to bring some fun, bright, feminine clothes for special dinners, a cookbook or favorite recipes, herbal teas, and my own bath towel, among other things. I was enormously grateful for their suggestions, especially later.

When I wasn't working or preparing for the trip, I was either studying for the written boards, or dealing with a growing medical crisis in my own family. Although my dad had been strong and healthy all his life, he was now seventy and starting to slow down. And there had been some alarming medical exams. Everyone in the family was worried that his PSA levels had been progressively higher—indicating possible prostate cancer. As the medical person of the family, I was tasked to convince him to deal with it before I left for Antarctica.

In October he agreed to a biopsy of his prostate. What should have been a routine procedure became an ordeal after he lost so much blood that he nearly went into shock. Then weeks went by with no word from his doctor. When I called the office, the nurse wouldn't give me the results over the phone, but she told me enough. Suddenly, all thoughts of going to the South Pole vanished. If my father had cancer, my family would need me here.

I called Mom to walk outside with me. We sat in the woods and I told her what I suspected. My mother could handle anything the world threw at her, except this. I have never seen such horror in her eyes.

"I can't bear to lose him, Duffy," she said. "You know that."

"Oh God," I said. "I can't leave you now."

"Oh yes, you can," said my mother, with the same voice she had used when she talked about duty and honor to a child across a batch of folded laundry. It was a voice like silk drawn over hard steel. "You made a commitment. You have to go."

First I had to find my father's doctor and learn the truth. He confirmed that it was indeed cancer. Dad would need an operation, and judging from his difficulties after the biopsy, it could be dangerous. I had to tell him. We sat at the kitchen table over a cup of tea. He listened carefully to what I said, and then nodded, as if affirming an inner voice.

"What will be, will be," he said, just as I had known he would. "The worst thing, Duff, is to see your mom so sad."

The whole family took Dad to the hospital in Cleveland. The night before, we hung out in the hotel making brave jokes. None of us could stand the thought of losing him. It was inconceivable. He was the anchor in all of our lives.

The surgery lasted much longer than expected. He had to remain in the recovery room because he had lost too much blood and had gone into shock. Now his blood wasn't clotting properly and his kidneys were failing. We were not allowed to see him.

When I finally talked my way into the recovery room, more than twenty years in medicine had not prepared me for what I saw. He didn't look like my father. He looked so old and his skin had the pale, flat color of death. With a weak voice, he managed, "I love you, Duffy," and that was all.

It was time for Mom to be with Dad. I knew she was being torn apart by the sight of him, but an outsider would never have seen it on her face. She held his hand and kissed him, and told him everything would be all right.

As always, we got through it together. My brothers and I wouldn't leave him. We were the family from hell, a nurse's greatest nightmare. In shifts, we stayed by the bed, worried when he couldn't breathe, constantly calling for one thing or another. The doctor daughter was feeding him tea against orders, the engineer son was questioning everyone about how the equipment worked, the building contractor would simply adjust the complex medical equipment himself, having watched what others had done when alarms beeped and the oxygen wouldn't work. It was a miracle they let us stay with him at all.

I was increasingly anxious about my plans, and more and more inclined to drop everything. In four days I was supposed to leave for the Ice, and I still had to take my ER boards. At my family's insistence, I drove to Detroit, where the test was given, and returned to Cleveland that night to take my shift at the bedside, relieving a very tired Eric. The next morning Dad looked worse. Too many doctors came in to tell us that there was hope. His drains were now filling up with urine from a leak in his urethra. He might have to return to surgery, but maybe they could stop it by increasing pressure in his catheter. Everyone in the family watched my eyes for a sign of what I was comprehending, since I could read through all the medical language and posturing. I used everything in me to appear calm. Then I went to his bathroom, where my mother couldn't see me, and wept. How could I leave now?

My brothers brought me back to the bedside. Dad, missing nothing, as usual, wanted to talk to me.

"It is time for you to go to Antarctica, Duffy," he said quietly. I had to lean close to hear him. "You made a promise to those people, you have a responsibility."

At that moment everything that my parents had trained me to be, and every value that I had learned at their table washed over me in a wave of anguish. All of my instincts, the visceral love a child feels for a parent, told me to defy him and stay. But I knew there was no point in arguing. This was the family I had been born into, and I might as well have tried to change the color of my eyes and the set of my bones as to neglect my duty. It was, at last, my turn to charge up the hill.

I couldn't say good-bye. I was still holding on to him and my brothers were taking my hands off my father and pulling me out of the room.

"Good-bye, Duffy dear," he said. "I love you. Now go."

As I walked down the echoing hospital hallway, I heard the door swing shut behind me.

And so, the eve of my great adventure was also the loneliest day of my life. My children were lost to me, and now I felt like an orphan as well. I suppose this was how sailors often set to sea: walking away from tears, heading into a fresh breeze, charting a course to a new world.

* * *

I flew to Denver in a daze. I completed the final paperwork for the trip, then different people handed me things to carry to Antarctica: some papers, some computer software, and a Styrofoam cooler full of flu vaccines and tuberculosis tests. Then I met the people who would be traveling together to the Ice: a woman cop, a plumber, a tinsmith, and a heavy equipment mechanic. We sized each other up tentatively, like teenagers from different schools glancing across the dance floor. I felt a bit giddy and awed: These people were all going to be *there* before long. It was exciting just to breathe the same air.

Before we left there was a final briefing to remind us of the lofty purpose of our adventure on the Ice: to support science. The array of scientific research in Antarctica was staggering. The previous year there had been 187 U.S.-supported projects on the continent, from studying fish with a natural antifreeze in their blood, to monitoring global warming through the behavior of glaciers. Some of the most exciting work was being done at the South Pole, where the unsullied atmosphere was perfect for astronomical observations and for detecting changes in greenhouse gases.

As a future resident of the South Pole station, I was also reminded of the other, perhaps more important mission this year: to support construction. After almost three decades of service, the facilities at the South Pole were in desperate need of repair and modernization. A huge construction project was underway to build a new station alongside the existing structures. It wouldn't be completed until 2005.

We flew from Denver to Christchurch, New Zealand, with stops in Los Angeles and Auckland. On the first leg of the long journey, I sat next to Mandy Anderson, the police officer. She was from Breckenridge, Colorado, where she had met Toby Anderson, who worked for years as a firefighter in McMurdo, the largest American station on the continent. He loved Antarctica, and when they got engaged, he convinced her to live with him on the Ice. Despite the absence of civilian police officers on the American bases in Antarctica, she agreed to go, taking a job as the night cook in the galley at McMurdo. They had been married for only two days when Toby was deployed. Mandy waited in the States for the next four months until it was time for her to leave. They planned to hon-eymoon in New Zealand and Fiji when they got off the Ice. Needless to say, she was looking forward to seeing him in a few days.

In Los Angeles we all went through Customs and waited together in the passenger lounge for our flight to New Zealand to be called. We were already forming a tight group of friends. We talked about our lives and what we would be doing on the Ice. I told them that I had taken a road that I would not return on, that I already felt I was no longer of this world. I knew that I had made a major decision in my life, and that things would never be the same again. I told them I felt like Alice going through the looking glass. As we boarded the Kiwi Air flight to Christchurch, my sense of wonder only deepened, and it never really left me.

My rush to reach Antarctica was so intense I had virtually no time to learn much about the continent that would be my home for the next year. As I eased back into my seat on the jumbo jet, I leafed through U.S. Antarctic Program *Participant Guide* issued by the NSF. A lot of the information had been covered in the ASA briefings, but I was interested in learning more about the history of the continent. There weren't many books about Antarctica in the Cleveland book-stores, but I managed to pick up a Lonely Planet guidebook that had some good information.

Antarctica was an idea before it was a place. Sailors from ancient fleets could not get past the ice floes and fog banks and storms that shrouded the southern edge of the world. Greek philosophers deduced there was a landmass there, but nobody could prove it until 1820, when Fabian von Bellinghausen, a Russian navy captain, spotted an island off the Antarctic peninsula. Whalers and seal hunters from all nations swarmed the coastal waters and outer islands during the 1900s, but no one attempted to explore the interior until the turn of the century.

It seemed that Americans had only recently developed a passion for the mysteries of Antarctica. In the United States, *polar exploration* usu-ally meant the Arctic adventures of Frederick Cook and Robert Peary in their quests to attain the North Pole. The Americans had been left out of—and mostly ignored—the great race to the South Pole that obsessed Great Britain and the Scandinavian countries in the early twentieth century.

That contest spanned ten years, and produced some of the most tragic and inspiring stories in modern history. In the end, the dash to the South Pole was won by a fastidious Norwegian named Roald Amundsen, who used skis and dogsleds to cross the polar plateau and plant his country's flag at the bottom of the world on December 14, 1911. At the same time of Amundsen's machinelike expedition, another, less efficient, party of discovery was approaching the South Pole from a different direction.

Robert Falcon Scott's Terra Nova expedition was his second stab at claiming the Pole for England. He was a dashing, romantic figure, much loved by the British public, but not the best tactician to attempt the Pole. For one thing, he refused to employ dogs, because it was unsporting, not to mention cruel (the Norwegians ate their dogs along the way). So Scott and his crew of four intrepid Britons "man-hauled" their supplies across hundreds of miles of treacherous terrain. They reached the South Pole on January 17, 1912, only to find Amundsen's abandoned tent and Norwegian flag rising above the plateau like an extended middle finger.

"Great God, this is an awful place," Scott wrote famously in his diary that day, "and terrible enough for us to have laboured to it without the reward of priority."

The dejected team headed back toward their base on McMurdo Sound. They were low on supplies and starting to show signs of scurvy. Then they ran into bad weather. Edgar "Teddy" Evans was the first to die, quietly, in a coma. Lawrence "Titus" Oates, a strapping cavalry officer, was the next to go. He had terrible frostbite and gangrenous feet. Rather than slow his companions down, he stepped out of the tent and walked into a blizzard, never to be seen again. It was his thirty-second birthday. His last words were "I am just going outside, and should be some time." (As I read about his fate, I thought

Oates would have fit right into my family. If these were the sort of men who went to the Pole, my mother would approve.)

Only three remained: Scott, his good friend Edward "Bill" Wilson, who was also an artist and physician, and Henry "Birdie" Bowers, a short, cheerful man with great stamina. They got within eleven miles of a cache of food and supplies that would have saved them, but they were pinned down by another blizzard and perished. A search party found their frozen bodies six months later, and buried them on the Ice.

More than forty-five years passed before another human being returned to the South Pole. Admiral Richard Byrd, the American explorer famous for his Arctic expeditions, claimed to have flown over the Pole in a private aircraft in 1929, but the accuracy of his navigation has been challenged. He made another undisputed flight in 1947.

It wasn't until after World War II, when the U.S. military was looking for footholds all over the globe to stop the spread of Communism, that the American government took an official interest in Antarctica. According to the NSF booklet, in 1946–47 the U.S. military launched the largest single expedition to explore Antarctica, dropping more than forty-seven hundred men on the continent. In 1956, the U.S. Navy landed an aircraft on the geographic South Pole and established an American presence there. Construction soon began on the first South Pole station, which would eventually be named for Amundsen and Scott.

The Cold War was raging by then, and the Soviet Union, which had a long-standing franchise on parts of coastal Antarctica, made its own push into the interior, establishing a base at Vostok, eight hundred miles away from the Americans, in a high-altitude region even colder and more isolated than the South Pole (the coldest recorded temperature on earth, minus 129.3 F., was reported at Vostok in 1983). Luckily, a military buildup on Antarctica was averted when twelve nations, including the U.S. and the Soviet Union, signed the Antarctic Treaty in 1961, setting aside the land and waters below sixty degrees south latitude as a zone of peace, devoted to scientific discovery. Since Antarctica had no indigenous people, there was nothing to prevent the world's nations from claiming it for everyone. Since then, another thirty-one countries have ratified the treaty. Eighteen of the signatories maintain more than forty scientific bases on the Ice or on islands in the Southern Ocean. Although a few nations, such as Chile and Argentina, claim sovereign territory on the continent, no one else takes them seriously. There has never been a war fought on the continent.

Further protocols and treaties (collectively known as the Antarctic Treaty System) have shielded Antarctica from all kinds of exploitation, including mining and nuclear testing. The Antarctic environment is extremely fragile, and in recent years extreme measures have been taken to protect it. Special protected areas with extraordinary ecological or scientific value have been set aside and are off bounds to unauthorized visitors. People can face large fines or imprisonment back in their home countries for bringing contaminants to the Ice, for harming or harassing penguins, seals and other wildlife, or for taking away rocks or shells as souvenirs from the Antarctic islands. While there is no legal body with authority over the whole continent, visitors are expected to obey the rules of each station, and of the Treaty System. Lawbreakers can be detained and deported, and sometimes prosecuted in their own court system. While Antarctica is still the most remote and pristine destination on the planet, about ten thousand tourists a year come to cruise the coastline, ski on virgin snow, or climb the immaculate peaks.

At last, after several hours of happy absorption of Antarctic lore in the dim, crowded aircraft cabin, the excitement of the journey subsided and exhaustion kicked in. I drifted off to sleep and woke up in another hemisphere.

The airport acronym for Christchurch, New Zealand is CHCH, hence its nickname: Cheech. This charming, leafy city on the temperate southern coast of New Zealand is the gateway for most North Americans traveling to Antarctica, since it is closest to McMurdo. Other points of departure for the huge continent include Capetown, South Africa; Punta Arenas, Chile; and a few other antipodal ports. In

Cheech I found that ASA had booked me into a fancy, expensive hotel, apart from my traveling companions. I suppose they thought a doctor would expect a luxury suite, but I was horrified. The last thing I wanted was to be separated from the group. So I invited Mandy to share my room with me.

The next morning we all reassembled at the International Antarctic Center out by the airport, a large, modern complex that serves as an operations center for the New Zealand, Italian, and U.S. Antarctic programs. The National Science Foundation and ASA had offices there. Our first stop was the CDC—Clothing Distribution Center. Men and women were ushered into separate rooms to try on the ECWs or Extreme Cold Weather gear they would wear on the Ice. Every item was government issue; it would all be returned (probably for burning) at the end of the season.

The warehouse was brimming with racks of geranium-red parkas, insulated Carhartt outerwear—familiar to me because they are a favorite with construction workers—and shelves upon shelves of fleece, wool, and microfiber clothing and accessories. Your choices depended on where you were going on the continent and whether your job was primarily inside or outside. Mandy and I had to take more clothing than the men because we would be wintering over on the Ice. I had the most of all because I was going to the Pole.

The guys finished quickly and soon started taunting us to hurry up. But since Mandy and I were built like women, much of the all-male clothing didn't fit, and we kept trying new ensembles until we felt comfortable. My standard outdoor attire would start with underwear, then long underwear, then a fleece jumpsuit, then a fleece jacket, then full-bib Carhartt's or lined wind pants, then a red goose-down parka. The red parkas were made in Canada, with a nylon shell and feathers mixed into the down for loft, and were widely believed to be the warmest coats on the planet. You could also get a green and black canvas parka with SOUTH POLE stitched on the breast pocket. These were referred to by Polies as their "colors," but I was told they were not as warm as the red ones.

For head protection I got a balaclava, a neck gaiter, a full face mask, hat, UV goggles, and a down hood. There were glove liners, wool gloves, then leather or fur gloves for the hands, and for the feet two pairs of wool socks, waffled boot liners, and two different types of boots. The warmest were the white rubber "bunny" boots that looked like something Mickey Mouse would wear. They were specially made for polar climates and insulated with inflatable air bladders. Not as warm, but much more comfortable, were the leather "blue boots." They let your feet breathe while the bunny boots, I had been warned, turned your socks into wet mops. I was issued a pair of each. Then there were the indoor outfits. . . .

In the end, I had stuffed three huge orange bags with my government-issue clothing. Next we watched a movie about how to survive in Antarctica that included helpful hints about how to avoid hypothermia ("if your feet are cold, wear a hat"), how to tell if a blizzard is on the way, and how to take a two-minute "Navy" shower, which was all we would be allowed at the Pole.

Then we lined up to pass through Customs and get our passports stamped. We were given a sack lunch, herded onto a bus, and driven out to the airport, where a New Zealand Air Force C-130 was waiting to take us to Antarctica. Normally, planes operated by the U.S. Navy or the New York Air National Guard ferried American scientists and staff to the Ice. But it was late in the austral summer, and almost everybody was already in place at the three U.S. bases. So for our trip to MacTown—what everybody calls McMurdo—we piggybacked on a Kiwi supply flight.

We had to wear our ECWs in case we crash-landed somewhere on the Ice. It was hot and uncomfortable, but soon we were strapped into rope seats in the cavernous fuselage of the cargo plane. After takeoff I was able to shed my parka and stretch out on top of the pallets stacked in the center aisle for the duration of the eight-hour flight. To put us in the mood for a trip to the Great White South, the Kiwi flight crew blasted a rousing performance of Wagner's "Ride of the Valkyries" over the intercom. We were totally stoked and ready for our big adventure when the pilot announced that we had reached the "Point of Safe Return" and unfortunately weather at McMurdo had deteriorated. We couldn't land safely, so we had to turn back to Cheech. We were being "boomeranged"—a common occurrence in Antarctic aviation, I soon learned. Everyone was disappointed, but I was secretly relieved. Halfway through the flight I realized I had forgotten to bring the cooler full of vaccines I had hauled all the way from Denver. When I arrived at the CDC the day before, I'd handed them in to be stored in a refrigerator, and in all the excitement of leaving, I'd forgotten to retrieve them. My first mission, and I screwed up!

Four hours later we were back in New Zealand. There was nothing to do but wait for the weather to clear. Customs would not return our checked baggage, since we had already been processed out of the country, and we had to be ready to leave on short notice. Luckily I had left a spare bag of warm weather clothes at the CDC (awaiting my return in a year) so I had something to wear in town. The men in the group had checked everything. They ran around town that night in lined bib overalls and bunny boots.

We showed up at the airport every morning for almost a week, only to be sent back into town. It was a wonderful chance to explore Christchurch and some of the surrounding countryside. Mandy and I wanted to invite our traveling companions to come along with us, so one morning I called the rooming house where the men were staying. The desk clerk refused to rouse them, so I used my professional clout. I told the clerk that I was the doctor traveling with them to Antarctica and needed to speak with them. The clerk's voice brightened.

"So you are the American Ice doctor?"

"Yes."

"Then come over and deal with this crazy guy we have here. He got off the Ice months ago and he is, well, strange. And all the *women* coming and going!"

I had heard about the difficulty some people have readjusting to the world. There are those who hole up in a hotel in Cheech for months, avoiding anyone they didn't winter with. Others wander the mountains. This man's love life was none of my business, so I declined to visit him.

A large group of us rented a van and drove into sheep country one day. We hiked, saw whales, and swam with dolphins.

The Kiwis have a strong attachment to Antarctica, and most people in Cheech have either been to the Ice or have a close friend or relative with Ice time. Everyone we met was friendly and accommodating; they were used to seeing Americans stranded by the weather, and they made us feel welcome.

We ran into only one rough patch during our visit, when a burglar slipped into our hotel room one night. In retrospect, it was funny rather than scary. Our intruder had picked the wrong room to burgle: what he found was an angry ER doctor and a policewoman. We screamed at him and cornered him. Mandy demanded to know what he was doing in our room, assuring him, "I start nice so I have somewhere to go." The poor guy sputtered something about needing to give us new shampoo, that he worked for the hotel. We knew he was lying, but we let him go. We didn't want to spend time talking to a hotel manager or filling out a report in a police station. Our instincts were good. That very morning, at four a.m., we got a call telling us that the weather had cleared. We were going to Antarctica.

As we started our descent to McMurdo, I peered out a porthole window in the C-130 Hercules. My first view of Antarctica was a panorama of dark blue seas thick with icebergs under a blazing summer sun. MacTown occupies the southern tip of Ross Island, a mountainous knot of land in the Ross Sea that is attached on one side to the Antarctic mainland by a thick shelf of ice. (Scotsman James Clark Ross first sailed into this body of water in 1841 on HMS *Erebus;* Lt. Archibald McMurdo commanded the sister ship, *Terror.*) The U.S. base is located where the water, ice, and land meet to form McMurdo Sound. Above it all looms Mount Erebus, an eleven-thousand-foot active volcano near the center of Ross Island that belches a plume of steam and showers ash onto the fragile, puny buildings below. Even from the air, McMurdo station looks like a Klondike mining camp, crisscrossed with muddy roads and rows of tin-roofed huts glinting in the sun.

We touched down on a long ice runway, frozen solid enough to accommodate the hard rubber wheels of the big cargo carrier. There was no one to help carry my luggage off the plane. In fact, the MacTown "bag drag" is a traditional ordeal for newcomers. It took forever to haul those seventy-pound sacks of dead weight into the shuttle bus, particularly since I was carrying a cooler full of live vaccines, along with a delicate Celtic harp.

It was cold enough at McMurdo that day—probably ten below zero F.—but I was outfitted for an expedition to the Pole. I was overheated and exhausted by the time I reached my accommodations at the infamous "Hotel California," a dumpy hostel for people passing through MacTown. The rooms, strewn with empty bottles and sleeping bags, seemed to sleep five or six. I quickly called Mandy and asked if I could stay with her until I caught my flight to the Pole.

Poor Mandy hadn't seen Toby since their wedding. Now she had finally arrived only to find that her husband had been sent to the South Pole for a few days to maintain the fire extinguishers. I took advantage of the situation and moved in with her for the duration.

MacTown was like a small city in the summertime, with a population of twelve hundred. It was the largest U.S. station on the continent, and the logistics center for the South Pole and outlying research camps. MacTown was the seat of government for Americans on the continent, with a U.S. magistrate and federal marshals to enforce the law. There was a barber shop, a two-lane bowling alley (set your own pins), a coffeehouse, and two bars, all housed in shoddy prefab boxes. The whole settlement was architecturally impaired. Only the NSF offices, in an A-frame chalet, and the chapel resembled any actual buildings.

On my first afternoon in town I took a tour of McMurdo General Hospital and was introduced to the McMurdo medical staff. I was surprised that inside this nondescript building was a well-equipped clinic. Best of all it was filled with military and civilian medical personnel. My favorite person of all was Betty Erickson, an experienced nurse from Wyoming. I was impressed by the way she explained things, with an easy confidence that came from wisdom. In the coming months she would be my main contact in MacTown, and I came to think of her as my "fantasy nurse"—someone who intuitively understood me and shared my approach to medicine. I looked forward to seeing her again.

I hoped to spend a few days in McMurdo working with some of the medical people there to pick up more training in x-ray, lab, and dentistry. But Gerry Katz, ASA's physician advisor for Antarctica, who was there to help me adjust, told me I had to get to the Pole as soon as possible to relieve Will Silva. I understood and accepted this. But I was disappointed to find out that I wouldn't get survival training, at what we called Happy Campers School, which qualified people for trips outside of MacTown. It was where you learned how to make ice caves and set up propane heaters, just the kind of thing I loved. I asked the human resource office for survival training before I went to the Pole. They looked at me and said, "You don't get survival training when you're a Polie. If you end up outside in the night, you die." More reality training.

In the end, there was no time to worry about it, because on my second morning in MacTown, I got a space on a flight to the South Pole.

CHAPTER 3:

Great God, This Is an Awful Place

From: Jerri Nielsen
To: Mom and Dad
Date: 21 Nov. 1998 11:24:45
Subject: I have arrived

Dear Mom and Dad,

I have arrived at South Pole. It is strange and beautiful. The sun is bright like a welder's torch at 3 a.m. They drive bulldozers through the house. Nothing is like anything or any place on earth.

I am too tired to write more but wanted you to know that I am here and safe. Let boys know.

I love you all so much.

The Duff

It's not easy landing sixty-five tons of sheet metal on skis. The LC-130 cargo plane touched down on the icy landing strip with flaps pulled back, propellers in reverse, and all four engines howling like angry animals. I was one of a dozen passengers strapped in the dark belly of this aircraft, confined to a windowless bench seat. I had hoped to watch our descent over the polar plateau and catch a glimpse of the continent's most famous landmark, the geodesic dome at the center of the Amundsen-Scott South Pole Station. Still, I could picture the ice-bound world beneath us, as I had visited it in my imagination so many times since I was a child.

The LC-130 was a standard Hercules-class transport plane outfitted with special skis for landings on unstable polar ice. We barreled along the taxiway until the plane bounced to a stop near the Dome. Bundled again in my brand new ECWs, complete with big fur gloves and colossal white boots, I felt very much like the Michelin Man as I hauled my carry-on luggage up to the passenger door.

I stepped out into a blinding light, into the whitest world under an impossibly blue sky. The naked sun seared me right through my polarized goggles. The next thing that hit was a cold so deep and complete it was surreal. My first breaths torched my throat and chilled my lungs. It was cold from another dimension, from an ice planet in a distant galaxy. And this was *summer* in the Southern Hemisphere.

After a few stabbing gulps of thin air I was quickly reminded that I had gained almost two miles in altitude during the three-hour flight from McMurdo. While the plateau was flat as a griddle, it was also as high as the Austrian Alps. The South Pole station rests on a nine-thousand-foot thick slab of ice soaring ninety-three hundred feet above sea level. I immediately felt light-headed, lead-footed, and slightly nauseated, but I still had to drag my bags and the cooler of vaccines to the Dome. I forced my body to move, even though it felt like I could not. Then I noticed two figures in bright red parkas walking up to the plane, waving and laughing—presumably at me as I struggled down the stairs.

The Pole is a great physical leveler. At first glance, everyone looks the same dressed in twenty to thirty pounds of almost identical clothing, with heads and faces completely covered. They were almost in front of me when I recognized one of the figures as Mike Masterman, the winter station manager. With him was Will Silva, the doctor I had come to relieve. I couldn't hear them over the noise of the engines, but they were shouting and pointing up to the sky. I looked up and saw the sun was ringed with a brilliant halo of ice crystals and framed with an array of sun dogs like blazing outriggers. Will slapped me on the back and smiled. As we walked together toward the entrance to the Dome, I felt like I was finally coming home.

Will and Mike guided me down an icy ramp to a tunnel that led to a small town of orange-red metal buildings under the geodesic canopy. In the early 1970s, when the aluminum Dome was being constructed, its ice floor was flush with the level of the plateau. Almost thirty years of storms and blowing snow had nearly buried the structure, which was 165 feet wide and 55 feet tall. Bulldozer and tractor operators were fighting a continuous battle to keep the entrances open and to prevent the ice from closing around the Dome. Deep snow canyons ringed the structure, which, I was told, created a safety hazard in the dark months because people tended to fall into them.

The Dome itself was unheated and the indoor temperatures were nearly the same as outside—thirty-five below zero on this summer day. In fact, the Dome was merely an elaborate windbreak that protected the heated buildings inside from the elements. Three prefabricated structures, each two stories high, made up the nerve center of the station.

The galley, to the right of the entrance, was the first building. It was just like a Navy ship's galley, no surprise, since the Seabees had built it in the 1970s. The kitchen and dining room were on the lower level, with a smaller dining area upstairs, and the 90 South Bar. Unlike American oil rigs and aircraft carriers, this ship was not dry. Smoking and drinking were permitted at the bar, on a bring-your-own basis. Predictably, the galley and the bar were the focus of social life at the Pole.

Separate from the galley but accessible from a second-floor walkway, was the "freshie shack," a building heated to the temperature of a household refrigerator and used for storing vegetables and other DNF (do not freeze) items, such as beer and soda pop. The next building housed the communications center on the ground floor, and the library, pool room, offices, and South Pole store on the top level. The third and largest prefab structure held the computer lab, the science office, and on the top floor, dormitory rooms and the sauna. A berthing annex had been attached to this building to house still more people. A hydroponic greenhouse (with artificial lighting) rested on its roof.

My home—the Biomed building—was sheltered under a steel archway that branched off the entrance tunnel just before it reached the Dome. Biomed was an orange metal shack insulated with two-foot-thick foam. Boxes of office supplies and other commodities were stacked high against each wall. The front entrance was a huge white freezer door, the type found in a meatpacker's warehouse. As a twist, this freezer kept the cold out, not in. The building housed the station's two-bed hospital, examination and equipment rooms, as well as the living quarters for the doctor, the South Pole Area Manager, who would leave in the winter and be replaced in Biomed by the crew members with the most Ice time, and the winter site manager. We all shared one bathroom.

Compared to other living arrangements at the base, these accommodations were luxurious and private. The station was built to house seventeen people in winter and thirty-three in summer. Our winter crew would be forty-one because of the year-round construction project to build a new South Pole station. Now, at the height of summer, more than two hundred people were working, eating, and trying to live in harmony at this facility. Most slept in Jamesways, canvas Quonset huts with wooden sides, in "Summer Camp," a quarter mile away from the Dome. But all of us would take meals in the same galley and compete for space in the bar or gym or TV lounge at night.

Will showed me to my quarters. He had already moved out to a tent in Summer Camp, and although I felt a little guilty displacing him, I was grateful to settle in right away. The room was cozy and comfortable. I had my own bed, dresser, humidifier, bookcases, computer, and an assortment of wall hooks for my skis and cold-weather gear. I stowed away the live vaccines, stripped off a layer of clothing, and changed into the shearling boots I had bought in New Zealand. Most people wore lightweight boots around the Dome, since they were more comfortable than the heavy boots we had been issued. A long nap would have felt good about now, but there was so much to learn and only five days before Will had to catch a flight out of here.

Will, a wiry man with long dark hair, a scraggly beard, and quick, kind eyes, reminded me of an intelligent gnome. I already liked him very much from our email correspondence before I came down. He seemed to be a man from a different time and place. He was an intellectual rock climber from Harvard who was passionate about the violin, back-country skiing, and "his people" at the Pole. After Harvard, he had gone to med school at the University of Rochester in upstate New York and then put in years of private practice as an internist in Seattle, Washington. Like me, he'd had enough of the "'bean counters" controlling his medical decisions. Listening to him talk, I knew that I was finally with my own kind, a doctor who wanted to devote his time to healing rather than climbing the corporate ladder. Will, too, had left the "business" of medicine to find the same thing I was looking for. He had tested himself and survived.

Now Will was weeks overdue to leave the Ice, and he looked it. After thirteen months at the Pole, his clothes were filthy and torn to shreds. His eyes and the spirit within were now completely "of the Ice," a state I could not understand then but would come to know intimately. He emanated an aura of calm, an aura of contentment that comes from knowing who you are and precisely where you belong.

After he had me somewhat settled, Will walked me to the upper galley for my South Pole orientation. Bulldozers, snowmobiles, and forklifts were running between the buildings in a greasy frozen fog. While the outside environment was the most pristine on earth, inside the Dome was appalling, with worse air than an L.A. freeway during rush hour.

As I walked to the briefing, it occurred to me that the South Pole seemed designed to disorient human beings, like a world reflected in a fun-house mirror. Up was down and down was up. When it was winter back home, it was summer down here. *Summer* described the season of cold, incessant light, and *winter* the season of colder, incessant darkness. There was only one day and one night each year (admittedly with a protracted dawn and dusk). Time was practically irrelevant. The South Pole sat at the convergence of every time zone in the world, so the station managers picked whichever one was convenient. In the summer months, October through February, the schedule had to be synchronized with supply flights coming from McMurdo. McMurdo was serviced by flights from New Zealand, so the Pole operated on New Zealand time, which was a full day ahead of the U.S. When the planes stopped coming with the arrival of winter, the Pole switched to U.S. Mountain Time for the convenience of the ASA bosses in Denver. The extra day would vanish without a trace.

The extreme strangeness of Antarctica, and particularly the South Pole, fostered a sense of separation from the rest of the planet. Polies shared a camaraderie that reminded me of the Vietnam veterans I treated in Ohio. For Polies, there was Antarctica, and there was "the world."

Dave Fischer, the South Pole Area Manager, fondly known as the SPAM, greeted me and my fellow arriving Polies and introduced us to polar etiquette. No newcomer ever remembered much of this, due to the sudden elevation of altitude and concurrent memory loss, but an attempt was made to save us from committing social faux pas.

Since the walls between living spaces were either light pressboard or canvas, you should never talk in the halls or above a whisper in your rooms. There was a right and a wrong way to close the refrigeratorlike doors so as not to wake day sleepers. Basically you needed to be as unobtrusive as possible in a small, overcrowded environment where people lived too closely for too long. I would come to believe that expansive houses and standard, nuclear families served to isolate the human soul, and that tight, tribal communities were infinitely more suited to our natures, but I wasn't ready to feel that yet. We had to be introduced slowly to the notion of giving more than you have and using less than you need, of living without outward privacy, of knowing that all you really own are your own thoughts.

Another big issue was communication, within the world of the Pole as well as the outside world. Dave described the hard-wired communication system for the base called the "All Call." You could dial an in-house phone, found in most rooms, and make a direct call within the station, or make a public announcement on an intercom. (This was used in a fairly military and businesslike manner in summer, but toward the middle of winter it became a source of great public humor.) There were also handheld radios, which I learned to monitor like a police band so as not to miss any of the excitement on base during my daily routine.

Our main contact with the rest of the planet came through email via the Internet, which was dependent on the availability of satellites. Comms Tom Carlson, who ran the Comms shack, was a wizard at keeping track of the eclectic assortment of satellites skimming along the edge of the sky. This was not easy, since satellites appeared only a few degrees above the horizon at the South Pole, and were rarely visible for more than a few hours at a time. The email transmissions were sometimes slow and spotty and tended to arrive in the middle of the night, but I was amazed that they arrived at all. When satellites permitted, some people used AOL Instant Messenger for real-time conversations with folks back in the States. There was also a special voice-only satellite line that we could sign up to use, but only on Sundays. The South Pole was also part of a ham radio network that could patch us into the U.S. telephone system for calls home. Later in the summer, we were shipped special Internet phones that used the same satellite connections as our email.

I viewed all these ingenious forms of communication as a mixed blessing. Later, when I would open my electronic mailbox and find sixty unanswered emails blinking at me, I often wished that I had been born into an earlier, unwired era.

Dave Fischer went on to explain our power, heat, and water. Power was created by diesel engines turning giant generators that burned JP8 aviation fuel. The fuel, the same type used by the Hercules aircraft, was delivered to the station in their wing tanks. Everything at the Pole was imported by cargo plane, and seventy percent of everything used here was reused and or recycled. Even heat. The fluid used to cool the engines was flushed through a closed-loop system: Hot coolant from the diesel engines was piped to the buildings in the Dome. Each room had pipes running in and out of small radiators, with a fan to disperse the heat. Once discharged of heat, the fluid returned to cool the engines. The heat from the engines' exhaust was run through a heat exchanger that heated another system, a Rodrigues well or "rodwell," which melted the ice to make our water. The ice being melted for water today had fallen as snow sometime during the fifteenth century.

The materials recycling system was quite elaborate, with more than a dozen separate bins for different types of metals, papers and plastics, burnables and biodegradables. Some people never got it right. It became comforting to not waste, but at times it was awkward and difficult, making quick, easy jobs take hours to finish. For instance: What do you do when a piece of equipment arrives in a wood-framed box with plastic sides and bottom? Unpack the box, break down each piece, get dressed for the outdoors, and carry the wood and the plastic to separate triple-thickness cardboard bins, called triwalls, at designated places in the Dome. Return to workplace. Remove outerwear. Repeat as necessary.

Because there was so little storage capacity for water, and it took so much energy to make it, rules about its use were strict. Each person could have two two-minute showers per week and wash one load of laundry. You flushed the toilet only when it was necessary. There were four bathrooms in the Dome area. Mine, in Biomed, had the only bathtub in American Antarctica. I imagined that it was originally installed to treat hypothermia, but it was useless for that purpose since the tub rested on the freezing floor and the water quickly became cold. Our hot-water tank held only forty gallons. This bathroom was used by the four Polies living in Biomed, the patients, and anyone in the Dome who needed it. We had one flush toilet and a sink, and there was another flush toilet and a sink in the galley. In the annex dorm, which slept eight, the bathroom was almost too small for one person. There was one toilet, two sinks, and a single shower, but no door. The "upper-berthing" bath, our largest, had two showers, two toilets, and a urinal. This was also the site of the station's sauna, which we visited to warm up after working outside (and which I used to treat mild hypothermia cases).

All bathrooms in the Dome were coed. It took quite a long time for me to get used to sitting on the toilet while watching a man in the urinal beside me. There was a men's and a women's bathroom with a shower in the elevated dorm, for the use of those living "in the suburbs." All other buildings had "pee barrels," barrels with a funnel on top into which you emptied your personal "pee bottle." Tall men could go directly into the funnel, while very agile women learned to hang above them while holding on to overhead pipes or other equipment. There was a communal pee bottle next to each barrel, in case you forgot your own. Pee bottles were whatever could be scavenged. Women liked wide-mouth plastic peanut butter jars. (I willed mine to another female Polie when I was rescued.) Men had more options.

Solid waste had another protocol for disposal, but I will spare you the details. The sewage lines, as well as electrical cables and heating loops, ran under the ice through a network of steel utility corridors called "utilidors." All waste water flowed to "Lake Patterson," an empty water well that was now being slowly refilled. Human waste was the only byproduct not sent back to the States for recycling. It remains on the continent, like a huge Fudgsicle, so to speak.

We stored all our provisions on the roof and around the buildings in the Dome because there was so little inside space. Everything was frozen and covered with frost, which wasn't harmful because conditions were so dry. You just brushed the ice crystals off with your glove. Supply locations were detailed on Mapcon, a complicated inventory-tracking system. Everyone hated the computerized program, but it was necessary to keep a precise record of supplies at such a remote location. Office supplies and—for some unknown reason—entertainment, like puzzles, games, and costumes, were stored on the roof of the hospital, along with ancient medical supplies. I felt like I'd won the lottery the day that I found a small neglected medical whirlpool bath for sprains and strains, amid the clutter.

Food was stashed everywhere. We called taking a sled into a food cache "going shopping." Large items and seasonal equipment were stored on the berms outside, far from the Dome. I was surprised to find Christmas decorations a quarter mile from the base in a box out on the plateau. Wonderful things brought down in the fifties were still there, frozen, waiting to be uncovered by an innovative person.

All supplies and utilities were finite at the Pole. Conceptually, I could understand this, but in time, I came to live it. It was good that we all had less than we could use. It made things more precious and life less messy. Later, I would come to deeply understand that the human resources on the base were also finite. As there were no spare parts for the machines, there were no spare people, either.

When the briefing was over, Will collected me and took me to my bedroom in Biomed. "Just remember," he said with a wink and a grin, "the bedsprings squeak." I had to laugh! I was twenty years older than most of the kids here and hardly expected to worry about squeaking beds. I was more concerned with my pulse ox—the oxygen saturation in my bloodstream. When I checked it was 88 percent—well below the normal 95 to 100 percent. It took a while to adjust to the lack of oxygen at such a high altitude. No one slept well on arrival at Pole. I flopped on my bed, sucking air like a trout in a creel, then fell into a fitful dreamless sleep.

I spent the next five days in intense study with Will. There was so much to learn about the duties and bureaucratic procedures that went with the job, along with what supplies were on hand and how to get to them. Most difficult—and most satisfying—was learning to do the work that I had spent two decades relying on expert technicians and nurses to perform for me. It was back to basics: I had to relearn how to hang IV bags, how to do blood tests the way they were performed by physicians forty years ago, but now in the world, simply sent to a nameless specialist in the lab. I learned to use a blood analyzer and how to sterilize equipment in a terrifying autoclave, a contraption that looked like the washing-machine-of-the-future at the 1939 World's Fair. I experimented with an ancient cauterizer by practicing on a chicken leg. I even developed my own x-rays.

The x-ray machine belonged in a museum for old, balky equipment. It had produced nothing but problems for years. Will had given up at one point and x-rayed extremities using the dental x-ray machine. In fact, most of the medical gadgets seemed to be left over from Vietnam—or in the case of the cauterizer, possibly from the Korean War.

The South Pole station first served as a U.S. Navy installation during the Cold War in the fifties, and the supplies reflected a certain mindset. When Mike Masterman and I were inventorying an emergency cache we realized the Navy must have thought that the Russians were going to march over eight hundred miles of frozen nothingness to get us. Biomed was already running out of antibiotics for the season, but we had enough combat surgical packs to treat a major battle.

Just moving the x-ray machine out of its storage space was a major enterprise. Will let me practice my technique on a frozen sturgeon. I developed the negatives by hand, and did a fair job. Back in the real world I would have called in the radiologist for a better set of images. Unfortunately the nearest radiologist was more than three thousand miles away in New Zealand, and we were dangerously low on film. I was already feeling like a frontier medicine woman, setting up my practice on a vast ice prairie.

In between lessons, we saw patients when they wandered into Biomed. I'm sure Will is still laughing at me for reflexively telling one patient, "The nurse will be with you in a minute." The nearest nurse was my beloved Betty Erickson in McMurdo, 850 miles north. I quickly learned to keep the head of my stethoscope in my bra to avoid giving my patients frostbite when I lifted their three to five layers of clothing. Fully undressing patients was impractical here.

Not that everybody adopted the standard Polie uniform. That afternoon, while Will was showing me how to fill out accident reports, a very large man burst into the exam room dressed in only a T-shirt, leather jacket, shorts, and Sorel rubber-soled pac boots. He was from Southern California, of course.

"Hey, Will!" said Big John Penney. "I'm gonna fly my model airplane tomorrow. Want to come?"

"Oh, great!" said Will. "Hey, come over here and meet the new doctor!"

Will introduced us. Big John was the station's heavy equipment mechanic. After graduating from college he had spent more than a dozen years working on offshore oil rigs. I came to think of him as having lived his life as a sailor without a ship. When the oilfield work slowed down, he had labored "on the yellow iron," heavy equipment. Like me, this was his first time on the Ice. Big John was only average in height but powerfully built and with an enormous presence. He was in his early forties—a "graybeard." Most of the Polies I had seen were kids in their twenties, so I was happy to meet another grown-up who'd be wintering over.

Big John was a passionate builder of radio-controlled model airplanes. He was trying to get into the *Guinness Book of World Records* for the world's coldest model airplane flight. Although it would also be the very first such flight at the South Pole, Big John explained that Guinness would accept only records that could be broken—and "firsts" don't count. Neither would the southernmost flight. But the coldest would qualify. I was now invited as well, and I accepted.

"Way cool," said Big John, slapping Will on the back with a hand hard as a waffle iron. Big John had the countenance of a Viking, the voice of a late-night FM disc jockey, and the vocabulary of an English professor, albeit one who grew up hot-rodding on the West Coast.

"Later, dude." He turned to me. "Nice to meet you, Doc."

That was it: I was now, and forevermore, "the Doc." Before long, I was signing my email letters "Doc Holliday." I soon shortened his name to "Big." Later, Big told me that I had looked very serious that first day, with the concentration of someone new at her job, my blond hair wrapped in a no-nonsense bun, amber-brown eyes peering from behind horn-rimmed glasses. He was somewhat intimidated by the appearance and general aura of a "lady doctor," something that he would later see as funny.

Will did his best to prepare me for what to expect during my tour. Respiratory infections and injuries were widespread. Frostbite was so common that few took off work or even came in from the cold for it! Most people treated it themselves with ChapStick or Neosporin. Then there was Dr. Wennen's Frostbite Cream from Fairbanks, Alaska, of which John Wright, a frostbitten miner we called the Master Blaster, would later ask, "What's this? Snake oil?" We never learned the ingredients, so it may well have been. But it sure worked.

Common medical supplies such as adhesive bandages were useless here. They wouldn't stick. Duct tape sometimes worked, electrical tape was great because it stretched. Nosebleeds were a real problem because of the altitude and low humidity, but silver nitrate turned to powder in this climate. Will stood by and laughed at me while I attempted to mix it into a paste and put it in a guy's nose.

"That's exactly what I tried to do when I first got here!" he giggled. Will was definitely ready for his climbing trip in New Zealand.

There was no cocaine in stock (I guess we weren't to be trusted with it) so I ended up using cardiac epinephrine to stop the bleeding—but then worried about the blood supply to the poor man's nose at minus 30 F. It worked just fine. But I decided that if things got really bad I would cauterize bleeding noses using a surgical instrument heated over an alcohol burner. I was still afraid of the "chicken" cauterizer, vowing never to use it on a human being, or in cooking for that matter. I emailed headquarters for a new one, or at least for the parts to fix the old one.

Summer months were intensely busy because there were so many people to treat. Sometimes I saw fifteen patients day. I was terribly apprehensive for my first three months at the Pole because, on top of my patient load, I wanted to check all my supplies and equipment so I could requisition necessities before the last supply flight in February. I felt someone's life might depend on my ability to complete an inventory.

Meanwhile, I had to absorb everything I could learn from Will before he redeployed. He explained that wounds don't heal well at the South Pole during the months of perpetual sunlight (although they do better in the wintertime, for some mysterious reason). On my first day I saw a woman who broke her fingers while unloading cargo. When she asked to spend the night, I remember telling her that she couldn't be hospitalized, "because she didn't meet criteria for hospitalization."

Will pulled me aside. "What criteria? This is all your show. No hospital utilization committee here, Doc."

It would take me some time to abandon the tenets of third-party-payer medicine that had controlled my life and judgment for so many years. The woman stayed in Biomed where there was a bathroom and I could change her dressings with fresh water.

Two weeks later, when I removed her stitches, the lacerations popped right open. She ended up going to Christchurch to recover. The lower altitude and warm climate in New Zealand restored the healing process and she was able to return before winter. As so often at the Pole, seeing her daily for wound care and physical therapy helped me really get to know her. We would talk while I rubbed her finger wounds with vitamin E oil.

Skin, particularly on the hands, tended to dry out and crack into deep, hard fissures that refused to heal. Will said the only thing that closed them was superglue. I was skeptical at first, since I knew you shouldn't repair broken teeth with superglue because of toxins that could kill the nerve. But I soon learned that Will was right: it worked and did no obvious harm. Like so many problems particular to the Pole, the safety had not been studied but the procedure was taught to each doctor by his or her predecessor. In fact, Big John had developed an enormous fissure on his forefinger, surrounded by thick skin as hard as rhino horn. I had to surgically ablate the dead skin, cut below it to loosen and stretch it and repair the wound, and *then* apply superglue. It finally healed, to my relief. Before long I was emailing my mother to send me boxes of superglue for the winter.

There were other weird medical phenomena: Hair would grow amazingly fast or not at all. I last shaved my legs in Ohio before I headed to the Ice. Weeks later I still had no hair on my legs or underarms, but my fingernails were growing like claws. I had never been able to grow my fingernails. Now they were long, hard, and difficult to cut. My toenails were like talons. Later, in the winter, a mysterious but painless crescent of blood would form under the nails. Friends and patients reported similar strange conditions.

The effects of chronic hypoxia, a syndrome caused by oxygen starvation, and hypothermia at the Pole have never been adequately studied. Since enzymes and coenzymes work properly only at certain temperatures, it would be interesting to find out what happens to the chemical reactions in our bodies when our core temperature never rises above ninety-seven degrees, as seems to be the case here. The little research that has been done shows that metabolisms speed up in constant daylight, while the cold enlarges thyroid and adrenal glands. People become agitated, hyperactive, and easy to anger during the polar summer. With chronic hypoxia and no darkness/light cycles to regulate sleep, some develop the Big Eye syndrome, characterized by insomnia, general disorientation, and memory loss.

An organized study of polar health issues collecting all these medical anomalies would be very useful. But as far as I know, it has never been done. The best survey of physiological changes that I could find was the Navy's *Polar Manual,* last updated in 1965. More recently, Dr. Les Reed led a study of metabolic changes at McMurdo, which was helpful. Still, I always felt like I was reinventing the wheel. I graphed oral temperatures, learning that they were always below normal, even in those who worked indoors. I excitedly mentioned this to Betty, only to learn that this had already been studied and was well known in the McMurdo hospital. This was typical. Betty later sent me the Reed studies. But without a compendium of Antarctic medicine, you only knew what someone remembered to tell you, or what you figured out for yourself. Almost all current data was anecdotal. Just as in tribal times, when healers passed information through oral tradition, symptoms and remedies were transmitted along the polar-medical grapevine from season to season. Soon enough I came up with a plan to form the Antarctic Medical Association and to create a database of information and statistics from all medical officers on the continent. But first I needed to get some rest.

My first day of work ended at 11 p.m. After sending off a few emails, I settled into bed with Will Silva's medical report from the past year at Pole. He had seen 380 cases: an average of three per day during the summer, and .4 per day during the winter months. Will had two medevacs, seven hospitalizations, thirty-five accident/injuries, and three deaths. The deaths were all visiting skydivers who failed to deploy their parachutes. No one would ever know what happened, but it was speculated that the divers passed out, or were dazzled by the featureless white plateau, and lost all sense of depth perception as they plummeted to the ice.

For such an unforgiving place, the Pole has claimed relatively few human lives: five in the past century (although dozens more have died on the continent). Other than the unfortunate skydivers, the last death at the station had been in 1980 when a man was killed shoveling snow from a shaft and the walls caved in on him. Prior to that, in 1966, someone had been crushed to death by a pallet while unloading a cargo plane. Nevertheless, the ancient embalming kit and the collection of over twenty Navy body bags in Biomed gave me shivers. I found and read a file called "decedent affairs" outlining procedures for caring for the deceased in winter. They would be cleaned, packed, and frozen. At the time of station opening in October, the body was to be moved to the freshie shack (we would be out of vegetables by then anyway), where it would be partially thawed but kept cold until the first flight in the spring. Perhaps this was to help investigators examine the body. The manual didn't specify a reason.*

From what I could tell, the statistics were just a matter of luck. The Pole was a dangerous place and the medical system necessarily sparse at the end of the world's pipeline. I would frequently say to my patients, as they looked around my hospital with questioning eyes, "Hey, this isn't the Mayo Clinic."

I hated to think what might happen in case of a major catastrophe here, like a plane wreck or a fire. And during the eight-and-a-half months of winter, when there was no way in or out of the Pole, I would be the only medical officer available. What if something happened to me? A famous story recounted how, in 1961, the doctor at Vostok had operated on himself with a mirror to remove his own appendix. He lived. But ever since then the Russians have staffed their base with two doctors.

The first doctor to reach the Pole died on the way back, in 1912. Edward Wilson, Scott's closest friend, served as the artist, geologist, and physician on both the Terra Nova and the earlier Discovery expedition. He died in the blizzard with Scott and Bowers, so near the cache of supplies that could have saved them. Before Scott froze to death, he wrote to Wilson's wife that right to the end, his friend had "a comfortable blue look of hope" in his eyes.

A framed picture of Wilson hung on the wall in my room. Beside it was a photograph of Frederick Cook, the first physician to winter in Antarctica. I called them, fondly, my dead doctors. I would look at

---

*After I left the Ice, there was another death at the Pole: an Australian astronomer named Rodney Marks, who collapsed and died of unknown causes shortly after station closing. He was only thirty-two years old, a cheerful, brilliant man and a good friend of many of us, including Big John and Will Silva. As of this writing, his body is still at the South Pole, awaiting evacuation in the spring.

them and wonder how different their time here was compared to mine and yet how very similar. They worked alone, caring for their friends with no one to consult and few resources. For them also, there was no way out. They were already becoming a source of inspiration to me.

Meals at the Pole were always a great social occasion, interrupting the monotony of endless days. Food was served buffet style, in a room with rows of modular cafeteria-style tables. The pillars supporting the second floor, where the bar and extra galley were located, had been decorated with intricate rope patterns, perhaps by a sailor who missed the sea during a long-ago winter when the station was new.

The food at the Pole was reputed to be the best in American Antarctica. I had hoped to lose weight but now saw little chance of that. The meals were varied, enormous feasts. One of the cooks was Donna Aldrich, a woman near my age from Vermont. She had come to the Pole with her fiancé, an electrician named Roger Hooker. Her specialty was down-home cooking. Everyone loved her meat loaf and, as Floyd Washington, our genius utilities technician, would so frequently point out, she cooked "food that the guys all recognized." She gave us the comfort food remembered from childhood, stews on cold days, fried chicken, and wonderful roasts.

Wendy Beeler was a younger woman who had learned to be a chef on the Ice. She had already wintered at the coastal station, Palmer, and had worked in remote field camps on the continent. A world traveler from a Peace Corps family, she was a wizard with international and vegetarian fare. She was also a great high-altitude baker.

Being a cook in Antarctica is one of the hardest jobs offered on the Ice. It takes ingenuity to cook for the same people for such a long period of time and still keep meals interesting. Much has to be substituted or made from scratch. It is also a physically demanding and somewhat dangerous job. The food is frozen on pallets within the Dome. Heavy items must be lifted, dragged indoors, thawed, and processed in a small, confined kitchen built to serve far fewer people. I had the pleasure of getting to know both women very well, but unfortunately, it was because they often needed my professional services.

Shortly after I arrived at the Pole, I took a walk on top of the galley. Things were stored out in the open on the roof: pots, pans, mixers, cans of food, entire cows cut up. I counted twenty turkeys. The food was frozen from fifteen to a hundred degrees below zero, depending on the time of year. Humans were the only animals at the South Pole, so there was no risk of vermin. A bug once came in on some transported food, but it promptly died after being kept in a jar with some greens as a pet. Even microbes froze to death or became dormant in this environment.

The second day Will and I took a short break from work to watch Big John fly his model airplane. It was minus 38 F. He launched it on the taxiway in front of the Dome. We cheered as he guided the plane, which had an eighty-five-inch wingspan, into a loop and roll. The little electric plane circled the bottom of the world several times, sailing around the Ceremonial Pole, an actual barber-shop pole topped with a shiny silver ball and ringed with the flags of the nations of the Antarctic Treaty. This was the place where visitors posed for their "hero shots" to commemorate their trip to the South Pole. The actual, geographic pole, yards away, was marked by a brass plaque that is moved annually, to correct for the flow of the ice.

Big John's flight lasted five minutes and forty seconds and was duly documented for the Guinness record book. Unfortunately, on the landing approach, the plane flew too close to the elevated dorm, which is festooned with high-energy radio transmitters. They overpowered the radio receiver on the plane, and Big John lost control. The plane crashed into the ice, nose first. Big looked anguished, as if a friend had broken his arms and was writhing in pain. Big John believed that machines had souls, which is why he had such a magic touch with them. I tried to console him, and he quickly cheered up. It was still a record-setting flight, and there would be many months to repair the damage to the stricken plane. Will and I helped him gather up the pieces, and then we went back to work.

Along with his many other talents, Will Silva was a skilled violinist who had brought his instrument to the Ice. One night before he left the Pole he performed a Bach solo in the galley after dinner. There he introduced me to Dorianne Galarnyk, a cook who would be wintering with me. We sat together and talked. She was thirty-eight and from Wisconsin, where her father was a doctor. She liked medicine and wanted to be my assistant during her time off from her job in the galley, an offer I quickly accepted. She had a fistful of education and literature degrees from the University of Wisconsin and had taught for a while at Cornell. Like so many Polies, she had signed up as a laborer just to experience Antarctica.

Dorianne quickly became my best friend that summer. She made me laugh, and I like to laugh. She was a tender sort of person—very kind and spirited, but disappointed with her job in the galley. She had not been warned about the huge workload and the regimented hours. I spent time trying to convince her that we would have a splendid winter together, but I suspect she had already made up her mind to leave. Dorianne managed to make her disgruntlement seem like dinner theater. It was she who pointed out to me that on a desktop globe, Antarctica was the place where they put the screw. Her concept of marriage, she would say, was "for better, or until it gets worse." But in fact, she was in love with a man back home, and her longing for him was pulling her back to the world.

Dorianne was a great social organizer, and through her I got to know some of the people who would become my closest friends at Pole. We had a group who volunteered to work during the summer months in the station's greenhouse (where the only viable nonhuman life-forms at the South Pole could be seen, enjoyed, and later eaten).

Loree Galpin was a friend of Dorianne's who soon became a close friend of mine. In her early twenties, she came to the Pole as a meteorologist after doing similar work in the Air Force. She had a great interest in the Orient, particularly Asian literature, and planned to teach English in Japan when she left the Ice. We women would spend evenings in her room, covered in a wonderfully warm, soft comforter that she obtained during a tour in Korea. Here was one of the few places at the Pole where we actually felt warm, and we spent hours talking and getting to know each other. Loree was very smart and good natured, never saying an unkind thing to anyone. There was a strong spiritual side to her. She was very pretty but seemed oblivious to the obvious interest in her from a number of the guys at the Pole.

Andy Clarke was Loree's closest friend. He was a tall, slender thirty-something man with reddish hair and a wide-open smile and a wry sense of humor. Andy worked as a science technician for the National Oceanographic and Atmospheric Administration, or NOAA. All of the researchers in Antarctica were called "beakers," and Andy referred to himself as a "blue-collar beaker"—like a noncommissioned officer, as the old saw goes, he worked for a living instead of giving orders. He had spent time in other interesting weather installations, including ones in Barrow, Alaska, and Greenland. He knew what it meant to live in the cold and dark and came well prepared. I bought a great Alaskan beaver hat from him, which he had brought to the Ice to sell to less-seasoned Polies. He enjoyed most things and all outdoor sports. He even found a bicycle that he mounted on blocks to exercise on through the winter. I wondered what a bike was doing at the South Pole, but we were always finding strange, incongruous things stashed away.

Joel Michalski became another close friend. A physicist by training, he went to the Pole in a management capacity, as the NOAA officer. He was in charge of the Atmospheric Research Observatory, known as the "clean air facility," where he and Andy studied gases that affect global climate change. Joel, also from Wisconsin, had spent a lot of time on ocean research vessels. He promised to teach me to use a sextant and to disco dance, which was his favorite pastime. Most Polies seemed to have multiple interests and talents. In his time off work, Joel liked to draw, read, practice yoga, and write a weekly newsletter to school kids back in the States. He even learned to play the banjo during his year at Pole and performed in an old-time music band.

The other meteorologist in the crew was twenty-six-year-old Dar Gibson, the "Weatherboy." He was very precise, which made him good at collecting and collating data. But it made him nuts that I consistently misspelled *meteorologist* in my computer records. Every time I brought up his file, he would ask me if I had fixed it. After the third time, I showed him the screen and let him see that he had now become, officially, the station's "weatherboy." We all laughed and he was forever known by his new name.

Every morning at ten or eleven o'clock Dorianne and I would walk two or three miles around the base and talk. We learned to tell time by where the sun was in the sky, circling above us in a perfect, small, clocklike orbit. In the morning it was in front of the Dome, and at night behind the rear door. There were very few places to actually walk *to* at the South Pole. The plateau was so flat and uniform, 360 degrees of empty horizon, that going anywhere felt like sailing on the open ocean, miles and miles from landfall. The ice itself was carved into waves by the wind. The forms, called sastrugi, were as beautiful and hard as marble. The different size waves of ice produced musical notes when struck, like glasses of water hit with a spoon. We would lie on the ice and look at the sky. Mostly we laughed and laughed for no reason, or every reason. It may have been our oxygen-starved brains, or changes in the adrenal hormone level that have been noted in the summer months. But being at the Pole was exhilarating enough. Living at the edge of your senses, in such an extreme environment, makes life's simple joys more intense.

We would pick different destinations each day: the end of the runway; the shell of an LC-130 that had crashed in the eighties and been buried by blowing snow; a partially constructed igloo, the summer project of a Polie from Alaska, now a warm place out of the wind where you could look up through the roof at the blue sky and feel a quiet so complete you could hear the blood slowly coursing through your veins.

The funny thing about the Pole was how quickly you came to accept it as your home. You didn't think about the fact that you were at the bottom of the earth and that this was the coldest, the most hostile environment imaginable. You just thought, *Oh, I'm going for a walk today.* Or, *Oh, there's my friend with ice over his entire face, his eyelids are frozen shut, he's got icicles hanging from his mouth. Doesn't he look great?*

Neither of us was acclimated to Antarctica when we began our walks, but I was getting into it faster than Dorianne. She was always cold. I couldn't imagine how she was going to get through the winter, because she was already wearing all of her layers in the middle of summer. One day it was probably minus 20 F. when Dorianne and I were taking a walk to Summer Camp. The wind picked up and she wheeled around and said, "Oh my *God*, it's *cold!*" She looked at me incredulously, like she couldn't believe it was happening. "What the heck is *this* about?"

I looked back at her and said, "Dorianne, it's *An*-fucking-*arctica!*"

We both started laughing and couldn't stop. We really had forgotten where we were. From then on, when anything screwed up at work or annoyed us, that's how we referred to the place. Interestingly, when my housemate Liza Lobe, an Alaskan bush pilot with months of Ice time and who had already wintered at Pole, heard me say "An-fucking-arctica" one time, she gave me a funny look.

"What?" I said. "It's a joke."

"I wish you wouldn't talk like that about the Pole," she said. "It's my home."

I didn't get it. I thought, Well, it's my home too, and I like it, but it doesn't seem so sacred. Later, I would remember what Liza was trying to say to me when the Ice truly became my home

Meanwhile, as Will packed up to leave, I started to wonder if I hadn't made a huge mistake coming to the Pole. I felt I had been misled about the workload and about the nature of the job. It was so much more than I had expected, and it never, ever ended.

From: Jerri Nielsen
To: Mom and Dad
Date: 24 Nov. 1998 12:46:57 +1200

Dearest all,

It is late and I am so tired all the time that I can hardly cope.
My pulse ox is up to 90 now. We are all very slow moving
here and tired as we are hypoxic, hypothermic, and weighted
down with clothing.

Today I finished work at midnight. The amount of data that
I must learn in a hypoxic state is staggering, and all the
while people keep coming in with their fingers cut off and
whatever.

Basically, I totally run a hospital. I wash it all down, keep a
running inventory and monthly reports on just about everything on a computer that I can't yet run. I have to scrub the
floors and wash all the surgical drapes and sheets and blankets
and towels in the washing machine. Make the beds. When a
patient comes in, and they do in groups all day, I have to find
the chart, do the vitals, do the history and physical, chart
everything, play pharmacy. Write down what I gave them and
take it off a central roster, count the pills, put them in a bag,
label them. Then do all kinds of accounting.

When I fix a crushed hand, as I did today, I undress the
patient myself (ten layers of extreme weather gear), get out
all the equipment, examine, suture, reduce the fracture as
usual. Then I get out an alcohol lamp and paper clip to
drain the hematoma under the nail, then get the meds out of
the cupboard myself, write it all down, give them water,
wash the bloody gloves they were using, take them to the x-
ray, get out film, look up the exposure, take the x-ray, then
go to the darkroom. I spend 15 minutes in the darkroom,

praying, then take the films to the dryer, dry them. Then read them, then dress the wounds, and splint them. Completely dress my patient (ten layers). Then do more charting. Take all my used materials, put them in four different recycle waste containers, carry them outside (34 below zero) to the central bins (after dressing myself in ten more layers). Scrub all my instruments with a toothbrush in solution that I had to look up how to make. Put them all in a new clean suture kit that I make up, make ionized water with a big machine in someone's bedroom, looking up that procedure also. Then, put it with other goodies I made up in an autoclave, which is like a big pressure cooker and just as scary. And cook the suckers. And then I am done with that patient.

Next!

This must be what it was like crossing the prairie in the winter in a wagon train. The medical care couldn't be much different than my one-man show. Except for the autoclave.

Love you all,
Byrd, Doctor of perpetual sunlight

I was exaggerating about the ten layers of clothing. It was five, max.

My fear of the autoclave arose from fear of pressure cookers. Growing up in the Ohio dairy farm region, my friends and I would be chased from the kitchen by our grandmothers during canning time. The reason: the pressure cooker was on and it could blow up any minute. My autoclave sounded just like Mrs. Krizay's (my neighbor's Yugoslavian grandmother) cooker and seemed to accomplish the same thing. She had used hers for years and made us play outside in the barnyard every time it was on the stove. She was old and knew about such things.

Eventually I would lose my fear of mechanical things while here, but I was not yet ready.

My mother finally figured out how to use email, and I started getting news from home. In one letter, Mom asked if I'd heard that the president had been impeached. Not only had I not heard, but since we didn't get TV or radio broadcasts, I had to think to myself: what president?

One piece of news from the world was very welcome, indeed: My father's test results came back negative for advancing cancer. He was already healing from the complications of his surgeries, and it seemed more and more likely that he would fully recover. It was a tremendous relief to all of us in the family. Our father was the rock, the foundation on which we built our values and our lives. Life without him was unimaginable.

Suddenly one day, Will proclaimed me ready to go on my own. He could get out before the cargo flights stopped for Thanksgiving break if he left tomorrow. We did our last big job together, the transfer over of narcotics, in what was now my room, while playing Bach on the stereo . . . loud.

When we were finished he walked to the door and said formally, "Rodney and I have been hoarding the last two pints of Guinness since midwinter for a special occasion like this. The occasion is that this is my last night at Pole."

Will wanted to spend the evening with his great friend and last remaining crewmate, Rodney Marks, a witty astronomer from Australia. I was not invited. I was part of the new winterover team, they were the last remnants of the old. Will and I were both physicians, but only those who had wintered at Pole were his true colleagues. I had not yet earned the right to be his equal, but the baton had been passed.

CHAPTER 4:

The Hard Truth
Medical Centre

From: Jerri Nielsen
To: Mom and Dad
Date: Dec. 13 1998 00:59:35 +1200
Subject: Another day

This place is like a space station or like a penal colony on an ice planet. I can't tell which. It is without time, without days or nights, and without any sense of being on the earth . . .

Doc Holliday

On Thanksgiving Day we all piled into the TV lounge to watch football games that had been taped weeks ago and shipped from the States. Nobody seemed to mind. The holiday dinner was truly magical and most civilized. Turkey was served with all the trimmings on tables covered in white linen. Wine was poured in crystal glasses. After dinner we danced to lively Spanish music and toasted each other's toughness and wisdom.

It was always customary for Polies to dress up in their best clothes on special occasions. For men that meant shirts with buttons and collars. Women, who were first allowed to work at the Pole in 1973, generally wore skirts or sarongs. I thought the Polie women who told me to bring pretty clothes were joking. Now I was happy that I had thrown a few dresses into my suitcase, along with a lipstick and a slinky silver blouse I added at the last minute, at the expense of extra fleece undergarments. In McMurdo my friend Mandy had given me glow-in-the-dark nail polish when I left for the Pole. She kissed me and said, "You Polie women are going to need this during the dark winter. But be careful—I used it on my toes once, got up in the night, and scared myself."

Getting cleaned up on occasion was a good morale-booster. Most of the time we looked like refugees from a NASCAR grease pit. Our hair and clothing were dirty due to water rationing. Anything torn or tattered couldn't be replaced, so our overalls and boots were held together with duct tape. When my shearling boots finally went south I stitched them up with a large abdominal needle and surgical catgut. On the other hand, a newly arrived English scientist wore a tweed jacket and white shirt every day. No one could help but stare at him. One day Joel, the dancing NOAA officer, remarked, "He must have gone through the wrong door on the wrong bus."

"If your travel plans do not include the South Pole," I added, "you should disembark this aircraft immediately."

Nigel the Brit was one of the people whose company I sought at the dinner table, as he and his fellow astronomer, Al, were so smart and funny. He wasn't about to abandon his English attire just because he had fallen off the edge of the world. He made me think of the Victorian empire-builders bringing their customs with them, for better or worse, over the globe.

Formal dining to mark time had been a tradition on the Ice since the British explorers arrived in Antarctica. The high point of this custom was Scott's famous solstice party in 1911, when his men dined on seal soup, roast beef, plum pudding, and vintage Champagne. The feast was followed by liqueurs and brandy, voluminous toasts, speeches, and loud, manly singing.

We did our best to honor these traditions by faithfully celebrating all holidays, and inventing some of our own. The Friday after Thanksgiving marked my introduction to another hallowed polar ritual: slushies. Every Friday since the 1970s, when NOAA erected a building to monitor atmospheric conditions upwind of the Dome, Polies have made a weekly pilgrimage out to the Clean Air Facility. There, the purest snow on earth is shoveled into a cooler and brought inside for the devotees to scoop into glasses and soak with their favorite beverages, which ranged from Coca-Cola to Bailey's Irish Cream to Wild Turkey. Since I was basically on call twenty-four hours a day, I did not feel free to fully indulge in this polar practice, but it was fun to relax and talk and laugh after a hard week's work. Joel loved disco music and was a great dancer, so as the NOAA officer, and therefore the host, he turned slushies into a disco dance party.

Soon after Will's departure, a string of visitors started arriving from MacTown. Some were medical staff who came to train me on particular items of equipment, others just came to visit. I felt it was my job to entertain them, so I would take them around the station and bring them to social gatherings. Once a delightful chaplain I met at McMurdo came to visit and, because of bad weather, was stuck at Pole for the weekend. I figured that just because he was a preacher he shouldn't miss out on one of the most famous of polar traditions. I told him where and when to meet me. When he didn't show up on time, I had him paged on the All-Call. Officially, the system was supposed to be used only for emergencies, or for official announcements, such as "Aircraft on deck, please clear the skiway" or "Attention South Pole! The fire team will meet at thirteen hundred hours." But often, particularly on Friday or Saturday nights, the overhead address system was more like the loudspeaker in *M*A*S*H*. That night everyone broke up laughing when they heard: "Pastor Dave, you are late to slushies. Call 249, Pastor Dave!" The announcement certainly attracted the chaplain's attention, and he seemed to enjoy his Pepsi served over the cleanest snow on earth.

Unfortunately, later that summer, some partiers got so raucous that for the first time in South Pole history, the SPAM canceled slushies for the season. Alcohol and altitude are not a great combination. The effects of drinking are magnified in the thin air. This, I suspect, was the cause of my first medical emergency at the South Pole.

Let me start by saying that it was a great party, the first real bash of summer, hosted by Big John and some friends in the heavy machinery shop. They covered the floor with sawdust, hung an orange-and-white parachute from the ceiling, and built a large bandstand behind chicken wire for a Texas-roadhouse feel. We danced to a terrific thirteen-piece all-polar rock band called "You Guys Suck." Paul Anthony Kindl, a thirty-five-year-old electrician from upstate New York who became known as Pakman, was the only winterover in the band. By this time, I knew that the Pak and I would some day be great friends. He had a special spark. He wore an enormous striped top hat and sang rock 'n' roll while he worked. He also played the bass quite well, and the band rocked all night. Everyone crowded onto the dance floor, with women usually dancing with two or three guys at once due to our unusual population pool here.

A barbecue of burgers and bratwurst was served. I donated the large white Styrofoam boxes that had transported medications to the Pole as coolers—to keep the beer from freezing. A contest was held to name the new CAT tractor that dragged snow to keep our ice runway smooth and flat. Halo Bob, aka Bob Gleenler, a beaker who researched the halos that sometimes surround the polar sun, won the prize by dubbing it the Drag Queen.

I was one of ten designated sober people on the trauma team, standing by, ready for trouble that never came. Until the next day.

That afternoon, I took Scott Jones, the dentist from Mactown who came to give me further training in dentistry, to meet the astronomers out by the telescopes. He had spent the past five days teaching me how to use my army-field-camp dental equipment and how to extract teeth, wire jaws, take and develop dental x-rays, and improve my root canal techniques. I remember my first dental patient watching me while I fiddled with the dental drill. I asked, "Are you afraid of dentists?"

"Yes," she answered.

"Don't worry," I reassured her cheerily. "I'm not one."

Scott and I walked to the cluster of telescope buildings in the "dark sector" of the base, the quarter mile away from the Dome, where astronomers probed the secrets of deep space. We were standing on the roof of the AS/TRO telescope when I got an All-Call. This one didn't sound like the others.

"Jerri Nielsen, call Comms, Jerri Nielsen, call Comms. Mike Masterman, call Comms . . ."

Mike functioned as "incident command," the man in charge if anything went seriously wrong. Paging us both at the same time was ominous. I tried to call in but the telephone line to our communications center was busy, so I radioed that I was walking back to the Dome.

Minutes later I saw a snowmobile speeding toward me over the ice. All I could make out was a flash of red, trailed by a white plume of snow, and a maniac seemed to be driving. When it got closer I could see that the driver was no ordinary maniac, but Mike himself, because he always wore a distinctive wool hat with braids down the side. Mike had been a fireman and had driven ambulances in West Virginia. Now he had that we-are-going-to-a-fire look in his eyes, the only part of him that I could see. He pulled up and without a word, I jumped on. It was a ride to end all rides. We were airborne, skimming the tops of sastrugi. I grabbed him as tightly around the waist as I could and held on. The cold froze my face solid, so I buried it in the down of his parka and looked out the corner of my eye to watch for bumps. Halfway there he told me that someone had had a seizure in Summer Camp.

As soon as we arrived I knew the whole story at once, just by seeing who my patient was. It was Nelson,* Big John's partner in the Heavy Shop and his best friend on the Ice. Nelson once told me he'd injured his head in a motorcycle accident years ago and had suffered

---

*who asked that his name be changed.

from seizures since then—although not in the past ten years. Still, I'd
been surprised that he was medically cleared for the Pole. After the
party he had been hungover, hungry, and dehydrated, and that combination probably caused the seizure. He had also recently changed
medication.

We found him lying on his bed in a post-ictal condition, a state of
confusion and flat affect that occurs after a seizure. He was talking
with other members of the trauma team, who were already evaluating
him and preparing him for transport. During the summer we had two
vans for moving people and for emergencies. We carried Nelson into
one of these and rode together to the Dome.

We got him to Biomed, where everything went amazingly well.
The trauma team worked together as if they had been at it for years. I
hung an IV without a nurse for the first time in my life! Strange
things like the fact that the floor was uneven and the instrument stand
took off across the room at high speed was just "South Pole." I had
already come to expect it.

Unfortunately, my patient's days on the Ice were over. We couldn't
risk another seizure. A plane arrived to take him to McMurdo and on
to New Zealand. We packed him up in an Army sleeping bag, tied
him on a Stokes stretcher, and carried him out of the Dome like pall-
bearers to the big Hercules aircraft.

Big John was devastated. I stayed up talking to him until two in
the morning. Big recounted how he'd had to pack his friend's gear for
him. "One of the toughest things I've ever had to do," said Big. "I
don't even like packing my own stuff, let alone someone else's." He
packed his friend's clothes, books, the unopened Christmas presents
from his wife. Then he ran across Clifford, a huge red stuffed dog
given to Nelson by a grade-school class back in the U.S. to include in
pictures he took in the locales he visited.

"I knew that Nelson hadn't taken any pictures of Clifford since
he'd arrived here," Big said. "So I got busy." All day, while I was
watching over Nelson in my hospital, Big had been racing around the
South Pole with his friend's camera and a stuffed cartoon dog. He

snapped pictures of Clifford on the Drag Queen, on a snowmobile, at the geographic and ceremonial Poles, at the entrance to the Dome, and a dozen other places. He put the film in his friend's hand before we carried him away.

Big man. Bigger heart. John Penney would definitely have been the most eligible bachelor at the Pole except for one thing: He was married. His wife was back home, living in the same town as his parents, just as she had all the years he'd been away on the oil rigs. It was not such an unusual marriage for a Polie. Very little about any of us was conventional. If there were, we wouldn't be here.

It was part of my job to tend to the emotional and psychological health of my colleagues. I spent a lot of time thinking about what type of person goes to the Ice. Many people here spend October through February at Pole and then follow the sun north to Greenland or Alaska. They are looking for a frontier when so little is left. Someone told me, "Here you don't ask people where they are from, you ask them where their storage unit is." By now we had all heard the famous polar adage: "The first year you come for the adventure. The second year you come for the money. The third year you come because you don't fit anywhere else."

I found the most interesting reading on the subject in a thirty-five-year-old Navy *Polar Manual,* which contends that motivation is the most important factor when selecting a crew for a polar expedition. The author divides the pool of applicants into five types: He likes men (there were no women at the Poles in those days) who "go with a specific interest, to be professional explorers, for scientific research, or the adventurous . . . type who has to go 'just because it is there.' Less desirable because they are easily disillusioned are the idealists, the ambitious, and the glory-seekers."

His second category is the "escape artist" who signs up to "evade family troubles with sweethearts, wives, or in-laws." Others go to escape financial or family responsibilities, or jobs they hate. This type "is either a good man or almost totally useless on the Ice."

There are also the "money savers," and "drifters" who go because they have nothing better to do at the moment. Either can be a good man "because the charms of isolation and beauty of polar regions puts reason in his being."

"Least desirable" and "most dangerous to themselves and others" are "martyrs, sadists, homosexuals" (this, again, was the early sixties), those with strong subconscious suicidal or masochistic complexes, "to whom a rugged life of isolation sometimes appeals."

The author concludes that the happiest candidate for the Ice is a type of escape artist—"the rugged individualist who finds modern urban life intolerable with its TV and newspapers, . . . world crises and crime. . . . Many men who have never met the Almighty in church meet him occasionally at the operating or delivery table, but really get to know him at the ends of the earth."

I wondered where I fit into the equation. Was I the escape artist or the adventurer? Maybe a bit of both, with some martyr thrown in for danger.

A few weeks after I arrived at the Pole, my hospital—previously called "Club Med"—was renamed "The Hard Truth Medical Centre." It happened after I examined one Polie—who shall remain anonymous—when he came in with an assortment of nonspecific symptoms. Basically, he felt lousy.

"Doc, what's wrong with me?" he asked. After talking to him for about an hour and completing a full physical examination, I was quite sure of the diagnosis. It was not leukemia or anemia, as he had thought.

"You drink too much."

He looked at me for a second, and blinked. "Jeez," he said. "You get nothing but the hard truth around here . . ."

Someone even made an official-looking sign for the door of Biomed: THE HARD TRUTH MEDICAL CENTRE.

Like any new tenant, I quickly started reorganizing the exam room and hung packets of emergency medical supplies on the wall, clearly labeled, so that I could access everything instantly, and so could anyone else if I wasn't there. I was getting used to the equipment, including the intimidating autoclave, and I now had neat little packs of very clean objects lying out all over the hospital. It reminded me of canning summer vegetables and the pleasure of a well-stocked larder.

My first solo CBC (complete blood count), done as it was done in the old days, took me two hours. I used a round metal wheel calibrated like an old-fashioned slide rule with a capillary tube for the hematocrit. I spun the plasma in a centrifuge, then laid it on a grid and counted the number of white blood cells. There were other, even more time-consuming steps to the CBC.

If I didn't have a medication, I sometimes made it. I enjoyed mixing up preparations, stirring my potions like some sort of sorceress. I made Cleocin (an antibiotic) gel and a 10 percent hydrocortisone cream to put topically on tendons. Those drugs were in stock, but not in the form I needed. I made a heel cup to treat heel spurs with a Kotex. I came to regard sanitary napkins in a new light; they were good for many things, including use as bandages. They were so good I added them to my apocalyptic medical cache in the emergency power plant that would serve as my medical center if the Dome burned.

Gynecology was another challenge. Since I couldn't find a speculum or stirrups, I improvised. I wrapped a metal wash tub in an Army blanket, put it in a pillowcase, and set my patient's butt on that. I did a pelvic exam with two kitchen spoons—and two women guarding the doors to Biomed.

Once in a while I could sneak away from Biomed to hide in Joel's room so that I could read a few chapters in *High Altitude Medicine,* a book that Will had sold to me before he left, to find out more about human physiology at ten thousand feet and beyond. Humans at the South Pole experience a phenomenon called "physiologic altitude." The centrifugal force of the earth's rotation causes the atmosphere to bulge at the equator and flatten at the poles. The mass of air at the equator weighs more than the air mass closer to the Poles, which means the atmosphere is thinner and lighter at the South Pole, ninety-three hundred feet above sea level, than at an equivalent altitude in North America, such as the eastern slope of the Sierra Nevada Range.

Lower barometric pressure decreases the blood's absorption of oxygen and can make the body respond as though the altitude is higher than it actually is. If a low-pressure system moves over the Pole, the physiologic altitude can climb to twelve thousand feet and more. When that happens most people suffer lassitude, decreased concentration, poor sleep, and sometimes nausea—the classic signs of mild mountain sickness. There are other symptoms as well: According to a study of climbers on Mount Everest, vision begins to decrease at five thousand to eight thousand feet; and conceptual reasoning goes at twelve thousand feet. Long-term effects are unknown.

It was interesting to see how much of this I had worked out by myself. It was like when I was little and figured out that the continents had all been connected at one time. It was disappointing to learn that someone had already thought of that, but cool that someone agreed with me. Again I was thriving in an environment that encouraged me—actually required me—to think.

Thinking was not particularly welcomed back in the world, and certainly not in the world of corporate medicine. So much of what I had done I call "reflex" medicine. We learned to memorize and think in "treatment pathways." In the fast pace of emergency medicine, this can be life saving, but it also precludes creative thinking, sending the physician to the most likely, but not necessarily correct explanation. Often I had been thankful for the time I'd spent during my training with old family doctors, the ones who'd taught me the little tricks and shared methods of treatment from another time.

One doctor who taught me surgery had been a missionary in India, along with his wife, who was an ob-gyn. The stories he told about how they managed to practice medicine in the Third World were part of my inspiration to work overseas. The old surgeon told me how he made retractors to open up body cavities with wire coat hangers and used spoons to make dissectors for slicing through tissue planes. Instead of cutting tissue, he had to separate it to reduce bleeding because there was no blood bank at his rural hospital.

Seemingly archaic information of this kind often came back to me as I tried to think of alternatives when my familiar high-tech response was not available. I was so glad that I had learned medicine before the advent of the CAT scan. Here, at the Pole, I was learning all kinds of things by trial and, thankfully, very few errors.

Health care was not my only job at the South Pole station. My other official titles were "storekeeper" and "postmaster." The doctor ran the store and post office two nights a week during winter and kept their books and inventory. All staffers had to take turns as "house mouse," helping out in the galley, cleaning, and busing tables. On weekends, when the cooks had time off, we had to prepare the meals as well. I was not exempt. Actually I welcomed the chance to do different things and get to know the people I would be treating. I spent one Saturday night making pizzas, cleaning up, and listening to some CDs I had brought from home.

The next day a visiting woman scientist walked into Biomed, vomiting and complaining of headache. She had been on the Ice for only two days, and she was convinced the food and the Willie Nelson music had made her sick! She had no idea her doctor was the country music fan who had made pizza for two hundred last night. I still think her problem was altitude sickness.

On top of my usual workload, I made a point of trying to attend as many lectures and social events as possible. One Sunday night the science lecture was "The South Pole and the Universe." The universe was a big topic down here.

There are stories in the ice and the sky—and scientists come to Antarctica to find narratives in the raw materials of our untouched world. Ice cores drilled at Vostok have revealed all the major climatic events since before the beginning of history. In the Dry Valleys, near McMurdo, where it hasn't rained in a million years, lakes formed by melted ice hold microscopic life forms unlike anything else on earth.

Hundreds of science projects were being conducted in Antarctica, but only nineteen of them were at the South Pole while I was there. You had to have a very good reason for studying something at this unique, remote station. And there were some passionate and eccentric scientists on our team. I went to slushies one Friday night with an analytical chemist who was so excited by the sulfur he had found in the ice that he was screaming, laughing, and jumping up and down. Apparently sulfides get trapped in ice after volcanic eruptions, and this allows scientists to date the samples.

Some of my best friends were beakers. Greg Griffin, a tall man in his late twenties, also known as Giant Greg, was a brilliant astronomer who was searching for the origins of the universe through the lens of the VIPER telescope at the Pole. I met Greg the first week when touring the three different telescopes out on the plateau. Analyzing cosmic background radiation to find the heat left over from the Big Bang, he was looking for differences of around a millionth of a degree or so in the temperature of celestial objects. Greg explained investigations of the Big Bang to me in a way I had never heard before. He understood it with such extraordinary depth that he could casually explain his research to someone out of his field. He encouraged me to think of temperature as color, explaining that for years the earliest universe looked, to astronomers, like a white sheet. "The universe sent us a twelve-billion-year-old message in a bottle and, when we popped the cork, there was just a blank piece of paper," said Greg. But in the past decade, he said, scientists had found incredibly subtle variations in the temperature of the primordial universe, and Greg was using those variations to try to read the message in the bottle.

Giant Greg was also a great jokester and fun to be around. He worked at the VIPER scope with "Middle John" Davis who, at sixty-one, was the oldest Polie in the winterover crew. Middle John, a scientist/mechanic who maintained the telescopes, had been a schoolteacher in Barrow, Alaska, and would tell us stories of whale hunts and isolation at the other end of the world. When he wasn't on the Ice, he lived on a farm in Indiana with his wife, Peggy.

AMANDA was the acronym for another experiment (the Antarctic Muon and Neutrino Detector). This one didn't look up at the sky but down into the ice beneath our boots. As Nuclear Nick Starinski, our resident Ukrainian-Canadian nuclear physicist, explained it, AMANDA was an array of more than four hundred holes melted into the ice, some more than two kilometers deep, into which were lowered strings of "photomultiplier bubbles." This array was located at the South Pole because the physicists were interested in studying neutrinos, subatomic particles that were minute enough to pass through the iron core of the earth. The sensors picked up muons—bursts of blue light emitted when neutrinos interacted with ice, which gave the scientists information about the nature of the particles and perhaps the Big Bang where they may have originated.

The other nuclear physicist on AMANDA was Bai Xinhua. He was from Beijing, where he was married to a dentist and had a small child. When he undertook the year of isolation at the Pole, he was isolated from his family not only by distance, but also from the others at Pole by a language barrier. I can't imagine the courage he had to muster for this mission.

The beakers all worked under the auspices of NOAA or the NSF, which was the lead U.S. agency on Antarctica. Their salaries and living allowances came from grant money. The ASA staff of maintenance people, mechanics, cooks, and one doctor accompanied them "to support science." But despite the importance of the research at Pole, no one here could forget that the station stood at the very end of the pipeline for all supplies. Our cramped, ramshackle facilities, the outmoded equipment, and the lack of spare parts sometimes made us feel less than significant. It was simply life on the frontier and we expected shortages and problems.

If something broke, particularly in winter, we simply had to fix it or make a new one. Spares were nonexistent. The medical shortages were frightening: We were already out of large x-ray film, and so was McMurdo. We had no ultrasound machine, and I begged for Mactown's old one as soon as they got a new one. Although welders and carpenters were grinding metal every day, I had no slit lamp to remove shards from their eyes. Fortunately, however, the pharmacy was surprisingly complete.

I was constantly bartering with visiting medical staff or sending and receiving goods through "Guard Mail," a system whereby you gave Navy or Air Guard guys a large bag of cookies and they hand-delivered goods to or from friends in McMurdo. There were other techniques for obtaining supplies. If patients didn't use all of their medication, I would barter to get it back. I traded a pillow to one guy for what was left of his cough syrup. There was a continent-wide black market for essential goods.

Well-traveled people told me the South Pole was a lot like Russia. It reminded me of *Mir,* the ancient, ailing space station hurtling through the heavens on the perpetual edge of calamity. There was a big difference, though, between *Mir* and the Amundsen-Scott South Pole Station. If a life-threatening emergency occurred in space, the cosmonauts could conceivably be rescued by a shuttle mission. But no one has yet invented a craft that can survive a winter visit to the South Pole. For eight and a half months each year, there is simply no way in or out.

The spare parts problem affirmed my reverence for people who could fix things. At the Pole the sorcerers of material innovation were known as utility technicians, or UTs. My housemate, Ken Lobe, was one of these geniuses. He was a wonderful craftsman and a former lab tech in Vietnam who worked as an Alaskan bush pilot when not on the Ice.

Floyd Washington, also a UT, liked to describe himself as the world's most southerly black man. He was so good at his work that, to convince him to stay on for the winter, ASA flew him back to the U.S. to visit his folks in Virginia, tie up his business, and collect his Nintendo Play Station. Floyd had learned his job in the Navy, and I knew he could fix anything when he actually rebuilt the tumblers in the lock to my drug safe. Floyd preferred playing Nintendo and surfing the Net to parties. "Solitude is not the same as loneliness," he explained. But he shared his sharp sense of humor weekly in his station newsletter, *South Pole at a Glance*. Polies would wait around the galley on Sunday afternoon, when he distributed his paper, to see which of their dark secrets had been uncovered. Sometimes the revelations were stingingly accurate. This is one of my favorite items, typical of Floyd's writing:

> *Yea though I live in the land of semi-eternal*
>   *darkness,*
> *I shall fear no mechanical breakdown.*
> *Utility Technicians and their tools protect me.*
> *Glycol and furnaces warm me all the days of my*
>   *time here,*
> *Well, almost all the time.*
> *They lead me through the utilidor, where green*
>   *pastures*
> *Would be if we had dirt here.*
> *They will anoint my head with blows from a dead*
>   *blow hammer*
> *If I make extra work for them.*
> *They are there when my toilet runs*
>   *over.*
> *Surely my days will be blessed if I do not*
>   *piss them off.*

Despite its dangers and its dilapidated condition, I was already fond of the Pole and the place we all called "Dome Sweet Dome." It was sad to think it would be abandoned in 2005, when a new, larger facility was due to be completed. The Dome was to be dismantled and shipped back to the USA for use as a museum or storage facility, so there was no need to spend money fixing up something that was doomed. A new station was being built piece by piece alongside the existing one, and the race was on to bring the huge project in on time and within budget. In the past year, the South Pole had transformed from a sleepy research station to a polar construction work camp. Most of the supply flights to the Pole—which were possible only from late October to mid-February in any case—were now dedicated to hauling construction equipment and materials. Anything else was considered of secondary importance, including, as we would soon learn, the fuel needed to power the station through the winter.

The additional construction crew strained the capacity of everything at Pole, from the sewage system to sick bay. The specific mission for our season on the Ice (outside of "supporting science") was to erect a new garage arch and shop for servicing heavy machinery. The work was dangerous under the best of conditions in the outside world; at the Pole it was treacherous. Coming from a family of builders, I had a special place in my heart for the carpenters building the garage arch. They scared the wits out of me every time I bundled up to do walk-throughs of the construction site.

I remember ruminating about what to be when I grew up. My dad said, "Make sure it's a job where you can come in out of the cold." Winter was what he didn't like about his work as a builder. I thought of him as I watched carpenters struggling with saws, and iron workers walking metal beams at forty below zero in clunky boots while cranes sent loads of steel over their heads. This was not America. If you dropped a wrench here, it broke clean. But these guys were so macho they wouldn't come in for simple treatment of frostbite or lacerations. They waited until they noticed their wounds weren't healing or became too painful for them to work.

The construction injuries kept me on call day and night all summer, from November through February, when the construction guys worked three shifts. I wasn't able to read, study, or even sleep. Worst of all, I almost never got to go outside. I could see the light from the plateau pouring through the open wooden doors to the Dome, but I was trapped, like a child in detention. I couldn't wait to see more of the continent, and I looked forward to the trips to McMurdo that I had been promised.

At last in early December I was able to take a driving class that qualified me to take out snowmobiles. I did so at every opportunity, buzzing around the outbuildings with the visiting medical personnel and VIPs I was often in charge of entertaining. These excursions were a nice break for me, but I wasn't permitted to stray too far away from the station. And I always wore my portable radio, a tether tying me to my work. As the only doctor, I was a precious commodity, a queen bee to be protected at all costs. I was trapped in the hive and often felt like a prisoner.

At the same time, being surrounded by so many competent people made me feel very safe. As a child, I felt secure because I believed that my parents would die to save me. Here, for the first time since adulthood, I felt just as safe. Even if I couldn't trust the supply line, or the weather, or the worn-out equipment, I trusted my colleagues. We worked as a team so that we could exist here. We would die for each other.

I was receiving a lot of emails from Will Silva, who was still in New Zealand waiting for the weather to clear so he could go climbing. I finally confessed to him that I was having trouble replying to "How's it going?" letters. It was going pretty poorly. Like Dorianne, I didn't think my employers had accurately described my job to me, and I was frustrated. I asked for his advice on limiting the workload so I could get something out of the experience here. He came back right away with some words of wisdom.

From: Will Silva
To: Jerri Nielsen
Date: Fri., 04 Dec. 1998 00:07:01 PST
Subject: Re: temperate greetings

Dear Jerri,

I know what you mean about people's expectations. You have to be all things to all people at all times . . . and this is not something any of us can really do. I suspect a combination of all-parties email and an announcement at station meeting may help, maybe make and post signs to the effect that usual clinic hours are from X to Y, please limit nonemergency visits to these hours. You can set your own hours, but you may have to fight for them. Trick is that people have inappropriate expectations. Clearly a limit-setting issue.

Do what you need to do, my friend, to take care of yourself for the long haul. My first blush impression was that people seemed sicker this year than last. Who knows. The trick will be to set the limits you need to protect yourself and keep your wits and humor about you.

Go well, and stay tuned. Cheers, Will

Meanwhile, Christmas was coming, and I was getting a dose of holiday blues. I kept writing to my children but never heard a word back from them. I wondered if they had even been getting my letters and email. I knew they had received some presents I had arranged—including a pickup truck for Ben's sixteenth birthday. While there was still mail service at the Pole I posted souvenirs and cards. I sent them all personal emails and copied them with letters on my "family and friends" list, but they never responded or acknowledged the gifts. The wounds of separation opened again and again as the people at the Pole asked me about my life back home, and my kids. I tried evasion, but they kept pushing for details, just to make friendly conversation. How could I explain what I could hardly believe myself?

I confided my feelings to my mother, one of the only people I could talk to about my children.

From: Jerri Nielsen
To: Mom

Date: 18 Dec. 1998 12:13:03 +1200
Subject: Mom to Daughter chat

I have been really sad about the kids for the past two days. I don't know why. I just can't believe that I lost them all. I can't understand it and it hurts so deeply. I can't look at their pictures. Everyone here has pictures of loved ones taped to walls in their rooms. I can't. I put them up then took them down.

Have you heard from Ben about the truck?

Don't they ever think of me?

Love, Duffy

The one thing I was looking forward to was a weekend trip to McMurdo for training, hanging out with my friends, bartering for medical supplies, and just getting away from the endless stream of patients at Pole. I was most excited about going to Happy Campers School, where I'd learn how to make an ice cave and an igloo and live outside in the wilderness for a couple of days. Maybe I would even get to see penguins and seals.

Then one day the SPAM walked into my bedroom/office and told me that I couldn't go. Denver hadn't informed him in advance, so he wasn't authorizing it. He made me feel like I was trying to pull a fast one, even though the ASA medical director had set up my trip. It was so mindlessly military and political. I had been told that being on call 24/7 for months had beaten up previous doctors, and a weekend off was a reasonable solution. I wouldn't have cared so much if I hadn't been promised the trip.

Meanwhile, I was told I was not permitted to ask for help with medical procedures without a filling out a work order. Why, then, had I taken the time and trouble to train the trauma team to help me? It seemed like the Pole was just like the rest of the world, full of decisions not necessarily made for the benefit of the community. This was not how it had been described to me.

The only thing that stopped me from giving notice was the unwavering hope held by all winterovers that "once we get all these summer people out of here, things will be great." Besides, what would I tell my parents? I had a fax from home with an inspirational message for me tacked to my wall: "Press On," it began, "nothing in the world can take the place of persistence . . ."

So I put on a brave front and poured out my disillusionment in letters to friends and family, some signed, Jerri Nielsen, Physician, the Penal Colony on Ice.

My family was relentlessly encouraging. My mother was determined that this year would be the best experience of my life. My brothers were proud of me, particularly Scott, the wild child, who understood something about living in the badlands. We had always been close, but now we were writing each other regularly and his letters were extraordinary. After I wrote a sad letter about my loneliness, he answered with this:

From: Scott Cahill
To: Jerri Nielsen
Date: Wed., 16 Dec. 1998 20:11:45 -0500
Subject: Re: Polar Love

I am very proud of you, and we all think of you a lot. This is not summer camp—but then—who wants something that anyone can do? Of course you miss the outside world—everyone who ever sailed single-handed or explored the jungles or the tropics or the deserts or the open cold of the polar regions has missed the world and faced "the grim reaper," laughed in his face and then, when they re-enter this world—they are never quite the same. They understand things that they never saw all of their lives sitting on the bench beside them.

Take this from one who has sailed out away from the horizon alone at night a hundred miles out with the monsters and the angels and the solitude and the loneliness: You are where you are. You are very fortunate to be there. Enjoy and savor every minute of it. Feel the cold—when winter comes—feel the isolation and solitude—breathe it in, savor it—THIS IS LIFE—this is the edge—the edge is everything.

Scott Cahill

On Christmas Eve, my mother wrote describing the wonderful dinner she'd planned. There would be prime ribs and oyster bisque, presents and candles and Christmas music. My brothers and their families would be coming on Christmas Day. I felt so far removed from it all, I could hardly even feel homesick.

I tried to keep my mind focused on the present, and I soon found a friend to help me. His name was Ola Skinnarmo, a twenty-six-year-old Swede who skied alone across the polar plateau from Patriot Hills, a private camp at the edge of the Ronne Ice Shelf in western Antarctica. He covered more than six hundred miles, reaching the South Pole in forty-seven days. The South Pole managers try to discourage adventurers and tourists from camping out at the facility. When Ola arrived just before Christmas he was allowed to pitch a tent near the Dome but was offered only one meal from the galley.

When I heard about the handsome young Swede, I told Dorianne that I could get us into his tent. She dared me. So I walked over and welcomed him to the South Pole in Swedish. He invited us into his tent and shared some Swedish Army biscuits. I ended up sneaking him food and drink until the SPAM relented and let him join our community for Christmas, until a plane picked him up. We got to know each other well, and he came over to Biomed every afternoon to talk.

Ola had trained himself both physically and mentally for the expedition. He realized that mental fortitude was even more important than physical strength in determining survival. He found experts to help him train his mind to block out pain, cold, hunger, loneliness, and despair. We discussed this at length, because this was what I had also worked long and hard to accomplish.

On Christmas Day the "Race around the World" was usually the high point of everyone's summer at Pole. People walked, jogged, drove, or were dragged three times around the skiway—a 2.5-mile course circumnavigating the South Pole. One guy rode his snowmobile backward the whole way. The Drag Queen pulled an ice barge loaded with Polies lounging on living room furniture. It looked like fun, but I felt removed from the celebration, like a diver watching the world through a mask in deep water. I already felt the pull of winter. Summer traditions like the race or croquet on the skiway seemed designed for the visitors who would soon be leaving. I had not come for games. Summer was what we had to get through before we could do what we came here for: to winter at the South Pole.

From: Jerri Nielsen
To: Mom and Dad
Date: Fri., 25 Dec. 1998 00:59:35 +1200
Subject: Re: Merry Xmas Eve Dear little girl of mine

Merry Christmas all of you whom I love.

I have not been able to write to anyone as I am so busy that I fall into bed every night with my work half done.

I had a nice Xmas Eve. Today we built crazy contraptions and "raced around the world." Everyone on station did it. Some ran or walked. Others rode sleds and snowmobiles. I hope to go to a Christmas party tonight if I am not too tired. Thank you for the packages. I got the shirts and the hair dryer, electric blankets, cookies and fudge, and cover-ups for Xmas. The oranges and apples were wonderful.

Love, Duffy

A mutiny brewing at Pole was also weighing on my mind. In the last week of December, six people quit, including most of the cargo department and my best friend, Dorianne. I never really found what had happened in cargo. I knew I would really miss Dorianne. She wasn't prepared for the amount of work expected of her, and in many ways, I could empathize with her frustrations. But I really believed that once the station closed and all the summer people left town she would love being here.

I knew it would be foolish to talk someone into wintering at Pole—you have to want it without reservation. But I had to try something, to be sure she wasn't making a mistake. I invited all her close winterover friends to my room to discuss Dorianne's options. Andy the blue-collar beaker, Loree the meteorologist, Joel, and Big John all came. One of us would list the reasons to stay and then another would counter with reasons to leave.

Loree began. "We need you, Dorianne. The best friends that you'll ever have are in this room. We're all here to do this thing together."

"It will be the best year of your life," said Big John.

Then it was my turn. I had always encouraged her to stay with us, so to be fair, I laid out my own worst-case scenario.

"Do you know what I fear most?" I said. "What if one of us is terribly injured or sick and there's little that I can do? You might have to help me care for someone you love, unconscious with a bad head injury, all winter. We would have to sleep beside him in shifts, watching, waiting for spring, knowing that if we were home at a proper hospital, there would be some hope. One or more of us could easily die. If we lose power, we'll all freeze to death. If the Dome burns, life here will be horribly difficult, maybe impossible."

This wasn't something we often talked about, but it was just beneath the surface of our conscious thought. We were all constantly aware of potential disaster. I hated laying it out like that, but I couldn't bear talking her into this mission without acknowledging the risks.

"Dor, I have to know if I can do it, survive it. That means everything to me. How much does it mean to you?"

She would sleep on it and make her decision in the morning. But I already knew her answer. Now, sadly, I would have to face the winter without a close girlfriend who could make me laugh, a confidante in the dark days.

Just as she was scheduled to ship out, the weather at the coast deteriorated and no flights were coming or going from Mactown, dragging out the whole ordeal.

While Dorianne packed to leave, all her friends started begging for her stuff. We took everything she would part with: clothes, tapes, furniture. As she walked around the station, people pleaded for her hat or face covering. As the best friend, I did very well, coming away with a down comforter and a set of flannel sheets, some nice books, and food. I was still holding out for her down vest, hoping she would weaken in her last hours. Such was our culture. We would flip coins for your bedroom while you were still in it. People ripped things off your walls.

When Dorianne's flight to McMurdo was canceled, she had to borrow my clothes—she had nothing left to wear. She had no towel or soap. She wore my T-shirt to bed—and I watched closely to make sure she didn't leave with it! Someone took her slippers that night. You could walk into anyone's room and find little pieces of her everywhere.

When Dorianne's flight finally landed at Pole, I kissed her cheek and watched her climb Heart Attack Hill up to the taxiway. I was reminded of the "sin-eaters" of rural Wales and Ireland. According to tradition, during a wake food was placed on a corpse to represent the deceased's unconfessed sins. The sin-eater would eat the food and take on the sins to free the soul from purgatory. Then, at the time of the sin-eater's own death, someone from the village who really loved her had to eat her sins—or she would die with everyone's sins, a sure, horrible hell. That person would in turn become the sin-eater.

I have always felt that a physician is like a sin-eater. You hold all the pain and secrets of everyone else in your heart, with no one to tell, no one to care for you. Here at the Pole, the doctor was more alone with this knowledge than anywhere else I had been. Well, I thought as the Hercules lifted off into the cloudless sky, the sin-eater no longer has anyone here who loves her so much.

The day Dorianne left, Big John came over and said, "Doc, what you need is a motorcycle ride." We called the snow machines motorcycles—another example of Polarspeak—and Big was the monarch of the motorcycles. Because he was in charge of maintaining the vehicles at Pole, he had access to all the snowmobiles, and he had chosen the best one for his personal hotrod (even though it was officially assigned to one of the beakers).

Big John knew what it was to lose your best friend here, since Nelson had been medevacked out a few weeks earlier. I allowed him to abduct me from the station. I pulled on my parka and climbed on behind him, and we were flying. I just held on as the wind burned us and we sailed over the wind-carved waves of ice. We went straight out into the nothingness of the polar plateau.

At a point five miles from the station where you can see nothing except 360 degrees of horizon, we stopped and shut down the machine for a minute and listened to the absolute silence of the ice. The place was so beautiful, so clean and perfect. I was beginning to learn to read the subtle changes in color and texture of the endless horizon, the wash of the sun through a thin veil of clouds, the direction of the wind. It is hard to imagine how many shades of white and blue there are until they, alone, give the world definition. I began to feel a shift in my heart, like a key fitting into a lock. I was opening up to the emptiness, as it revealed itself to me.

To: Xpole
Date: Mon., 28 Dec. 1998 02:46:03 +1200
Subject: New Year's Day Celebration

Everyone Welcome . . .

Roger and Donna request your presence, New Year's Day, at 3:00 p.m. at the Ceremonial Pole to witness their exchange of wedding vows.

They would like all guests to encircle them, holding hands to form a ring "around the world" and around the bride and groom.

Pizza will be served at the reception to follow at or about 5:00 p.m. at "Sally's Galley," the finest restaurant on the plateau.

Live music to be performed by "The Icemen" of South Pole, Antarctica, at 7:00 p.m. No gifts required . . . bring your fun spirit and well wishes for the new couple.

RSVP required. ;-)

Donna, a winter cook and Roger, an electrician, dressed up in their best McMurdo-made matching polar parkas for their New Year's Day wedding at the Pole. They exchanged beautiful rings fashioned by the Alaskan bush pilot, Ken Lobe, from brass fittings in our shop. Ken also performed the ceremony. It is a little-known but charming fact that any Alaskan citizen can apply to be a "marriage commissioner" and perform a wedding ceremony. Apparently that law came into being because Alaskans live pretty much as we do here, with a distinct shortage of justices of the peace.

The other big event on New Year's was the annual moving of the Geographic Pole Marker. The Amundsen-Scott South Pole Station sits on a sheet of ice that shifts about thirty feet per year. The official marker moves with it and must be repositioned to remain over the true South Pole. I described these events to my family, as I tried to express the shift that was taking place in me.

From: Jerri Nielsen
To: Mom and Dad
Date: Wednesday, January 06, 1999 8:46 a.m.
Subject: January the beginning

Well, the mutiny may be over. Dorianne is gone and I miss her seriously. Her feather comforter comforts me. Her room was grabbed up by someone who was sleeping in a tent and life goes on. I have been spending more time with Big John and Joel, the dancing NOAA officer.

We had a wedding on New Year's Day. We also moved the Geographic Pole. By tradition, each crew member takes turns hammering it into the ice. We move the marker yearly and each crew signs it. I've sent you pictures. Our marker is inscribed with my favorite quote from Captain Scott: "Great God, this is an awful place."

It is awful and wonderful. It will kill you as it did Scott, or make you whatever is happening to me. It is not paradise. Nothing good is. I want to stay.

Love from the Ice,
Jerri Lin

CHAPTER 5:

Going Polar

From: Thom Miller
To: Jerri Nielsen
Date: 28 Dec. 1998
Subject: bad, bad, bad!!!!!

Hey Jerri,

It costs mega dollars to make water here. We have all heard
about your "Hollywood Shower" which set off the fire alarm
last night; there are rules here we all have to follow, even me,
and I make the water. 2 min. twice a week. Another subject I
heard rumors about is a sun-tanning light you have found.
That is definitely a NO-NO! Anything over a 100-watt
light is unacceptable for use. It costs us about 90 cents per
kilowatt hour (at home you pay 9–15 cents) to make electricity here and a light of that magnitude would be an
extreme draw on the power plant. We do monitor every
building on a 1-minute basis with our power monitor computer, so we will know if you have it on and will have to
remove it. I don't want to do that so please just don't use it!

(Don't worry—once all these people get the hell out of our little community, we will be able to do many more things, but for the summer we have to play by the rules!)

Thanks,
The Power Plant

I was innocent. The "Hollywood Shower" fire alarm was caused by a faulty smoke detector that was oversensitive to steam. I had not exceeded the two-minute limit; in fact I was religious about conserving water. But this didn't prevent my fellow Polies from calling me Doc Hollywood after the incident. (I have no comment, however, about the sunlamp.)

Showers were such a luxury that all I cared about was washing my hair. It was always so dirty that I wore it up in a bun even when I wasn't working. I didn't care about the rest of my body anymore. You can't tell *anything* about anyone's body underneath twenty-five to thirty-five pounds of canvas and down.

Our clothing was even filthier than our bodies. We wore it until it was just foul. We were on water rationing, so you carefully planned your one load of laundry a week. You couldn't use the water to wash the goose-down parkas, so they were blackened. Most of the men worked ten-hour days covered in grease and fuels. I was a "dome slug" so I was squeaky clean, relatively speaking. The Old West must have been like this. When people get dirty enough, they desquamate— shed skin—which is nature's form of dry cleaning. The only place I wouldn't tolerate dirt was in my hospital. Once I almost killed my roommates with chlorine fumes when I scrubbed the floor with industrial bleach. I had mixed in too much powdered concentrate and the solution blew up, shooting the rubber top off the bottle like a Champagne cork and spewing all over the ceiling.

In the weeks after New Year's a number of "distinguished visitors"— members of Congress and other government officials—arrived at Pole.

That entailed work for me and long hours. They were usually not well screened for the rigors of Antarctic travel and seemed to have more health problems than the average Polie. I treated many of them for altitude sickness, which meant they had to stay in my little hospital. The worst part, from my perspective, was that some of these visitors would be journalists. The last thing I wanted was publicity back in Ohio, knowing it would incite my ex-husband's jealousy. He had always been resentful of any attention I received, and when he was angry with me, he took it out on the children. I had made the decision long ago that flying below the radar, trying to be invisible, or at least to be a moving target, was the only way to escape his rage.

The following message was sent to all hands at the Pole at the beginning of the year:

From: South Pole Area Manager
To: #everyone
Date: Thu., 7 Jan. 1999 19:03:15 +1200
Subject: MEDIA GUIDANCE

Polies,

Pole will host a number of journalists this month; the message below, from NSF, gives tips and pointers. Please take the opportunity to talk to these folks while they're here.

----- Forwarded Message Follows -----

During January, McMurdo and South Pole will welcome journalists from five different media organizations. These journalists are here at the invitation of NSF. They are here to report chiefly on science—although some may also do related "human-interest" stories about life on the ice.

They are one of our best conduits to the American public, and help us to tell the story of Amazing Antarctica.

Should you talk to them? Absolutely. NSF has no objection to anyone talking to these journalists, including contractors and military personnel, and in fact encourages you to do so. However, we do ask you to refer any policy questions to NSF, and to stay within the boundaries of your own area of expertise.

Some general tips regarding the news media:
— AVOID JARGON.
— BE BRIEF.
— BE CONCISE.
— BE YOURSELF (and show enthusiasm if that's how you feel).
— TAKE YOUR TIME ANSWERING QUESTIONS; THINK BEFORE YOU SPEAK.
— DON'T BE AFRAID TO SAY "I DON'T KNOW" (and refer the question to NSF).
— KNOW YOUR LIMITS.
— ALWAYS CONSIDER YOURSELF "ON THE RECORD" (even during casual encounters in the galley or bar).
— NEVER SAY ANYTHING YOU DON'T WANT TO SEE IN PRINT.

Jerry Bowen, a CBS News reporter, and his crew spent several days swarming all over the station, putting together a story about life "at the bottom of the world." They were in the galley at mealtimes and in the Jamesways and the research facilities, cornering people for interviews. I avoided them. I told my family about our visitors in an email home: "I am going to try to not talk to them. I don't want Dan Rather at my door."

One very welcome visitor was Betty Erickson, my "fantasy nurse" from MacTown. She was sent to the Pole to train me in some remedial nursing techniques, such as how to run the IV pump and where to give shots without causing damage. With Betty around, I didn't feel so alone. There was no need to explain anything to her: She understood my wonder and my terror practicing medicine on the Ice. We laughed together while inventorying medication for liver flukes and malaria (many Polies also spend time in the tropics) while searching for basic antibiotics (eventually found). Again and again she demonstrated how incomplete a doctor is without a nurse, and why our professions developed in parallel, to serve each other.

I wanted to show her a good time during her trip, and we managed to squeeze in a spectacular snowmobile ride across the plateau. But, sadly, much of our time together was spent in the hospital—with Betty as my patient, in bed and on oxygen for altitude sickness. No one was immune.

Meanwhile I was enjoying the Pole more each day, partly because I was starting to make more meaningful friendships.

I met John Wright when he got frostbite. He was a summer guy, a hard-rock miner from the Colorado mountains, hired to dig ice tunnels at the South Pole. We called him the "Master Blaster" because of his efficiency with explosives, but he was an artist with ice. He carved one tunnel with a chain saw and a pickax. It was a thing of beauty and symmetry, created with techniques used back in the days of Babylon. Later he would employ dynamite, and then a prototype drilling machine, to see which was more efficient. But the frostbite on Wright's fingers was so bad he came into Biomed one day for treatment. I realized his ASA-issue leather gloves couldn't keep him warm enough, so I made my own design. I had brought a piece of possum fur from New Zealand, planning to sew myself a face mask for winter. I cut it up into small pieces and stuffed them into the fingers of his gloves. It was the only medical treatment I could think of to help him, and it seemed to work quite well. And we became good friends.

Big John was tight with the Master Blaster, and the three of us shared a love of poetry. After dinner or on weekends, we'd sit at a table in the galley, reciting poems to each other. Wright had a deep, stentorian voice and he could deliver long passages of Robert Service by heart. Big was also a Service fan. My favorites were Yeats, T. S. Eliot, Emily Dickinson, and Edna St. Vincent Millay. People would gather around to listen to us and to enjoy the banter.

Wright would recite a few stanzas about miners and big-chested lumberjacks, and then I'd read a verse about lost love and youth. Wright would sigh dramatically and say, "Oh, women's poetry is so needy!"

"Women's poetry isn't all needy," I shot back at him once. "I'll show you needy." Then I recited "Wild Women Blues," adapted from a blues song by Ida Cox:

> *I've got a different system*
> *And a way of my own.*
> *When my man starts kicking*
> *I let him find another home . . .*
> *I want to tell you something*
> *I wouldn't tell you no lie.*
> *Wild women are the only kind*
> *That really get by,*
> *'Cause wild women don't worry,*
> *Wild women don't have the blues . . .*

Everyone had a good laugh at that, and I believe I made my point.

The poetry contests would escalate all night and spill into the next weekend. Eventually, people started asking if they could bring their own poems to share. By the end of the summer we had started a new tradition of poetry slams at the South Pole.

This strange world at the end of the earth seemed more and more normal every day. Even the climate seemed ordinary, something I started to take for granted until it taught me a hard lesson one bright afternoon. That day Joel and I had decided to walk out to Wright's tunnel, about a mile away from the station. The blue ice tunnel was so beautiful and peaceful, we treated it as a tourist destination. But after we had turned back and were halfway home, deep in conversation and not paying close attention to the sky, the wind picked up from the plateau over hundreds of miles of flat ice, and within seconds we were engulfed in a full-blown ground blizzard. It was a total whiteout. We couldn't see a single landmark, and we lost our orientation to the Dome. For the first time in Antarctica, I felt my own mortality. I realized you could die in an instant—and the quickest way to go was to stop paying attention. Joel and I got down on our hands and knees in the blowing snow and started crawling. Incredibly, we found a set of recent tractor tracks, and like Hansel and Gretel following a trail of crumbs, we crept along the furrows until they led us back to the station.

I knew by now that I had changed profoundly since arriving at the Pole. For the first few weeks, I had clung to the idea that this journey was just a sabbatical. I would go back to Ohio and resume my life, a stronger, wiser person, but essentially the same. It didn't take long for me to realize that I did not want to return to corporate medicine. I was no longer interested in the money or status or false glamour attached to the job. I was sick of playing the political games needed to get ahead. I no longer wanted to get ahead. I was now thinking of joining the Peace Corps, or traveling in the Third World, seeing if I could find a way to use my skills in the poorest places. I knew now that my children would be out of my life until my ex-husband lost interest in them. They would always be welcome to join me, wherever I traveled, but I could no longer attach my future to false hopes. I searched for a way to explain to my family what was happening to me.

From: Jerri Nielsen
To: Mom and Dad
Date: Sun., 17 Jan. 1999 10:30:03 +1200
Subject: The latest from the ice

Dear Folks,

Enjoying the life here again. The world is so distorted here that it is not possible to keep your bearings. Time is totally meaningless. Time expands and contracts and even with a lot of attempts to keep it straight, there is no hope. Things that happened yesterday could have occurred months ago, yet months ago seem like earlier today. Everyone senses this. We also have such a short perspective as there is no outside input.

This must be how small tribes of people developed their own religions and belief systems before the age of communication and travel. Here, we are only physically connected through the movement of planes. But the planes are always the same ones with the same crews and the same loads. They are also part of this small world.

We scare most of the Coasties who visit us. I hear that after the year is over we scare everyone. That is hard to imagine now as everyone here seems normal while everyone coming in seems bizarre.

Now, I am a total Polie and I know that there is nothing out there that I need. Everything that a Polie needs is here. We have food. We have all the ragged clothing that we need. We hold our clothing together with duct tape that we heat with a heat gun so that it sticks. My boots are all taped up. Some people hold the legs to their pants with it. It is cool to use different colors of electrician's tape to hold clothing together but I save what I can acquire to hold together wounds.

We really do have what we need as we need less and less. After a while you almost stop thinking about sex.

All that I want is for the sun to go away and with it all these summer people. They are starting to feel like the guests whom you have invited and love with all your heart, but who really should have left three days ago. I am told that those who are ready to do winter always feel that way now. We have something that we came here to do and we can't do it until that last plane leaves. Then all this becomes so real.

I am ready for the reality of winter. At first we talked of it with a little fear. We were going to live through the cold, dark, lonely, hard, cold winter. Now we are looking forward only to the warmth of the Dome, full of friends and family— no matter how dysfunctional—solitude, rest, reflection, and isolation. I will be glad to see that last plane leave. Really glad. I am hungry for the darkness.

Love you all,
I am already never the same. Duffy

As January rolled along, the ASA people who would be wintering at Pole started taking their week-long R&R's in McMurdo—supposedly their last big social blowout before the isolation of winter. (The beakers, who were on more deluxe grants, got to go to Cheech.) Big, Mike Masterman, and a group of other winterovers took their leaves together in mid-January. Big John had elaborate plans for himself, most of them involving vast quantities of beer. Before long I was receiving spirited emails describing the entertainment in MacTown:

> From: guest10@mcmurdo.gov
> To: Jerri Nielsen
> Date: Tues., 19 Jan. 99 13:31:41 GMT
> Subject: Re: Keeping In Touch
>
> Hey Doc:
>
> I took a shower that lasted for 51 minutes! I sat in a chair and drank a six-pack of beer with the water running. Boy was that nice.

I just got home from the bar. These guys close at 1:00, they don't know how to live like we do. Well, I accomplished three of my goals already: I drank too much, I smoked too much, and I stayed up too late. We'll see if I can accomplish my fourth goal of sleeping in tomorrow.

And a few days later:

Hello Doc:

Wow, did we have a wild day and night. It all started in the barber shop tonight. I cannot tell you what went on, as I took an oath not to tell, but you will see when we return. Rest assured that I started it all. You can be secure in that knowledge.

Big John

When the R&R team returned from MacTown, every one of them, even Mike, sported a Mohawk hairdo. They looked fabulous! It was so good to see them all again. I didn't realize how much I'd miss them, and how incomplete the station felt with some of the "brothers" and "sisters" gone. I particularly missed Big John, who, of course, had the best time of all and regaled me with his exploits on the coast. He told me he had even managed to score some "boondoggles"—unauthorized and forbidden trips outside of base—including a helicopter ride to the Dry Valleys and a tour of a Coast Guard icebreaker.

I was totally jealous, because I knew I wouldn't have much fun when it was finally my turn for R&R. There would be no other Polies to party with, since I had to be switched with the doctor in MacTown, and it worked out on a week when no other winterovers had leaves. Even worse, I was expected to be on call at all times. Not much of a vacation.

When my time came at the end of January, I was happy to learn that at least I would be traveling to MacTown with Andy, who was going to Christchurch one last time before the station closed for winter. Andy and I boarded the LC-130 and headed for the cargo section to stretch out. I was lying on an empty pallet, staring at the ceiling listening to Tracy Chapman's "For My Lover" through earphones on my CD player, when someone walked back from the flight deck and tugged at my parka.

"Dr. Nielsen, are you Dr. Nielsen?" he asked.

"Yes," I shouted over the engine noise, thinking, *Damn, someone's sick on the plane and I'm going to have to work.*

"We need you in the cockpit, Dr. Nielsen."

I walked up front and, through the huge flight-deck windows, I saw that we were flying over the Transantarctic Mountains. The pilot grinned at me and said, "Dr. Nielsen?" I nodded. He said, "Hold on!" and gestured for me to grab a handhold. He then dropped the plane into a canyon right between two glaciers. "This is a present from Big John!"

I always loved to fly low and fast. As we dove, I could see two large glaciers, the Beardmore and a tributary, flowing together in a deep Y-shaped valley between rows of tall black peaks. The mountains poked up out of the endless ice like crocuses through March snow. I could easily make out the crevasses on the glaciers, large enough to swallow a snow machine, but from the air looking like folds in taffy. For the first time, I could feel the awesome scale of the continent and its fierce, seductive beauty.

The pilots let me ride all the way to McMurdo in the cockpit. They owed Big John a favor after he'd helped them out with a mechanical problem, and he had talked them into buzzing the glacier for me as a gift—the best I had ever been given.

MacTown at the end of summer seemed a lot like Casablanca during the war. Polar refugees were everywhere, waiting to get out on the next flight north. The weather had been bad for days, so flights were backed up in Christchurch. All these workers and beakers were trying to get on airplanes that never came, hanging out in the gin joints all night, like the patrons of Rick's Café.

When we arrived Andy couldn't get a flight out either, so we decided to go out on the town together. I was already homesick for the Dome, but since this was my first night in the "big city," I was still looking to have some fun. We walked into a bar crowded with strangers smoking and drinking hard. Andy said, "Where do you want to sit?" I pointed to a little table with two chairs in a dark corner away from all these people. "That's where I wanted to sit, too," he said.

Even though we didn't know it yet, Andy and I had already gone through a major change at the Pole. We ordered our drinks and I started analyzing the situation, out loud, which was my usual conversation style. "Isn't it interesting that we don't want to mingle?" I said. "That we just want to be alone? And chose to be over here, away from everybody, when this is our big time to party?"

"Well, you know," he said, looking over at the crowd, "they're just not Polies."

Then I noticed a table of guys sitting on top of guys, and girls sitting on top of girls, and people hanging on top of each other because there weren't enough chairs. At the center of the table stood a pyramid of beer bottles.

"Now, *they* could be Polies," I said, and then we started laughing. "Wait a minute! They *are* Polies!"

They were old friends from summer, doing the Casablanca thing on their way back to the world. So we went over and joined them.

Andy was stuck for a few days. He was living in Hotel California with a pack of crazed Russians from Vostok. He called them "the Russian ants" because they ran all over the place, day and night, drinking and laughing and playing pool. Who could blame them? They hadn't been on leave in *two years!* And from what I'd heard from friends who had visited the base, Vostok was in even worse shape than the Pole. And there were no women.

So, while waiting for their flight home, the Russians lived it up in this American oasis of consumer goods. The first thing they did was to sell or trade all their clothes. One traded a beautiful bearskin hat for a South Pole baseball cap. After they got rid of their Russian outfits they went diving for American clothes in the "skua piles"—named after scavenging seabirds. The piles were bins where you threw horrible stuff you didn't want to pack back to the States, and anyone could take whatever he or she wanted. So the Russians went cruising around MacTown in things like plaid jackets and bedroom slippers. They were trying to pick up chicks in bars—just wild and crazy guys who spoke no English. They were a big hit.

Everyone adored the Vostok crewmen and tried to help them out. One night I played pool with them. My friend Mandy, who worked in the night kitchen, fixed up a tray of sandwiches that I brought out to the pool hall to feed the Russians. One could speak English pretty well and he translated. They asked how many women were at Pole, and I told them there would be nine of us in the winter.

They discussed this in Russian for a while, then the translator turned to me and asked: "Do you share your women?"

I assured them that we did not.

They finally got out on the same flight as Andy. No one is allowed to board a military aircraft in an inebriated condition, but when the plane landed, these party animals were wasted. One was so drunk he had to be carried onto the aircraft. The crew took pity on them. Everybody, even hardened Polies, admired the Vostok winterovers, the toughest guys on a very tall mountain. So the loadmaster picked up the dazed Russian and strapped him in. Naturally all the other passengers, particularly Andy, tried to avoid sitting by this group. But Andy ended up smack in their midst. He reported that they woke up halfway through the trip, and, champions to the end, they started passing around more liquor. It was a long flight.

I never got to attend Happy Campers School. And, unlike some of the previous South Pole doctors, I never managed to visit the research field camps or the incredible Dry Valleys. Since I never knew when I was to be on call, I couldn't go very far. I even had to work at the MacTown hospital one day, since Hugh Cowan, the winterover physician at McMurdo, was at the South Pole to relieve me. After a few days I had seen most of what I wanted to see: I'd been to all three bars, including the coffee bar. I had toured the power plant and the site where fresh water was made by reverse osmosis, filtering pressurized sea water through a semi-porous membrane. I checked out the dive shack, where biologists in SCUBA gear swam under the ice to study exotic marine life, such as white-blooded fish that can live in below-freezing salt water because their bodies create an organic antifreeze. I visited the Crary lab, a state-of-the-art research facility with refrigerators that the scientists worked inside to re-create certain Antarctic temperatures. There was also a small aquarium with marine creatures from under the Ross Sea.

Next, I dropped by the chapel for juice and cookies with Fr. John Coleman, the Kiwi priest. We had become good friends during his recent visit to Pole, where he celebrated the last Mass before the nine months of winter.

When I first arrived at McMurdo it seemed very warm compared to the Pole, and I often felt overheated in my ECWs. The oxygen-rich air at sea level filled me with energy. One morning I put on jeans, hiking boots, and a T-shirt and headed out of my dormitory to visit the Discovery Hut, one of the continent's oldest historic landmarks. The hut stood on a small peninsula in McMurdo Sound, less than a mile from the base. I walked a trail along a half-frozen inlet, enjoying what seemed like a brisk but sunny spring day.

McMurdo was established as an American base in 1956, but Ross Island, on which it sits, had served as a way station for expeditions to the continent since the nineteenth century. The island's appeal was its position in the more or less navigable McMurdo Sound, abutting the massive Ross Ice Shelf, which reached deep into the Antarctic interior. The abandoned Discovery Hut, built by Captain Scott's crew for his first Antarctic expedition in 1902, looked out from its rocky promontory to the southern ice fields. Several later expeditions had used it for shelter. A mummified seal lay on the bright veranda, frozen and unmoved since it had been stashed there for food, perhaps by

Shackleton's crew or Scott's own doomed Terra Nova expedition, when he returned in 1911.

The door to the hut was locked, so I peered inside through the windows. Nothing decayed here. Nothing changed. The supply crates stacked against the rough wooden walls seemed ready for use, the rumpled blankets on the seamen's cots might still hold warmth from the bodies of sleepy, hopeful men.

Suddenly I shivered and remembered where I was. Antarctica had tricked me. This was not a spring day; the temperature was a few degrees below zero and I was standing here, alone, without a coat or hat. I held on to my ears and started jogging back to the station under a lovely blue sky. I ducked into the first building I encountered and sat in its manufactured warmth until I could again feel my face.

Before my R&R ended I took a shuttle bus to Scott Base, New Zealand's Antarctic station a few miles out of Mactown, to meet Jude Winter, the Kiwi medical officer, and to take her a South Pole hat. Scott Base was a lovely place, a cluster of lime-green buildings, clean and new inside. Jude showed me her hospital and medical system. Like everything in New Zealand, the dispensary was spotless and well organized. She invited me to dinner with her crew in their galley with picture windows overlooking the sound. From the dinner table you could watch seals surfacing through holes in the pack ice. Afterwards, they invited me to lounge in the bar and get to know everyone. All Ice people think that New Zealanders are the most hospitable people in the world. My visit reinforced this; I was made to feel like family. I met the Antarctic curator for a museum in Christchurch and promised to bring him back something from Old Pole, as they had no artifacts from the original American station, now abandoned and buried beneath the ice. I promised Jude that I would keep in touch by email all winter.

It was time for the last shuttle to McMurdo, but we were having such a great time that I stayed over at the New Zealand base. I still tell people I woke up in a different country. That was the highlight of my R&R.

When I was back in my temporary quarters in MacTown, looking out my window toward the spectacular volcanic mountains, the view was beyond beautiful. But looking at it made me so homesick for the flat white nothing of the polar plateau I couldn't stand it. I longed for it the way a young girl longs for her lover. I didn't want to be here, in a crowded, dirty town with amazing views. I wanted to go home, to the Pole.

I walked to the communications center, picked up a radio, and put in a call for Dave Fischer, the SPAM.

"Dave, this is Jerri, over. I want to come home, over."

As it turned out, an international rescue operation was under way to medevac a scientist across the continent after he suffered a stroke on a remote research vessel. He was being transported to Christchurch by way of McMurdo but would stop at the South Pole for stabilization. Hugh Cowan, who was substituting for me at Pole, could fly with the patient to McMurdo, making life easier for everyone. But I would then be needed on station, and so I was able to get the next flight to Pole.

It was now February and the world was changing—I could feel it in the air and see it in the long shadows creeping over the ice. The sun was slowly spiraling down from its peak summer position of twenty-three degrees above the horizon. The lower sky took on a pale pink cast and the temperature began to drop. Big John said he felt like he ought to be kicking through piles of dead leaves and cutting wood for the cold days ahead. It was autumn on the ice plateau, and a hibernation instinct seemed to be taking hold of the winterover crew. We were all sifting through our supplies and making want-lists for the last supply flights of the season. The station was due to close on February 15, before low temperatures and storms grounded all cargo planes in MacTown.

During the summer months, a huge shaft of blinding light penetrated the Dome through the open doors of the entrance arch. Every time I entered or left Biomed, I could see the sky and tell what kind of weather we were having on the plateau. But after a nasty blizzard blew over the Pole, it was time to close the doors to the Dome against the weather, a sure sign that summer was ending. Each wooden door was ten feet wide by fifteen feet high, big enough to drive a forklift through. But we wouldn't be needing the forklifts in winter, when the supply flights ended and there were no more pallets to deliver in the Dome. One of the huge entrance doors had a smaller door within it, so that people could come and go on their way to the telescopes or other facilities. From now on I would have to wear my ECWs to see the sky. When the doors groaned shut, we were thrown into darkness until our eyes adjusted to the feeble incandescent bulbs, spaced throughout the Dome, that would light our way through winter.

On February 4, the first meeting of the winterover crew, we learned—officially—that we didn't have enough stockpiled fuel to last through the winter. Thom Miller, the power plant mechanic and official observer of fuel levels, projected that to survive we needed forty-one tanker aircraft, planes carrying nothing but fuel, to land at the Pole in the next ten days.

Everything in the American Antarctic program—from tractors to aircraft to power generators—ran on JP8, the most highly refined jet fuel on the planet. (In comparison, Learjets run on JP4.) Hercules turboprop cargo planes have a ten-thousand-gallon fuel capacity in their massive wing tanks, yet they need only five thousand gallons to make an average round trip from McMurdo to the South Pole. The South Pole "fuelies" siphon off the extra fuel from each flight, storing it in huge tanks under the fuel arch. But the heavier the cargo, the more fuel was needed to run the plane and the less was available for us. Because of the New Pole construction project, the aircraft were carrying construction materials instead of extra fuel. And flights had become less and less frequent this month as the weather worsened on the coast. We were looking at a disastrous shortage.

This news did not go down well with the winterover crew. Some were angry and skeptical of ASA's commitment to keeping us all alive. A number of Polies were already packed and ready to leave if we weren't supplied with fuel by the fifteenth. Others, myself included, were ready to tough it out, no matter what. I couldn't leave my people, even if only one was left. There was talk of stopping all construction and sending the construction workers home, and leaving a skeleton support crew here to hold the base. Headquarters in Denver would soon have to make a decision on how to get us through the winter.

I wrote to my mother that night, explaining what was going on but trying to downplay my worries.

From: Jerri Nielsen
To: Mom
Date: Thu., 4 Feb. 1999 09:29:58 +1200
Subject: Soon the test begins

So much happens here and yet nothing ever does. Today we closed the doors to the Dome. Weather is getting nasty. I call it pulling up the moat and closing the doors to the castle. I feel what is coming, the death of the sun, the takeover of the darkness and wind. We are emotionally ready. We are expecting the experience of our lives and yet know that there could be an ugly dark side crouching in an unsuspecting corner somewhere. Two nights ago in my bed, I felt fear for the first time since this adventure began. It only lasted a few minutes but was intense and real. One of my friends said that it came to him in the same way, in the night . . .

Love, The Medicine Woman

* * *

From: Mom
To: Jerri Nielsen
Date: Fri., 5 Feb. 1999 08:39:11 EST
Subject: Hi Duffer

Dear Duffy,

It's scary for us thinking of you with only those big doors
and that wretched little dome between you and the ever-
lasting deepest cold on this earth. But, you have always been
a survivor in almost all areas of your life and I am sure you
are one of the strongest links in the little isolated chain of
life down there in the underworld. Duffy, we are so proud of
you.

MOMMA

A strange, anxious atmosphere permeated the station as closing
drew nearer and, one by one, we said good-bye to our summer friends.
I had by now acquired a videocamera, sent by my mother in a care
package. One of my snippets of tape from this time shows a Friday
night party in the 90 South Bar, with a seventies-style disco light ball
throwing strange shadows around the room, and Jim Morrison's eerie
baritone crooning "This is the end, my friend" on the sound system.

To our relief, more flights were making it in from McMurdo each
day and, according to Power Plant Thom, the winter fuel supply was
looking more promising. On February 14 the last Navy aircraft
landed at the South Pole. It marked the end of an era. The Naval Air
Squadron VXE-6, known as the Ice Pirates, had been supplying the
Pole since the beginnings of Operation Deep Freeze in 1955. But
over the past few decades, the U.S. military presence on the continent
had been gradually phased out—mainly for economic reasons. The
civilian-run National Science Foundation, which is in charge of the

U.S. Antarctic Program, had recently arranged with the New York Air National Guard 109th Airlift Wing to provide air support in Antarctica. Now, as the last Navy flight crew said their good-byes, the cooks in the galley brought out a special sheet cake decorated with a replica of the Dome and the Ice Pirates insignia.

On February 15, we held the traditional station-closing ceremony as the last flight to pick up passengers at the South Pole called in its approach. It was an Air Guard Hercules.

Almost everybody left at Pole—the last remaining summer staff and the hardcore winterovers—gathered in the galley. Welder Walt Fischel, a lively member of the construction crew, wore a huge top hat emblazoned with the Guinness label; one of my summer friends sat in the front row wearing a rainbow-colored Afro wig. Jerry Marty, the NSF representative, said a few words thanking us for serving our country and told us he'd see us again on October 25, the traditional reopening of the South Pole station.

My videocamera rolled as the crew sent him off with light applause. Then Jim Chambers, from ASA, stepped to the front of the room. "Only about twelve hundred people in history have wintered at the South Pole," he said, "so you are entering a very elite group . . ."

Just then a voice on the intercom cut him off. "Aircraft is on deck." We started whooping and hollering. Winter was suddenly very real. Chambers sped through his remarks. Dave Fischer, the SPAM, was returning to Denver for the winter. As of today, Mike Masterman would be in charge of the station. Fischer stood up to offer some more encouragement and words of praise.

"This is gonna be a different winter," he said. "Forty-one winterovers instead of the usual twenty-seven or twenty-eight. There's more of you and you've got more work than any winterover crew has had to do." He seemed to be avoiding eye contact with the guy in the fuzzy wig. "Please write, please call if you do need anything . . . you guys are taking on the toughest job in the U.S. Antarctic Program, and we are there to help.

"So for the winterovers—a round of applause!"

"Let's do it!" said Big John. *"Whooo-hoo!"*

"That's why we're here!" I yelled. "Let's do it!"

"Let's get these clowns out of here," said Dar the meteorologist, looking at the wig man. "Literally."

"You going or staying?" I asked Comms Tom from behind my camera.

"Wild penguins couldn't drag me away." He grinned.

We bundled up in parkas and bunny boots to send the summer folk off with a proper good-bye. All of my close summer friends, including John Wright, had caught earlier flights, and I was more than ready to see the rest of them off. We stood outdoors in minus fifty degrees, hugging our departing colleagues, dancing with each other to keep warm, and wishing they would just get on the plane and go already. Finally the Herc barreled down the skiway, lifted off with a roar, banked and circled the station, then climbed into the blue, cloud-streaked sky. The plateau was quiet again. Some people stayed on the deck to watch the plane disappear over the horizon. By then I was already back inside, sipping a cup of tea.

As the rest of the winterovers trickled back to the galley, a warm feeling of comfort washed over me. Those people who were borrowing our home were gone and life could now go on. The galley filled with friends. A few of us played Yahtzee and shared one of the last cans of mixed nuts on the planet—our planet. I had probably not been so happy since childhood.

That night we observed a recent South Pole tradition by gathering in the TV lounge to watch a double-feature of the 1950s sci-fi thriller *The Thing from Another World,* and the 1982 remake, simply called *The Thing.* They both tell the story of an isolated polar research station that, just as winter begins, is invaded by an evil creature from outer space.

The temperature was plummeting daily, but for four days after the official station closing, five fuel flights arrived daily to top up our winter supply. Having the constant stream of aircraft on deck all week took some of the drama out of station closing. But at least there was a chance to pack in a few more essentials before the big cutoff.

I had not yet received all of my medical resupply order. I was still low on x-ray film, my biggest concern. My pathology stains were so out-of-date I doubted they would be of use. Worst of all, I was short of contraceptives! I needed both pills and condoms. During the summer, I had put condoms in every restroom in the station for the taking. They had already expired anyway, but so had most everything here, and soon they were all gone. I thought they must have been used for water balloons. When one of the managers learned that the latest batch of condoms had been snatched up in one day, he jokingly threatened to call out over the loudspeaker that there would be no more condoms in the restrooms until the doctor got laid, as she didn't believe that they were being utilized appropriately. I was able to prevent this announcement.

As the last supply flight was being assembled for the Pole, Hugh Cowan, the doctor in MacTown, called to ask me which items were essential. The last two aircraft to land at Pole had been damaged by the extreme cold weather, and they were trying to determine if they should even attempt another flight. Much of the cargo was medical, although the shipment was also to include the last of our personal mail and part of the winter supply of cigarettes.

Hugh opened the resupply boxes and questioned me over the radio. Could I make do without Brevacol, oral contraceptives, and pathology stains?

"Hugh," I said, "we have to have contraceptives. My obstetrics skills are a bit rusty!"

He kept asking if I was sure, weren't there any alternatives? I finally blurted, "Yes, I could enforce abstinence . . . that would work here for sure!"

The radio transmission went silent. I think I actually flustered him! But face it, there were going to be thirty-two men and nine women marooned in a dark dome on ice for nine months. And as the officer in charge of the mental health of the crew, I was extremely concerned that their basic needs—including legal habits such as smoking and drinking—be met to get them through the winter.

"And we need more cigarettes," I added. "I'm not prepared to take care of twenty Polie smokers in nicotine withdrawal. I don't have that much Valium!"

In the end, my wish list didn't matter. The last flight was boomeranged, sent back to McMurdo due to bad weather, and with it our smokes, medical supplies, and mail. Two hours later, Mike was called to the Comms shack to talk to the commanding officer of the Air National Guard in MacTown. He had suspended all further flights. No one could reach Pole until next October.

"We can't make it," he said. "That was your last plane. You are completely on your own. Good luck."

As Mike later told me the story, the guys in the Comms shack just sat there for a few moments, looking at each other, letting the words sink in.

"There is no turning back now," said Mike.

I nodded gravely, out of respect for Mike's feelings. But inside I was churning with joy, thinking, *It's about time!*

CHAPTER 6:

An Irish Airman Foresees His Death

From: Jerri Nielsen
To: Family and friends
Date: 27 Feb. 1999
Subject: Last Days of Fall

The world is growing dark and cold and gloomy. The wind blows snow so that you can't see the station from outside. I am behind in my work every day as I have so much to do just to keep equipment running. I have never been so happy or felt more alive.

I am not afraid of anything as I spend my days with friends. And, I realize now, that I have already lived a lifetime in my 47 years. None of us fears death here, even though it is a sure thing with a long walk outside. Funny thing.

Love, Doc Holliday

Life was harder in some ways, but so much more enjoyable now that we were finally alone. All the winterovers had by now moved into the Dome or to the Elevated Dorm out in the suburbs. We held work parties in the lingering twilight to string flag lines between buildings so that people wouldn't get lost in the coming darkness. The routes that would be used during the winter were marked by six-foot bamboo poles, connected with rope and topped with color-coded flags that you might be able to see with a flashlight. Green flags denoted a safe route, red ones marked hazards such as drop-offs, and black flags meant "off-limits." As the sun set and the wind picked up we would pull our way along, careful not to leave the path. By now it was minus 55 F. inside the Dome, and you couldn't walk between the inner buildings without a coat. My hands would go numb taking out the trash. If I showered and then ran to the galley, my hair would turn stiff and brittle before I got there.

The setting sun threw long shadows over the station, and there was an eerie feeling everywhere, like a wonderful night animal was lurking across the ice. Behind it was more darkness, weeks and months of darkness. This was the beginning of our passage into an unknown world, and everyone in the crew seemed energized. It felt like the start of something magical.

There was a tremendous amount of work to do. First we had to close Summer Camp while we still had light. We all spent a day away from our usual duties to clean and vacuum the Jamesways, remove all the linen to be washed, and then close down the hatches. I took on the job of washing all the sheets and blankets. It took three days. I must have done a hundred loads of laundry that week. We hauled everything that wouldn't be needed until next summer out to the cargo berms.

Mike and I inventoried the station's cache of emergency medical supplies, kept at the emergency power plant in case the Dome burned or some other catastrophe forced us to evacuate. A stash of metal combat medical cases contained everything we would need: medications, bandages, dressings, IV bags, oxygen and airway supplies, surgical setups, and stretchers. I took careful note of what was needed and then returned to Biomed to add more supplies. I wrote the dosages and uses for the medication on the boxes and included medical books that might help others in case I was killed or disabled.

Mike and I checked the supply of extra sleeping bags stored on one of the berms. At the same time, Donna and Wendy were hard at work, in terrible temperatures, organizing and evaluating the frozen emergency food supply kept in metal containers called millvans.

Mike also ordered us to prepare our personal gear in case we lost the Dome in a fire. Although it had never burned, there had been some close calls. In past seasons outbuildings had been lost, and with no humidity to speak of, we always lived in fear of fire. Everyone had to pack one bag to be stored in Summer Camp. I wondered what to pack for Armageddon. What would the well-dressed Polie girl need? Should I give up one of my two wool sweaters? Would I want something to wear while I slept? Should I take my books? Candy? A bottle of good Scotch? (That could buy me a toothbrush at the end.) Did I want to give all that up for a pillow? In the end, I remembered my "take half of what you need and take twice as much money" motto. I would pack Glenfiddich in plastic saline bottles, a case of candy bars, a pack of cards, and some ladylike toiletries. I'd be able to trade for what I forgot. And to feed my soul, I threw in a book on the history of the world and a medical text. That, and all of my extra survival clothing.

Only a small window remained before we lost the use of the snow machines and tractors, none of which was specially fitted for these phenomenally cold conditions. JP8, the aircraft fuel used for all the heaters and engines, turned into a glutinous gel at temperatures below minus 80 F. Glass windows shattered easily, and hydraulic lines cracked in the extreme cold.

The snowmobiles were already complaining bitterly. They were difficult to start and had to be coaxed into speeds above twenty mph. Once they went down, we would have to man-haul supplies on sleds, just like the old explorers. Most of the heavy equipment had already been put into hibernation at a place called the boneyard. It was the mechanical wizardry of Big John, the Horse Whisperer of Machines, that kept them running at all. All winter long, Big John would drag the machines, one by one, from the open-air boneyard back into the garage for their big annual maintenance. He changed their fluids, lubricated their fittings, and peered into every nook and cranny looking for mechanical maladies to repair.

Meanwhile, everybody was sorting and logging in the last batches of supplies and parts that had arrived before closing. Boxes of medicines and other items were stacked all over Biomed, waiting to be entered in the dreaded, laborious Mapcon inventory program. This was it. What I didn't have now I would have to make, borrow, or steal.

This period just before winter was the best time of year for "skuaing" around the station. "To skua" was to glean what had been abandoned by others, a practice named for the gull-like skuas that flock to the Antarctic coast in the summer and pick through the trash bins at McMurdo. I found I had a real knack for the art of skua-ing. I enjoyed diving into trash bins for things that I could clean up and fix. I would find games and Halloween costumes stashed on the rooftops in the Dome, or art supplies out on the berms. When it came to medical supplies or equipment, I had no compunctions about appropriating them for the hospital.

The summer people had left behind myriad treasures for the skillful Polie skua-er. Cleaning the Jamesways had allowed me to sort through all the abandoned bedding and to cadge the best stuff for the winter crew and the hospital. I found some wonderful flannel sheet sets. I would hand the nice ones out as gifts and salvage the ratty ones to make covers for heating pads and ice bags. I found a one-piece bunny suit in the trash that looked like it would fit tiny Yubecca Bragg, one of our heavy-equipment operators. Some people had left vaporizers that I snatched up as an edge against the dry polar air.

My big score was an extra stash of little green notebooks that we all used to keep our notes and "to-do" lists. We called them our "green brains." Our memories were all deteriorating as chronic hypoxia ate away at our brain cells. Studies done in Antarctica showed a decrease in short-term memory of 13 percent in those staying through the winter. And that study was done at sea level! The effects on long-term memory had not been studied.

Nothing was wasted in our isolated world. And if we were negligent for a moment, James Evans, aka Pic, the man in charge of recycling at Pole, would remind us. Pic attacked his job with religious fervor. Whenever somebody misused the triwall bins, or committed some other sin against the strict rules of recycling, Pic would send a rocket to everyone's emailbox.

> From: James Evans
> To: #winter
> Date: Fri., 26 Feb. 1999 01:14:57 +1200
> Subject: We're talkin' trash.
>
> Hey,
>
> Let's go over a particularly difficult and confusing category of refuse. WOOD.
>
> First criterion of this category is that the object in question actually be MADE OUT OF WOOD!!! It comes from trees. Unfortunately, I can't point out a tree right now to clarify my point. However, wood does NOT look or feel like BLACK STYROFOAM, which is what I found in the wood box in the Dome a couple of minutes ago.
>
> Wood comes from forests. Styrofoam comes from hell.
>
> Got it?
>
> Thanx,
> Pic, tyrant of trash

Pic Evans's official job title, "Environmental Specialist," sounded too grand to him. He preferred to be called a garbageman. Recycling was as natural to him as breathing, and it was at the core of his life's philosophy. He hated waste and greed and had learned to need less and make use of everything during his years as a Peace Corps volunteer in Africa. He had traveled the Third World on three dollars a day as a young man, and could still get by with almost nothing. He started going to the Ice after Africa because he wanted to go from one extreme to the other.

"Comfort bores me," he told me. "Rich people bore me; it's the poor people who make my day." He was the quintessential Polie: He never took a job for the money. The harder the work, the worse the conditions, the better he liked it. In his previous life, he had been an Eagle Scout and a U.S. Marine. But he was no saint and he wanted everyone to know it. "Gandhi I ain't," he said. He had been an alcoholic, and he avoided parties at the Pole to maintain his hard-won eight years of sobriety. Pic now lived a solitary life, reading and practicing yoga and being our conscience of trash.

He was skinny as a toothpick, which is how he got his nickname. Like most rough travelers, Pic had contracted his full share of tropical diseases along the way. He showed people how to strain water through a handkerchief to prevent infestation with guinea worms in Africa. He suffered from chronic sinus infections because a Ugandan dentist had accidentally hammered a tooth into his sinus while trying to repair one of his crowns. Pic took it all in stride. When he returned to Biomed for more medications for his ailments, he would bring the small plastic bag I had given him before, washed, dried, tattered, and taped together.

Back in the world I would probably never have had a chance to know someone like Pic, or many of my other close friends at the Pole. One of them was Heidi Schernthanner, a woman in her thirties who became my buddy and confidante over the winter. Like Loree, the meteorologist, Heidi sent me short stories, sonnets, and affirmations as gifts of friendship. I gave her a collection of poetry that contained

"Wild Women Blues." She and Wendy Beeler, the cook, were known as "the twins." They were very close friends, having known each other back in the States. They even looked alike: tall and slender, with short blond hair.

Heidi had grown up in Idaho, the daughter of an Austrian ski instructor. The Ice was a family passion: She had two sisters in Antarctica this year, one at Palmer Station and one in McMurdo. Heidi had studied to be a physical education teacher, but ended up on the Ice, first as a laborer, and then as a heavy equipment operator. She had to struggle for her place in a "man's" job, and I understood the obstacles she encountered.

Toward the end of February, just two weeks after the station closed, I came down with my first illness on the Ice. It seemed to be bronchitis, and it left me tired and feverish. I stayed in the Dome for several days, since the winds outside were fierce and there was constant cloud cover and blowing snow. The infection must have been something brewing inside me, because once the station closed and planes bringing new people and new microbes stopped coming, there should have been no new diseases for us to catch. By now we had all been exposed to each other's germs and had developed the immunities we needed. The winterover crew was starting to function like one organism, with one big immune system, and in a way, one nervous system, too.

We developed a synergy that grew more and more intense as the weeks went by. If one person was sick or unhappy, the whole group could feel it. There was no way to avoid each other, even if we wanted privacy. There were few secrets at Pole. You could hear the people in the next room turn over in their bed. You couldn't crank your stereo loud enough to block out private conversations. Everyone knew where you were most of the time. If you tried to slip away, people knew you were missing. To escape, some tried to live opposite hours to everyone else, or they stayed in an uninhabitable place, such as a sleeping bag under a telescope.

This was a sign of "being toasted." Toastiness is actually a documented syndrome characterized by social withdrawal, staring into space, memory loss, and attention deficit. We had all seen examples of toasted Polies when we first arrived at the station and ran into members of the outgoing winterover crew. They would avoid eye contact with us and seek only each other's company. They would wander away in mid-sentence. I overheard two toasted Polies conversing in the galley; one asked the other: "What's that country, in the Mediterranean, you know, that's shaped like a boot?" And neither could think of the word.

I had read about this condition in the Navy's polar manual. The Navy thought it was caused by constant lack of intellectual stimulation and sensory deprivation. Some suffered more severely than others. They would shut down and do almost nothing. You would find them lost in no thought at all; looking out to a horizon that wasn't there. Generally, the symptoms started to appear in August. For our crew, however, signs of toast showed up much earlier. By the time we went to McMurdo for R&R in January, most of us were already becoming reclusive and feeling uncomfortable around non-Polies. (The symptoms can last for months after returning to the world.)

Joel, the dancing NOAA officer, started turning into a hermit almost as soon as the sun went down. Andy, who worked with him, noticed it first.

"Joel is turning into a dog," Andy announced at breakfast one morning. "All he does is eat and sleep and take his walk every day to the Clean Air Facility."

He wasn't alone. Pakman, the rocking electrician, would fall asleep immediately after supper. Others, referred to as the "walking dead," rarely slept at all.

To keep the monotony of sunless, identical workdays from taking its toll, we tried to stay as active and motivated as possible. Now that summer was over, we had more time and space to entertain ourselves. We set up tables in the upper galley for the hobbyists. Big John, Ken, and Charlie started building airplanes, and Mike was constructing a large Victorian dollhouse. Like some polar equivalent of the Walton family, Yubecca and Liza made a quilt, Donna and I sewed, and Heidi and Wendy knitted. Captain Kirk Spelman, head of the cargo department, made pinhole cameras with cardboard scraps, creating surreal black-and-white images of our surreal life.

To keep every day distinct, we stacked up weekly events. Every Tuesday was Bad Science Fiction Movie Night in the TV lounge. Some of the world's greatest telescopes were here, and with them came the world's greatest astronomers. Great astronomers have strange tastes in movies. One week we saw *Godzilla vs. Megagodzilla.* Another week it was *Journey to the Center of the Earth.* Our favorites came from the cult Mystery Science Theatre 2000 series. (I even named my x-ray machine "Tom Servo" after one of the characters.)

Saturday nights were dedicated to action movies. We arrived early in the TV lounge to get a place on one of the three couches, which we called bobsleds. Three to five people would pile on, often in a long row, with each person sitting between another's legs, using the other's chest for a back rest. The station was built to winter seventeen people, and we were forty-one.

On Monday and Thursday nights I ran "Pole Mart," the station store where you could buy sundries, snack foods, cigarettes, and certain beverages, including beer, wine, and other forms of alcohol. Some Polies brought cash, but like coal miners and sharecroppers, most of us used credit at the company store. I was a lousy storekeeper and found the job tedious. I didn't object to selling cigarettes and alcohol (whatever gets you through the night; I believe educated people need to make their own choices), but many of us were offended by some of the stock. We had been warned that the Pole was so green we had to bring rechargeable batteries and leave perfume at home. Yet here I was pushing ecologically incorrect goods such as thirty little pretzels in a *tin can!* Before we left the world we had all been asked to list what we thought we would consume in a year. Pic had requested the pretzels but couldn't bring himself to eat them because of the packaging.

Bookkeeping was the toughest part of the job for me. Fortunately,

Donna had run her own country store in Vermont, and Liza Lobe had worked at the store during a previous winter. At Pole, there was always someone who knew more than you did about almost everything, and they were always willing to help out.

Luckily for me, the store computer crashed during the first month of winter and I had to keep records on paper, which I found much easier. Even Lisa Beal, a computer tech and master with technology, couldn't repair the computer. Lisa was one of my best friends at Pole, and she often volunteered to help me with the store. We liked studying people's purchasing habits. For instance, right after station closing, everyone was buying as much Guinness as they could carry, for fear the supply would run out. After a few weeks, Lisa murmured one night as we closed up shop, "I think we have evolved from hunter-gatherers to drinker-hoarders."

There was genuine cause for concern. We all knew that the supply of good beer had run out early the previous winter. Last year someone in MacTown had taken all the Guinness intended for the Pole and sent us a pallet of a soft drink called Mr. Pibb disguised as Guinness. This was the impetus for the "Dome Brewers Association." Each Thursday, the brewers made beer with hops and other ingredients procured in Christchurch. There was also a still, ordered from New Zealand and brought in clandestinely on a military flight, that produced "South Pole Toast Juice," a form of moonshine, from whatever could be scavenged. Liza Lobe, who knew where everything was stored, found a load of off-inventory corn syrup that was programmed to be retro-ed (meaning returned) to the States. We were grateful to her for keeping the guys from using up all the frozen corn on station.

Like my lost friend Dorianne, Lisa Beal was always making me laugh. When we were together, the decibel level rose ten points. She was quick with retorts, and I was her straight man. This was Lisa's eighth tour on the Ice but her first winter. She had worked at Palmer station and McMurdo and had sailed on the research vessels. After thirteen months of Ice time, she had figured out what she needed. She didn't bring much extra clothing but lived in her Carhartts and bunny boots. She knew that everything she really required would be provided by the Antarctic program in her three orange bags. She used her weight allowance to bring an electronic music synthesizer, a personal computer, and an amazing array of hot sauces. Her dream, when she got off the Ice, was to build a storm-chasing van and track tornadoes in Oklahoma.

In winter, at last I had time to join some of the activities being offered by my fellow Polies. I passed on the swing dance lessons from Joel and the karate course from Nuclear Nick, but I attended the computer class Lisa gave every Thursday after the store closed. I also signed up for the ham radio class on Monday nights, offered by Comms Tom, who taught us to build radios out of toilet paper rolls. He also organized another winter activity: the first South Pole radio station, dubbed KOLD by Lisa. Somehow he and Nuclear Nick were able to build a transmitter (using, among other things, the Dome itself as an antenna) to broadcast random-play CD music to anyone with a receiver on station.

Tom Carlson was another of the "graybeards"—like Big John, Ken Lobe, myself, and others in the over-forty crowd, we brought half a lifetime's experience with us to Pole. Tom called the Twin Cities area in Minnesota home, but he had traveled in more than seventy-five countries before taking the position as the South Pole communications specialist. He was an electrical engineer by training and had done more than a few amazing things in his wide-ranging career, including running ground stations for Mystic Star, Air Force One's communication system. Now he ran our lifeline to the outside world. He also fixed the copier and was constantly working on my x-ray machine.

Comms Tom was bright and energetic, always full of fun and adventure. He was a professional musician who was at his best on the old-time fiddle. Comms was teaching Joel and Dar the clawhammer banjo in hopes of putting together a band. Like me, Comms Tom had been fascinated by exotic places since childhood. In fact, we had both been Rotary exchange students in 1969, experiences that eventually led us both to the Pole and started our friendship. We had met in Spanish Club during the summer. One night I was telling a story in my very bad Spanish when I became lost for words. Whenever I get mixed up in a foreign language, I unconsciously throw in words from the first language I learned as an adult, Swedish. Comms asked in perfect Swedish, "Where did you learn that?" He was of Swedish descent and had learned Spanish as an exchange student in Argentina, the same year I had gone to Sweden—in the same exchange program.

I was hoping to learn enough about ham radio from Comms to qualify for an operator's license by the end of winter (I eventually had to drop out). I was also very serious about learning Russian from Nuclear Nick, our renaissance beaker. Nick Starinski was a nuclear physicist originally from the Ukraine but now a Canadian citizen, with a wife and small child back home in Montreal. Not only was he a genius scientist, but he also had a black belt in karate, wrote songs, and could draw portraits.

I made it my mission to remember and celebrate birthdays as they came up. It was important to me that everyone have the best birthday of his or her life so far from home. When Andy and Choo Choo Charlie both had birthdays the same week, I threw a special M*A*S*H theme party in Biomed. Everyone was encouraged to dress in surgical scrubs. We used the gurney as a buffet table and served chips and dips in sterilized bedpans and instrument trays. I had gone "shopping" around the Dome and managed to find imitation crab with seafood sauce, cream cheese, and Triscuits. I dispensed red and white wine and martinis from IV drip bags. All scientists received a "beaker" as a glass as they entered the party.

The M*A*S*H theme song played in the background, and people laughed like teenagers as I walked around the room, offering everyone hits of pure oxygen out of a big green tank saying, "Welcome back to the Home Planet." At one point I considered retrieving from storage my portable hyperbaric chamber, and holding a raffle to "Win a Trip to Sea Level." But I decided it would be bad to inadvertently break someone's eardrums along the way.

I always tried to give a special gift to anyone celebrating a birthday at the Pole. Big John and I cooked supper for the crew, giving Chef Wendy the night off. Giant Greg got a science book by Carl Sagan that I had brought from home; another astronomer got an outerspace board game found on the roof. I would always wrap them as nicely as possible. My favorite wrapping paper came from cut-up emergency blankets that the Navy had left lying around in crates in the Dome. I couldn't imagine how they could possibly help save anyone from hypothermia at minus 100 F, but they did make attractive gift wrap, with a shiny silver side and a shiny gold side. Electrical tape and used IV tubing made pretty bows.

Other activities to keep us going through the winter were the card games and darts in the 90 South Bar, a small gym for those with the fortitude to work out, and a sauna. My favorite diversion was just relaxing in each other's rooms and talking with friends. Everyone had a story here, and I truly never tired of listening.

To an outsider, all the games and parties and silly nicknames might seem a bit childish for such a serious mission, but in fact all of them stemmed from a long and sensible tradition. The earliest polar explorers did the same sorts of things to survive in this harsh and isolated environment. Scott's men put on elaborate plays to pass the time and dressed up as women for some of the roles. Shackleton's men played football on the pack ice while their ship was slowly crushed. There is wisdom in the notion of laughing in the face of danger. It helps people cope.

Antarctic lore is also rife with nicknames, from "Birdie" Bowers to "Titus" Oates. Recent generations of Polies have been encouraged to keep up the custom, because it binds people to a group. You give up your old identity and assume a new one as a member of the tribe. During orientation in Denver before coming to the Ice, Polies gave themselves nicknames as part of a "ropes course" exercise to build teamwork. Some of them—like Choo Choo Charlie—stuck. One of my favorite nicknames belonged to a carpenter, Rich Higgins. He had grown up ski racing in New England, trained as an accountant, and when he moved West to Snowmass, Colorado, he became a carpenter and built custom homes. His original nickname was "Richie Rich" but while working at the Pole, Richie keep lacerating his fingers. First he was Nine-Fingered, then Eight-Fingered, and finally he became known as Seven-Fingered Richie.

From: John Davis
To: #winter
Date: Mon., 1 Mar. 1999 02:07:40 +1200
Subject: WHERE'S HOME

Hi folks:

When I got here one of the first things I did was figure out which way home was. I suppose most of you have already figured out which way your home is, but just in case you haven't, here is a really easy way. Just figure out when it is noon at your home. Go outside when it's noon at your home and look at the sun. Your home is right beneath it. If your home is on daylight savings time, your home will be fifteen degrees to the left of the sun.

That's it folks.

There's no place like home.
John Davis.

Middle John's memo arrived on my forty-seventh birthday. I suppose I should have been thinking about my life back in Ohio, but I found it hard to imagine any place other than here as my home. I was in daily contact with my mother, who had borrowed my laptop and soon wore out the keyboard writing me emails full of family gossip and long, beautiful descriptions of life back in the States as she saw it. She would describe everything in loving detail: the fat, hot raindrops in Florida where she and Dad had bought a second home and where Dad was convalescing; the delicious meals she was preparing; her trips to flea markets and antique shops in search of hidden treasures. She hadn't heard a word from my children, and neither had I, so there was little to say on the subject. Instead she talked about American politics, how the stock market was climbing, how my doctor friends were doing in their jobs.

I looked forward to her correspondence, but the subject matter became less and less relevant to me. I was living in the present tense with no real past and no predictable future in my world. All directions pointed north, but none of them led me home. Home was here and now.

For a birthday present, Big John took me on a "motorcycle" ride out to the rose-tinged plateau. He had managed to keep the snowmobiles running long past their usual winter bedtime. And so once again, we set off racing over the sastrugi, out to the edge of the world.

I was holding on from behind, using his broad shoulders as a windscreen. It was wild and joyous skirting down the manmade hills at the storage berms, riding as though each ride might be our last. Despite the speed, I always felt safe with Big. It was good to take your "personal mechanic" with you when traveling a long way from the base.

Still, we had some close calls together. One time my feet froze when I carelessly wore my summer boots. About five miles from the Dome I realized I could no longer walk or feel anything below my ankles. To my horror, Big John yanked off my boots and socks and stuck my frozen feet in his bare armpits until I could feel them again.

I had learned my lesson. For my birthday trip I was dressed properly as we skimmed along the waves of sastrugi. The sun was so low by now, and the light so soft and flat, that it was impossible to pick out changes in texture on the ice plain at any distance. Someone had made a pass with the tractor where there had never before been traffic, and we were right on top of a set of ruts by the time Big John saw them coming.

I felt him kick the snowmobile aside as both of us went flying through the air. I landed on my stomach, arms outstretched like a diving angel, and skidded along the ice, eating snow, for another ten yards. When I managed to open one eye, Big John was crawling toward me, shouting, "Doc! Doc! Are you all right?"

I pulled myself to my knees, spitting ice, checking to make sure my shoulder wasn't broken. It wasn't. I stood up and held out my gloved hand.

"Give me the keys," I said. "I'm driving."

Later I celebrated my birthday with a few friends out at the Clean Air Building. Joel and Andy had a five-hour videotape of a blazing log in a fireplace, which they played to conjure up a cozy atmosphere. Some of my favorite Celtic music was on the CD player. We each wore fake eyeglasses with rubber noses and birthday clown hats. Loree and Andy made coffee, and we told stories. It was the best birthday I had had since childhood. I was forty-seven and surrounded by friends, in a community that needed me, in a place that I loved, discovering more every day about what truly mattered in life. I understood that I could not control my past; it was gone. I saw nothing in my future but wondrous possibilities.

In the last days of Antarctic dusk, we were beginning to realize how isolated we had become. The only regular contact we had with the world was email and a daily radio check with McMurdo Station, eight hundred miles away. MacTown was also closed, with only two hundred Coastie winterovers remaining. Not a single airplane was left on the continent.

The Pole's skiway markers had been taken down so that blowing snow couldn't drift around them and make it even harder to plow the strip open when flights resumed in the spring. Snow and sastrugi had already covered the bright red edge-markings painted, for the sake of biodegradability, with strawberry Kool-Aid. The skiway was now indistinguishable from the rest of the polar plateau except for the occasional bamboo pole left to mark the perimeter. It was as good a reminder as any that, in the end, the Ice takes everything back.

The first thing you learn at the Pole is that if the power generators fail, you die. The three 475-kilowatt generators in the power plant not only supply the station with electricity but heat the Dome as well. Without them, everything and everyone in the main buildings would freeze solid within hours. To survive, we would have to evacuate the Dome and head to the Elevated Dorm, which had its own heating furnace and could be powered by the emergency generator. It would support life—barely—until we could be rescued at the end of winter (assuming that the generator didn't fail as well). For these reasons, we all took each emergency drill very seriously.

As the station's medical officer, my job in an "incident," such as a power failure, was to stand by in Biomed and wait for casualties. Manager Mike, Big John, and Power Plant Thom were to race to the power plant and restore electricity.

Thom Miller was a twenty-five-year-old Grateful Dead fan from Connecticut who had brought his snowboard to the South Pole. He was also one of the most solid members of the crew. This was his third season on the Ice, and his first winter. He had spent his previous seasons in remote field camps as a machinery mechanic, at one place rebuilding a bulldozer from scavenged parts. Like quite a few others, he was in contact with a grade-school class back in the States and had pictures of them in his office.

Thom was our regular bartender at the 90 South Bar and ran the Dome Brewers Association. In another life he had worked in a Pizza Hut, so he often prepared our Saturday-night pizzas. He was fun to be around and mature beyond his years, a "cool head." We trusted him with our power, which meant we trusted him with our lives.

We ran our first winter power-failure drill shortly after station closing. Everything went as expected, at first. As Big reported later, he got to the power plant and went though the series of procedures necessary to shut down the faulty engine, if it was still running, and get another one on line. Big fired up the second generator with no problem. Then suddenly the power plant filled up with what seemed to be thick white smoke. Everybody started running around looking for its source and quickly discovered it was not smoke but glycol fumes coming through the fresh-air intake from the roof.

A heat exchanger on the roof had sprung a leak. This device took the waste heat from the engine exhaust and transferred it to a pipe filled with glycol—the main ingredient in antifreeze. The glycol was pumped in a closed loop out to the "rodwell" where, like hot water in a household radiator, it was used to melt ice, and then heat that water to melt more ice for the station's water supply.

Big John called Power Plant Thom, who had gone out to the emergency power plant, to tell him the glycol loop was down. Thom ordered the main generators shut down until that problem was fixed and put the station on emergency power. This was now a potential crisis. We had to get the water well back on line as soon as possible. If it stayed down too long the lines would freeze, and the station would be without water.

While Big, Boston Bob the electrical foreman, and Mike were still trying to locate the leak in the glycol loop, Power Plant Thom called and asked Big to ride out to the emergency power plant. One of the two emergency generators there had shut down on an "engine overheat fault." Only one generator was powering the entire station, and one was not enough. If the situation continued for an hour, we would have to begin evacuating the Dome.

Big hauled himself out to the emergency power plant on his fastest snowmobile. When he arrived, things weren't looking good. The one unit still on line was running at maximum capacity. It would hold for awhile, but with no backup, there was no room for error. We were a half hour into the incident; time was running out. Big started digging into the circuitry of the "overheated" generator to locate the problem that shut it down (it turned out to be a loose screw in the thermostat). Luckily, the guys at the power plant called to say they had fixed the glycol leak, and we were going back on main power.

It was a close call, but everyone had done his job well and disaster had been averted. One thing still troubled us, however: Nobody knew why the glycol loop had sprung a leak, or if it would happen again.

We held our first winter poetry slam in the galley one Friday night, with Big John as master of ceremonies. He had kept his Mohawk haircut and wore his leather jacket and "dress" shorts for the occasion (a clean version of "work" shorts). The event was well attended, and the range of poetic styles was astonishing.

Loree began by reading a heartfelt love poem by Keats. She finished to a round of applause, and Big hopped up to the front of the room like the emcee at a Vegas nightclub. "God, does it take balls to come up in front of this crowd or what?" he said, clapping heartily.

Next up was Pakman, who chewed on a slice of pizza while reading his original verse from a scrap of paper. "I'm not sure what to call this," he said.

> *We went to McMurdo for a holler,*
> *The big guy did not try to foller.*
> *I went this way and that,*
> *We did not go to camp,*
> *We got a ride on a copter,*
> *told a lot of people,*
> *But heard no one holler.*
> *We had a great time,*
> *Even though I might have been hard to find*
> *I loved my time with Big Johnner . . .*

Big John, giving Pakman a bear hug, was moved to make a short speech. "I'm really happy about the community involvement here. It's important that we get together and share things. It's so special, I just love it."

"It's heavy!" someone shouted.

"I love you, man!" yelled Dar.

Big John grinned and took a slug of Wild Turkey. It was his turn.

"This is a poem by Robert Service, sent to me by John Wright, the Master Blaster, a solid dude," he said. "It takes place on the opposite Pole, the other screw in the globe. It's cool . . ." And Big John proceeded to read "The Men That Don't Fit In" with great enthusiasm:

> There's a race of men that don't fit in,
> a race that can't sit still.
> And they split the hearts of kith and kin,
> as they roam the world at will.
> They range the field and they rove the flood.
> They climb the mountain's crest.
> Theirs is the curse of gypsy blood:
> they don't know how to rest.

After Big had growled the final verse, Nuclear Nick shyly took the stage with a poem by Pushkin.

"There are two things I would never do in my life," he said in his lilting Ukrainian accent. "I would never pay taxes, and I would never read Russian poems in front of an English audience!"

The crowd yelled, "Buuuuttttt . . ."

"*But* Big John asked me personally to do that. And then he gave me a glass of Wild Turkey—so I can cope with my embarrassment!"

Then Nick ran a hand through his long black hair and explained that the poem he would read "tells of oaks growing on the beach, golden chains on the trees . . ." He shook his head, giving up on a translation. "Just listen to the sound," he urged, and read the poetry of a man who could make the Russian language flow like music.

Then it was my turn. I had chosen my favorite poem by my favorite poet, and I tried to explain why: "I chose this one because I love to fly, and I'm Irish, and I really understand 'a lonely impulse of delight.' The poem is by Yeats, and it is called 'An Irish Airman Foresees His Death.'"

> *I know that I shall meet my fate*
> *Somewhere among the clouds above;*
> *Those that I fight I do not hate,*
> *Those that I guard I do not love;*
> *My country is Kiltartan Cross,*
> *My countrymen Kiltartan's poor,*
> *No likely end could bring them loss*
> *Or leave them happier than before.*
> *Nor law, nor duty bade me fight,*
> *Nor public men, nor cheering crowds,*
> *A lonely impulse of delight*
> *Drove to this tumult in the clouds;*
> *I balanced all, brought all to mind,*
> *The years to come seemed waste of breath,*
> *A waste of breath the years behind*
> *In balance with this life, this death.*

It was only March and we didn't know each other well enough for me to explain my attraction to these last four lines. Soon we would know each other intimately. We would understand each other's longing for "the edge," the demons of our pasts, the grace that had brought us to the bottom of the world. In a few months I would not have to explain why the years to come and the years behind seemed waste of breath, balanced with this life, this death. By then, everyone would know who I was and how I came to be here.

*   *   *

Not long after the poetry slam, perhaps just a few nights later, I found a mass in my breast. I was sitting in bed, reading a book, and absently rubbing my upper chest when my fingers stopped on a small, hard lump. It was near the surface of my right breast, at twelve o'clock. I palpated it, trying to decide how big it was and what it might mean. I had fibrocystic breasts and had found small breast lumps before. They were always related to my menstrual cycle and went away after a few weeks. Lumps ran in the family; my mother had the same condition and had even had a couple of biopsies done on benign masses. My mammogram had been negative only six months ago, so I wasn't particularly worried. I decided to keep an eye on this lump and wait a month to see if anything changed.

CHAPTER 7:

Three Shades
of Twilight

Roopesh Ojha, known as Roo, was one of my favorite dinner companions. He was from Darjeeling in Northern India, but he didn't drink tea.

"Here, Roo," I'd say, planting a fresh can of tea leaves beneath his nose. "Smell childhood."

The scent would tickle that part in his brain where the past was stored, and he would tell me tales of India: of mountains and small villages, of rivers where mourners set the dead afloat on brightly decorated rafts. His father had been a Brahmin doctor, and as his son, he seemed to understand me instinctively. Or perhaps it was just his keen sense of perception. He was a Harvard astronomer devoted to his science. He worked in the Dark Sector on the AST/RO radio telescope, looking at cold molecular clouds of matter to find the origin of stars.

Roo shared his many interests with all of us. He spearheaded a small investment club that disseminated information on high-tech stocks to its members' email accounts. Later, the club became a forum for philosophy and religion. It was fascinating to follow along as Giant

Greg, who spent his days looking for the footprints of the Big Bang, Nuclear Nick, who studied neutrinos in the ice, Loree, a meteorologist who detected the grace and redemption of God in the clouds, and Roo, the star seeker, pounded out detailed arguments on faith vs. science and the existence of God.

Amazingly, even though we slept so close together we could hear each other cough, roll over, and breathe, much of our real communication took the form of written words. In the information age, the art of a well-crafted letter to communicate with a friend had been revived here. With computers on each desk, we were entrenched in new technology while living on a frontier as inaccessible as it had been in the days of wooden ships and dogsled teams.

One day I asked, "Gee, Roo, you're an astronomer. When will it get dark down here?" He was so delighted by the question that he prepared what he called a "rough-and-ready" memo for us describing, in simplified terms, exactly what was about to happen in our dimming world.

From: Roopesh Ojha
To: #winter
Date: Mon., 15 Mar. 1999 07:35:24 +1200
Subject: Nightfall

Hello Polies

Our sunset will be at 1000 hrs. on March 21, Sunday. The bottom edge of the sun will hit the equator (which is our horizon) at about 0330 hrs. on March 20 (Saturday). The center of the sun will be on the horizon about 1840 hrs. on the same day. And the top of the sun hits the horizon at 1000 hrs. on Sunday (the official sunset mentioned above).

But when does it get dark?

There are three kinds of twilight, Civil, Nautical, and Astronomical, which begin when the sun is 6, 12, and 18 degrees below the horizon (respectively). To give you a sense of how dark each one is: at the end of Civil twilight the brightest stars are visible and the horizon is clearly defined. At the end of Nautical twilight the horizon is no longer visible, and at the end of Astronomical twilight the indirect illumination from the Sun is less bright than starlight.

For us:

Civil Twilight ends about 0500 hrs. on April 5.
Nautical Twilight ends about 1900 hrs. on April 21.
Astronomical Twilight ends about 2100 hrs. on May 11.
So we should be completely dark by May 11!

Your friendly neighborhood astronomer,
Roo

I was fascinated by the concept of twilight and its three discrete stages. Yet all I truly understood was that the world outside the Dome seemed more beautiful and more alien every day. Now the sky was deep purple with bands of orange on the horizon. I was outside watching the sky one day when I saw my first aurora. It looked like a shimmering green curtain rolling in a solar wind, with pink searchlights shooting into the atmosphere, like heaven's own movie premiere. The rest was silence, and space.

I was beginning to comprehend what Admiral Richard Byrd had written about the sunset in his Antarctic memoir, *Alone:* "Above me the day was dying; the night was rising in its place . . . This is the way the world will look to the last man when he dies." I understood Byrd's wonder and his fear. Antarctica was a place so hostile and alien to life, that life sang out, and every small breath was a triumph against nothingness. You were forced to re-create yourself again and again or risk being swallowed in the emptiness, and to do that you had to know what you were made of. The route to the Pole was, after all, an inner journey. Antarctica was a blank slate on which you could write your soul.

Ever since the glycol leak in early March, when we had switched to emergency power, the station's "Uninterruptible Power Source" had been interrupted. No one knew why. The UPS was a collection of twenty deep-cycle lead-acid batteries in the Comms shack that were supposed to keep our communications systems operating in the event of a power outage. Comms Tom was simultaneously trying to recharge the batteries and looking for the source of the failure. Now, if we lost power, we also lost contact with the outside world. Nobody would even know what had happened to us.

Meanwhile, the station was plagued by a string of strange accidents. By mid-March, the office in Denver started calling our sit-reps "disaster of the week at Pole." One week, in particular, was a succession of strange mishaps:

It started when Wendy lopped off the fleshy end of a finger while chopping chives. She walked into Biomed with the fingertip wrapped in a napkin. The severed part was nonviable and she would retain more feeling in the fingertip by just letting it heal. I dressed it and sent her back to work. (We needed her; it was nearly dinnertime. Harsh continent, as we would say.)

An hour or so later, I went to the galley to check on her, only to watch in horror while she slipped and stabbed herself in the nostril with a very large fork. It was a superficial forking, but the punctures bled profusely, and because she had bruised a facial nerve, a couple of her teeth went numb.

By this time, supper wasn't going real well. I helped drain the pasta and deal with the baked chicken while she stemmed the hemorrhage and pulled the meal together.

Suddenly Lisa came running in, not looking like her playful, funny self.

"Doc, you'd better drop the chicken and go to Comms," she said. "They're over there playing in sulfuric acid!"

I sprinted across the Dome to the Comms shack. The place was covered in baking soda, as if hit by an Arm & Hammer blizzard. Manager Mike and Pic were running around dressed for a nuclear accident in their Hazmat suits. Comms Tom was nowhere in sight—he had already run to the dormitory annex and jumped in the shower.

Liza and Donna, still at their computer terminals in the Comms shack and uninjured, were able to recount what had happened: Comms Tom was working on the UPS system in the next room when several batteries exploded. A ferocious blast sprayed acid everywhere. Fortunately, Tom had just ducked down behind a steel cabinet door to adjust some wiring. Had he been standing, he would have taken the blast in the face. Luckily he was also wearing a long shirt, jeans, a hat with a bill, and glasses, and because he reacted quickly he got only a small acid burn on one arm. His jeans, riddled with holes, were later put on public display, tacked to the wall of the galley.

At this point we made the decision to abandon the UPS. It was too dangerous. (Within a couple of weeks, Comms had rewired a series of less-powerful, jury-rigged back-up units for the radios and other communication systems.)

A few days later I awoke to the sound of Comms Tom beating on my bedroom door. I shouted for him to come in while I grabbed for my glasses.

"Mike told me to get you up and ready and tell you myself," said Tom, trying to catch his breath. "Big John just fell through the roof of the Heavy Shop and they're bringing him in."

Oh dear God, here comes my greatest fear, I was thinking as I walked the short hallway to my examination room. The terror of a doctor in Antarctica is that one of your friends (and that includes everyone) will be seriously sick or injured and there won't be much you can do about it. And now, my first real trauma case was my best buddy and personal snowmobile driver. I was just setting up my equipment, turning on the hypothermia blankets and oxygen, when the trauma team arrived. It was encouraging to see that Big John was able to walk in the door with the help of Roger Hooker and Bill Johnson, the construction foreman. But my relief didn't last long. He was talking but he wasn't making any sense. Something was very wrong.

I assumed he had hypothermia—everybody did to some degree, even if uninjured—and I slapped the electric warmers on him as we got him onto the examining table. I stripped him down as I looked for head injuries and other trauma. There were bruises but no obvious fractures. I wanted to test his mental status so I ran through a list of questions

"Big John, count down from one hundred by sevens."

"Ninety-seven . . ."

I looked into his eyes, hard, and he must have seen my concern.

"Uh . . . ninety-three!" he said.

"Okay, continue."

He thought really hard for about fifteen seconds. Then he frowned. "Wow," he said. "Can I have another one?"

"Okay. What does it mean when I say it's better to have a bird in the hand than two in the bush?"

Big John said, "Um, I don't like questions like that, can I have another one?"

Now I was really starting to worry. Slowly, he started to come around. We x-rayed him with the temperamental machine, wrapped him up, and put him to bed.

Soon he was able to tell me the whole story:

Big had been having a fine morning, happily working on Cassie Rose, one of his favorite loaders in the Heavy Shop, not a care in the world. When he needed a new part, he went shopping where parts are stored on the roof of the building. Although the Heavy Shop was inside the garage arch, the temperature up on the roof was nearly as cold as on the plateau. Since he wouldn't be outside for long, Big put on his medium-weight Carhartt jacket, grabbed a flashlight, and climbed up the side of the metal building. He found the part he needed on an elevated shelf, but as he reached for it his right leg dropped through the roof. Someone had covered a hole in the ceiling by nailing a piece of plywood from inside the shop. It was pitch dark, and Big thought he was free-falling. He grabbed the shelf with his left hand, wrenching his arm as he fell. The hole wasn't wide enough for the rest of him, but his leg was stuck up to the groin. He thought he must have hit his head on the way down, but luckily he was wearing his thick beaver hat.

He lay there for a minute or two, assessing the damage. He didn't feel right at all. And he was getting cold. He had his radio with him and tried calling Manager Mike. When he couldn't raise him he called Captain Kirk.

"Yeah, Big, what's happening?" said the Captain.

"You know, I think I'm messed up . . ." Big said.

"Really? What's going on?" Still trying to sound casual.

"Well, I fell through a hole in the roof, and I'm not thinking real good. I think I need some help."

"Okay. . . . You just stay right there. I'll get Mike."

Big talked to Mike, then put his radio down. Lying there in the killer cold, his mind a fog, he finally heard the sound of feet running on the garage roof and men calling his name in the dark. It took three guys from the trauma team to extricate him from the hole. They had planned to haul Big down on a stretcher, but he wouldn't let them, fearing that someone would be injured manhandling his two-hundred-forty-pound frame down the ladder. Years ago he had been lowered in a Stokes basket into a boat from an offshore oil rig. Although he had been badly burned in an electrical explosion, he found the transport off the rig more frightening than his near electro-cution. So this time he managed to stand up, and, with arms draped over two of his brothers, limped into Biomed.

I never found any physical sign of head injury, so his confusion was still a mystery. I attributed it to hypothermia. His other injuries were painful but not serious: He had a sprained knee, torn tendons in his shoulder and elbow, and minor back injuries. He was confined to the hospital.

I watched him closely throughout the day. He slept for about twelve hours. When he woke up I brought him a meal from the galley, and Lisa gave him a stack of videotaped Westerns to keep him happy. Loree had left all of her CDs for his entertainment, and Larry Fordyce, one of the carpenters, brought a fifth of Wild Turkey (which I confiscated). Comms Tom dressed his five-foot-tall inflatable penguin, Monica Penguinski, in a nursing dress and put her in bed next to him.

"How do you feel, Big?" I asked.

"Like I've been in a street fight and don't know whether I won or lost," he said, grinning. "That's my story, and I'm sticking to it."

He had trouble breathing that night, and I worried about a pulmonary embolism. His pulse ox was a mildly disturbing 88 (97 to 100 is optimum). I kept a nasal canula of oxygen on him, which helped immensely. He stayed in the hospital for three days packed in ice to reduce the swelling with an electric blanket over him to keep him warm. Who said medicine has to make sense?

I would have kept him longer, but the most incredible thing happened: When Big John got hurt, the machines stopped running and nobody could fix them.

Power Plant Thom and Ken Lobe, both skilled mechanics, tried to cover for Big in the shop while also performing their regular tasks. Thom was calling five or six times a day, asking where certain parts were and how to get things running. I would only allow the most important calls to go through.

"Wow, Doc, we can't get the Baldersons working," Thom would say. "Can I talk to Big?"

The Baldersons were attachments on the loaders that allowed the operator to change from forks to buckets and back. After the second day, I let Big walk over to the shop for a few minutes at a time. If he stayed too long, I'd go down there and drag him back to bed. But eventually I had to release him for work before we lost all the tractors and snowmobiles. It reminded me of the children's song about the clockmaker, and how his clocks stopped, never to go again, when the old man died. Big John believed those machines had souls. There was something very special between him and machines, as if he could feel how they worked or understood so well the thought processes of those who had made them. I had never been so closely exposed to that kind of thinking before. Maybe machines did have feelings. As soon as he went back to work, they all started right up.

Big was well enough by St. Patrick's Day to join in a celebration at the 90 South Bar. The owner of Bailie's Pub in Christchurch had donated a keg of Guinness for the occasion, which had been shipped to the South Pole on a cargo flight to Welder Walt. Bailie's was a favorite hangout for Ice people from all countries. You could count on running into Ice folk from Italy, Russia, New Zealand, or wherever, to raise a pint or shoot a game of pool among friends.

As planned, we wore our "colors"—the special green South Pole parkas that weren't very warm and nobody liked—to a ceremony at the Pole, where we tapped the keg and posed for a picture for Bailie's wall. We all walked out to the Pole with banners, the keg, Guinness umbrellas, and a table with chairs. Walt wore his Guinness top hat. After the picture was taken, we immediately returned to the Dome for the party. It was eighty-six degrees below zero.

Knowing there would be a fine party at Bailie's that night, we Irish and virtual Irish at the South Pole did our best to hold up our end of the bargain. The Guinness flowed freely, as did shots of homemade "hooch"—South Pole moonshine.

As the night wore on, people began playing the spoons, beating on drums, and batting inflated condoms around (I had predicted as much . . .). Comms Tom brought Monica Penguinski as his date. Now she wore a beret and held a cigar in her beak. Larry tried teaching Roo an Irish jig, while Reza followed the music on his harmonica.

Reza was another one of my favorite Polies. He was a science tech who came from a remote village in Bangladesh. He ran a number of experiments in Sky Lab, a three-story building attached to the Dome by a small arch, where there were windows for observation and a cosmic-ray lab, and in the seismology vault out beyond the Dome. As a devout Muslim, he couldn't drink or smoke, but he was still the life of any party. Part of the fun was to pin him down, force him to hold a beer for three seconds, and snap a digital picture to send home to his mother. But in reality this was an idle threat since his mother lived in such a remote village that there was no Internet—or phone for that matter. He sent his money home to support his large family. Although it was his parents' hope that one day he would have a wife, he was forty and had never married.

I got to know him well because he couldn't sleep. I tried to help him, but at first nothing worked. The tremendous low-pressure systems that hovered over the South Pole made the human body respond as if we were at 11,000 feet or higher. Everyone had trouble sleeping, but Reza was the champion insomniac. I think he must have gone for two months without more than a few hours sleep at a time.

The St. Patrick's Day bash would have been a good time for me to bring out my Celtic harp and join the band, but I hadn't played it in months. I never had time to practice, since I was overloaded with lessons and community events. The harp hung on my bedroom wall, untouched and somewhat out of place, like a souvenir from a past life.

From: The Seismic Vault
To: #winter
Date: Thu, 19 Mar. 1999 22:14:41 +1200
Subject: Ice Booms

Everyone,

The last few days we've been getting very loud booming noises outside which we think are movements of the ice. If you hear one, could you note the time for us, please? We'd like to see if we can identify these events on the seismometer traces. We're seeing things on the charts that may be these events, but without reliable times, it's hard to be sure.

Your Friendly Science Techs

The temperature on the plateau was plummeting. By now it was minus 90 F. and falling, a new record for mid-March. One night I was watching a video with a friend when we heard the most horrible booming noise.

"What's that?" I said.

He said, "Oh, it's just the building settling."

It sounded more like the building collapsing. We heard more of these ungodly booms over the next few days as the ice heaved in great cracks under the Dome. People were having more trouble sleeping. Sometimes it sounded like the roof was falling in or the floor was caving or people were stamping their feet overhead. Sometimes it sounded like guns or cannons.

The ice was breaking around us everywhere. Large cracks ran from the front of the galley and then spider-webbed out to the Dome perimeters. There was a foot-wide crack over the ice road and a crevasse split what was left of the skiway.

Mike told us the cracks were not at all life threatening, but it was hard not to worry. The scientists speculated that the ice had never before gotten so cold so fast and the temperature change was causing it to buckle. I was afraid our electric lines and sewer pipes might break, so I started loading things in a backpack by my doorway in case we had to run. I collected emergency items and a supply of all the medications for chronic conditions such as hypothyroidism and high blood pressure that some crew members needed daily. Just in case.

Actually, we were so accustomed to standing by for evacuation that it was becoming second nature.

In addition to the planned drills, we averaged around four false fire alarms each week because the fire-detectors were so sensitive. With literally no humidity at the South Pole, the static electricity problem was awesome. The computer techs had to discharge the static before they touched their keyboards and blew out their circuits. You could light a whole room by rubbing a stuffed animal until it glowed, which was how Felix, Big John's plush toy cat, became known as "Felix the Electric Dude." One night Dar, the meteorologist, got into bed too fast and set off a fire alarm at 3 a.m. We ran to each alarm as if it was a matter of life and death. Which it was.

Before the darkness obscured all visual references on the polar plateau, almost the entire station set out for some outdoor fun. There were two archaeological sites to visit on the outskirts of our world. A Hercules aircraft had crashed back in the 1980s and was buried in snow at the end of the skiway. If you could find the entrance, you could follow tunnels into the fuselage and cockpit.

The second was our favorite and most forbidden destination: "Old Pole," the station built in the 1950s by the Seabees and abandoned when we moved into the Dome in 1975. The original South Pole station had been a collection of bright orange metal buildings, much like the ones inside the Dome, except that they were exposed on the polar plateau. Before long, the drifts that eventually cover everything at the South Pole threatened to bury the station. The Navy tried to save Old Pole, or at least postpone its demise, by building a roof overhead.

Once they abandoned the station, the ice took it quickly and it was now completely subterranean. The buildings had shifted, the floors were bowed, the roof was collapsing in many areas, and some of the archways were buckling under the tremendous pressure of the ice overhead. Old Pole was dangerous and therefore off-limits. Of course, that did not deter every winterover group from making a pilgrimage. The attitude was "Don't ask, don't tell." And this would be our last chance: a demolition team was slated to blow Old Pole to smithereens next summer and sink it in the ice.

We used the remote VIPER telescope as our base of operations for the expedition. The hardest part was finding the entrance to Old Pole. It was covered with a metal manhole cover, buried in a foot of snow, a third of a mile from the telescope. Luckily several Polies remembered its location. The temperature outside was minus 88 F. that day.

We were organized in teams of four that were checked in and out for safety by a special designated safety team. Each person carried at least three flashlights, as batteries died quickly in the brutal cold and there was no natural light. The manhole cover opened up to a small vertical tube ten feet deep in the ice. We descended by ladder to a long, sloping tunnel marked with a rope to pull oneself along, in the dark, to the main part of the station. This fit my personal definition of claustrophobia.

My first thought was *You don't want to do this.*

My next thought was *Of course you do.*

I often thought of the stories my Dad told about the Navy during World War II, such as crawling into ships' water pipes to scrape and paint them. They were so narrow you had to back out because you couldn't turn around. The idea horrified me, and I never thought I'd be able to force myself into such a tight squeeze. Well, here I was, in another tunnel built by the Navy. I got on my knees and crawled ahead.

As soon as I reached the station, I felt very comfortable. It was just like our home! The roof was held up by wooden beams instead of metal, but here were the same familiar refrigerator buildings. Boardwalks had been set between buildings for streets, and picket fences surrounded gardens of plastic flowers. Nothing is so welcoming as the smell of your own home, and there it was: the unmistakable odor of JP8 fuel.

We toured the Comms shack, a Biomed, berthing areas, science areas, shops, and the original 90 South Bar. Frozen provisions had been stored everywhere. The galley was particularly spooky. The tables were set, there were hot dogs frozen in the refrigerator and dirty dishes in the sink. It looked like the previous inhabitants had left in a hurry.

"Wow, this is like ghost ship," said Comms Tom as he beamed his flashlight over a half-eaten plate of food.

It felt more like *Planet of the Apes,* or the Dome after a neutron bomb attack. The fact that it was all so familiar, yet deserted, was what made it so creepy. It was like Scott's hut on McMurdo Sound, rustling with phantoms.

As I had promised, I brought a few items back for the polar museum in Christchurch—a table setting, some medical equipment, and newspapers—but it was slim pickings. Over the years, the place had been ransacked by every succeeding winter crew. Ours would be one of the last groups of grave robbers. We did find some frozen coffee cans and other provisions for ourselves, though. Donna and Roger Hooker rescued the picket fence and plastic flowers to install in front of the galley back in the Dome. And Joel found something worth saving: an unfinished letter, dated October 25, 1974.

Hi Honey,

Well I hope everything is fine at home? I'm fine as usual. Well, everything is going wrong it seems like. One of the tractors caught on fire yesterday . . . it burned the fan belts and quite a bit of wiring. The Nowell went down, the D-8 went down. This just hasn't been our week. However I did get the supply tunnel opened a day later than I had hoped.

Old Pole was just like home.

From: Jerri Nielsen
To: Mom and Dad
Date: Sun., 22 Mar. 1999 07:44:06 +1200
Subject: Sunset

Today the sun set without us. We saw it dipping at the horizon yesterday, thinking that we could relish the slow end to our four-month day. Instead, we woke to an Antarctic storm, which obscured the horizon and the long-awaited setting sun. The world was altogether different today. It is the world that I came to experience. There was an eerie twilight around us. The 360-degree circle of flat ice and horizon is washed with pink all along the edge of our world. Otherwise, it was quite dark, not yet night, but no longer day for 6 months. The wind had picked up the snow into the air so that everything was blurry. It looked threatening yet so wondrous. It was more of what I thought life here would be like.

There are those among us who speak of huge knots in their stomachs as they think of the quickness of the coming darkness. I can imagine how they feel and how natural that reaction must be. For me, the coming of the terrible and terrifying darkness is exhilarating! Today was the most beautiful yet in this great landscape.

I will love the night.
Love, Duffy

Ever since I arrived at Pole, I had been doing things I never thought possible. How surprised I was when I found myself sitting on the floor, surrounded by pieces of my former vacuum sweeper. Had an alien inhabited my body? No, the vacuum was making terrible screeching noises and smelled like fire, so I ripped it apart from stem to stern without thinking, knowing I would be able to put it back together again. How foreign that would have been to me six months ago. But just this week I had learned how to back up and park a tractor, I helped tear out the axles of a bulldozer, and I rebuilt a cupboard by myself. I failed to fix a timer that had been built in 1951, only to have Floyd Washington, the fix-it wizard, agree that it was past its useful life. And if Floyd couldn't mend something, it was not repairable. I had entered a new phase in my life: I had come to know my mechanical self. The genetics that made my little brothers an aeronautical engineer and a contractor who enjoyed only projects no one else would tackle may not have passed me by, as I once thought. These abilities were simply dormant, waiting to surface when my life depended on them. Such was the South Pole. You came here to conquer one dragon, only to confront others you didn't know were on your tail.

One big challenge to my mechanical self remained: The power plant generators still frightened me. They were all that stood between the possibility of life and the certainty of death. I wanted nothing to do with the responsibility of dealing with them, but there was no way to avoid it.

There were three generators in the power plant, and only one was on line at any given time. They had to be "rotated"—one shut down and another brought on line—every five hundred hours. Since I worked in the Dome, near the power plant, I was obliged to take my turn rotating the generators. I didn't believe I was the best person to do this—there were more qualified people who knew what they were doing. When I brought this up, I was told that if you can learn to practice medicine and to fly an airplane, you can safely rotate the generators. I just didn't want to kill everyone, but there was no way out of the job.

One day late in March, my number came up. It takes about an hour to turn off one generator and turn on another because they have to be synchronized. The process was very complex, and it involved dealing with a lot of big, hot, noisy machines and a bunch of gadgets and gauges and whistles that meant nothing to me. The whole distressing experience was somewhat redeemed, however, by my realization that the best place to warm someone with serious hypothermia would be under engine number one.

I was twisted up in a weird position on a ladder, turning off the water supply to number one and turning on the supply to number two, when I felt a little spray of something on my arms. This seemed wrong, but then everything in the power plant felt dangerous and not quite right. But the spray got stronger and soon my hair was wet. I looked up at the ceiling and saw that all the big six- and eight-inch

pipes running into the generators had sprung leaks and were shower-
ing the power plant with scalding glycol! Before I could react, four
large men came flying through the door, yelling over the terrible
noise, knocking me off the ladder and pushing me out of the way. I
thought that somehow I had broken the power plant.

In fact, it wasn't me but the same problem that had cropped up a
few weeks before, when the station lost both regular power and emergency power during the drill. I was lucky that the electricians and the
plumber were returning from break and saw huge clouds of steam
spewing from the power plant's walls. Roger Hooker and Pakman
scaled the wall, jumped on the roof, and stopped it in some miracu-
lous way. Then Dennis Aukerman, the plumber, replaced the pipes
and presto, we were back in business.

The glycol ghoul was raising its ugly head again, and we still
didn't know why.

A month had come and gone since I first discovered a lump in my
breast. I had hoped it would disappear after my period, as others had
done before. But it was still there and had grown slightly bigger and
more irregular. I could feel the beginnings of another mass just below
it. I decided to wait a while longer before telling anyone, as nothing
could be done about this. I wanted to see if other changes occurred. I
knew it could be cancer, but I wasn't prepared to believe that yet, and
I didn't want to raise the alarm by telling anyone at the Pole. There
were so many other possible explanations for the mass: It could be a
cyst, or a benign tumor. If it was a malignancy, I assumed I could not
get any sort of treatment for the next seven months until the station
reopened. This meant I would die, either on the Ice or soon after leaving here.

Strangely, thinking about the possibility of dying didn't bother
me that much. I had already lived through one of the worst catastro-
phes a mother could endure. Death didn't seem nearly as terrible as
losing my children. Besides, I had understood the risks when I took on

this mission. Until I knew more about the mass in my breast, all I could do was to get on with the business of living my life and keeping my people healthy.

Around this time, Joel wanted to send a photograph of me along with the weekly newsletter he sent to his pen pal high school science classes. He took my picture in the treatment room of Biomed, sitting between the photographs of Frederick Cook and Bill Wilson, my medical predecessors on the Ice. In my portrait you can see exhaustion in my face, a touch of sadness in my eyes, and a wry smile on my lips. I deliberately chose the spot between my Dead Doctors; it was a grim joke only the three of us shared.

CHAPTER 8:

Darkness, Darkness

In early April, just as our astronomer, Roo, had predicted, the brightest stars appeared in the near-dark sky. As the visible limits of the ice plateau grew smaller, the sky expanded in power and depth, and drew our eyes upward from the plain.

About the same time, I discovered my equipment to treat hypothermia had frozen solid. I no longer even found this to be ironic. The cold had filtered in through holes in the floor of the storage cabinet, and now "glaciers" were growing there. Patches of ice had also formed in the ceiling corners throughout Biomed. It was so cold now that I wrapped myself in my electric blanket at my desk when I worked on the computer. One night I dropped a towel in my bedroom and it froze to the floor.

The air was as dry as the Sahara, and our vaporizers were breaking down at record speed. When I woke up in the morning, my tongue was stuck to the roof of my mouth. Everyone's skin was extremely dry, flaky, and painful. At the same time, the barometric pressure was dropping, and we had been experiencing a sudden increase in physiologic altitude. We had gone up the equivalent of a thousand feet and everyone could feel it. Some were short of breath, dizzy, nauseated, or thirsty. Most folks were just very tired, and many were not sleeping. Those who did sleep reported strange Technicolor dreams and vivid nightmares. I made myself the dream-keeper, asking everyone for details. Some people claimed to be dreaming in colors that were not in the human visual spectrum, brilliant colors they didn't know existed. Andy saw horses running over the polar plateau. Nick dreamed of aliens and nuclear war. Invasion and attack were common themes. My dreams were more practical: One night I dreamed about ophthalmologic herpes and that I tore the cabinets apart trying to find the cure.

Concentrating in such an environment was difficult, reading was impossible. I found myself staring at a page, reading the same sentence over and over again. I often glanced forlornly at the shelves weighted with the fiction and poetry I had shipped here in the summer. In reality, I read very little outside of my medical textbooks.

One of the few books I was able to tackle during this time was *Endurance,* the story of Ernest Shackleton's incredible, failed expedition to cross Antarctica in 1914–15. He never achieved his goals, but he never lost a man to the Ice. His survival skills and leadership abilities were legendary. One of my favorite Shackleton stories took place after his ship, the *Endurance,* was trapped in the pack ice on the Weddell Sea. The crew had to abandon ship before the vessel was crushed, and the men could bring only their barest necessities. Shackleton set an example for them by pitching a handful of gold coins onto the ice while tucking a small book of Browning poems into his pocket. "I throw away trash," he announced, "and am rewarded with golden inspirations."

This gallantry reminded me of a bit of verse written by a medieval Persian who was a favorite of my Aunt Eva. As a fourteen-year-old, she had escaped the Hungarian Revolution by leaving her family behind and crossing Europe with only her best friend. I kept a copy of "Hyacinths" tacked on my wall at Pole to remember her back home in Ohio:

If of thy mortal goods thou art bereft
And from thy slender store two loaves alone to thee are left,
Sell one and with the dole,
Buy hyacinths to feed thy soul.

Sheikh Moslih Eddin Saadi, the author of that poem, understood what matters. So did Shackleton, who entered so much hard-earned wisdom in his diaries. Now that the darkness was upon us, I was drawn to one passage describing the Antarctic winter:

In all the world there is no desolation more complete than the polar night. It is a return to the Ice Age—no warmth, no life, no movement. Only those who have experienced it can fully appreciate what it means to be without the sun day after day and week after week. Few men unaccustomed to it can fight off its effects altogether, and it has driven some men mad.

Thankfully, no one in our crew had yet gone mad at the South Pole. But the station was falling apart, spiritually, as it did once before in the summer, at the time of the near-mutiny. As the doctor I was in the thick of it. People brought me their problems as a matter of course, and I was often cast in the role of mediator. I could treat their bodies, but their souls were another matter. Some people were getting cranky and petty, focusing on imagined slights and the minor social gaffes of others. For many, every insignificant detail assumed great meaning and things that shouldn't matter turned explosive.

Consider the "color of the paint in the bar" incident. Some folks took it upon themselves to paint and recarpet the 90 South Bar. The place was a pigsty, and as far as I was concerned, any change was an improvement. I felt that we should support anyone who wanted to spend his or her free time working to improve common areas. Other Polies disagreed. They were upset by the deep blue color (we had so little paint that the options were limited) and thought the choice of color should have been a community decision. Words were exchanged, tempers flared, and for a few days old friends refused to speak to each other. The incident drove home how fragile is the veneer of civility, especially when there is no escape from even the best of friends.

Like the old village sin-eater, I felt I had to absorb the pain of the whole station. Listening to everyone's complaints was exhausting, and sometimes dispiriting, but luckily my friends sustained me, particularly Lisa and Big John. We were enjoying the winter by making the most of what we had. For us, the darkness and isolation only magnified what was truly important in life: shelter, warmth, food, companionship, and something to think about.

For me there was a great advantage to living in a sensory deprivation tank on ice. With the lack of extraneous sensation, the perceptiveness and intuition that had served me well in emergency medicine developed to an extreme. Since everything in the world of ice was very much the same, I noticed that subtle differences became more acute. Every "Polie" looked alike dressed in red parkas and face masks, so I had quickly learned to distinguish my friends by the way they walked or how they stood. By now I was able to feel slight changes in my environment: the difference in a few millibars of barometric pressure, or five degrees of temperature, and to recognize the unique sound of the snow beneath my feet during different weather conditions. Toward the end of my stay on the Ice, I would no longer need speech to communicate with many members of my "pack" of Polies. All of this convinced me of what I had long suspected: that humans have many innate talents for survival and communication that are dormant in technical society. It was interesting to see how easily these buried skills could surface after a few weeks of darkness. Perhaps we had simply incorporated them, without acknowledging their origins in our tribal past. I wondered, is this how the ancients silently organized the hunt, with a glance or a grimace? Did they ostracize others by looking at the ground or sky, or request support by lowering the head or rubbing the brow? I noticed a body language developing among the Polies that incorporated these gestures. It helped us cope with the overcrowded conditions in which we lived, and it was part of the bond between us.

While our basic needs were satisfied, by this time in April we were also starting to experience shortages. Our freshies had all but run out. The last of the apples were about to shrivel, so Donna baked some of them with raisins and brown sugar for a wonderful dessert, and put the rest of the uncooked ones in a box on the table for general consumption. They were surprisingly good.

I had not had a salad since the end of summer, and that's what I craved most. It was a shame. The folks running the greenhouse in the summer had been able to keep us in enough lettuce for one salad a week, and that with a crew of almost two hundred. But for whatever reason, the person who had taken over the greenhouse operation for the winter was using much of the space to grow tomatoes and cucumbers. Resentments over vegetable cultivation also caused friction among the crew.

Besides salad, coffee was also becoming a problem. The special Swedish coffee I had sent to myself in the summer was almost gone. The cans of coffee we had skua-ed from Old Pole were at least twenty years old, although it was amazingly good while it lasted. I have never been a coffee snob. I even relish the sludge at the bottom of pots in hospital waiting rooms. But the stuff here was so nasty that all I could drink was tea. It wasn't worth it to me to make an issue out of food, but some people took their meals very seriously.

When Donna closed the kitchen for breakfast as an April Fool's joke, one of the carpenters snapped, "I signed up for three square meals a day, not this crap." He complained to Mike Masterman, who assured him that lunch would be forthcoming. All was forgiven when Donna made us "Happy Meals" with cheeseburgers served in big paper airplanes with our names on them. She even put in everyone's favorite drink and pudding. But April Fool's Day was not over.

That night, while Mike and I worked in the store, we were held up at squirt-gun-point by two masked intruders who looked a lot like Donna and Liza. They thrust a piece of paper at me saying, "Hand

over the booze or we will shoot." We gave them bottles of Crown
Royal and Captain Morgan's rum, but they hosed us anyway!

It was a good thing winter was only seven more months, or we
might have run out of diversions.

For a few days the temperature warmed up enough for Big John to
take me on a snowmobile ride out on the plateau. Now there was only
a hint of twilight over the polar flats and the night sky was blazing
with stars. For the first time in my life I saw the Southern Cross, the
kite-shaped constellation that sailors use to guide them across southern oceans. We rode far out into the black plain and looked back at the
twinkling lights surrounding the Dome. I was so glad to be outdoors
again. You need the chill of winter to know the meaning of warmth.
In some ways the feeling reminded me of winters in Ohio, where you
spend autumn preparing for winter, and then the terrible cold hits.
Only then can you feel good about curling up by a fire, wrapped in a
comforter, to read a good, long book. I love to get into a warm bed
from a cold room, or feel my back freezing while my face is burning
from the fire. The contrasts were so much like that at Pole. We traveled back and forth from the dark, frozen, lonely wasteland to our cozy
society with its laughter and warmth and light bulbs.

Observing our little city from a distance was like seeing a space
station in a science fiction movie. It was an oasis that sustained human
life and culture in a hostile, uninhabitable world. It looked so surreal,
shimmering above the black horizon. And it was as surreal on the
inside as it appeared on the outside. I was reminded of the scene in
Star Wars where Luke Skywalker, after crossing a desert planet to
escape his enemies, walks into a cantina full of aliens. The patrons
seem just like any hard-drinking crowd in an Old West frontier town
except that some have reptilian skin and eyes growing on stalks.

In many ways, our South Pole station was like a caricature of
America: a small colony holding on to the traditions of a faraway
homeland, but just a few degrees off-center. It was as though, remembering our roots, we could reproduce that culture but had forgotten
certain elements. After a while, we didn't know what was American

and what was Polar. We had our own customs and social rules, and we were progressively developing our own language.

The new vocabulary was a rich Creole of English and American slang, and included words all our own. My favorite originated in a story Andy told us: Andy had a friend in Alaska who owned a large Husky named BoBo that he left with the veterinarian one weekend. The vet's husband had just bagged a caribou and had hung it in the garage. Unaware of this, the vet left BoBo in the garage all day. When she returned, half the caribou was gone and BoBo lay barely conscious on the garage floor, panting, his tongue sticking out and one leg in the air. She tried to pump his stomach but the chunks of meat were too large. In the end, to save his life, she opened his gut with a knife and removed more than fourteen pounds of caribou meat.

From then on, the Polie verb for gluttony was *to BoBo,* as in "He really Bobo-ed that apple pie." We also asked each other, "How many caribou will you have?"

Like space travelers on a dark planet, time had no meaning for us. Every day was different, of course, but all were exactly the same. Yesterday was totally gone and tomorrow didn't exist. Your work was there until you quit. Your friends were there until you turned and walked away. It didn't matter if they were there tomorrow. They were here now.

After months of living this way, a Polie might think she was still an American, but in fact, she was now part of a different community, a subset of America with different values.

This may be one of the reasons it takes Polies so long to readjust when they redeploy. So many of us travel for months on our way back to the States. You could change your ticket for an extra five hundred dollars and stop all over the world on the way back as long as you kept traveling in the same direction. I was already writing to friends and family that I planned to spend several months in Asia and Africa after leaving the Ice. I could read between the lines of my mother's cheerful but cautious replies that she was afraid I was joining some sort of cult. Perhaps I had. I did my best to explain what was happening to me.

From: Jerri Nielsen
To: Mom and Dad
Date: 18 Apr. 1999 23:35:57 +1200
Subject: Hi

I have changed a lot. Mostly, I now know what I want and who I am. I am back to believing in myself. It is hard to doubt yourself here; you'd die.

This is a perfect society here as you get back what you give. You are judged by your soul, not how thin or cool you are. I am tired of trying to be acceptable to people, when I think that I am just fine as I am. I am tired of angry people who aren't as happy as I am telling me how to live. That is why I love the Ice.

I love it here so much that I don't ever want to leave. I guess they make you. I don't belong in the world, never have. And now I belong even less.

Love, Duff

P.S.: I am learning how to weld. (As in sparks and a helmet.)

Meanwhile, the temperatures were falling again. We could watch them plunge on a video monitor in the galley, where a digital readout constantly registered changes in the South Pole climate. When, in the last week of April, the mercury dropped to minus 98.5 F., we all started speculating about when it would be time for the 300 Club.

The 300 Club was another of those time-honored polar traditions. To qualify for membership you wait for the outside temperature to fall below minus 100 F., then sit in the sauna at +200F. When you can't stand it anymore you dash outside the Dome—an instant drop of three hundred degrees—wearing only boots and perhaps a neck

As an emergency room doctor, Ohio, 1997. (photo by Artistic Photography)

Standing between my brothers, Eric and Scott Cahill, on the beach in North Carolina, 1997. (photo courtesy of Diana Cahill)

Entrance reads: "The United States of America Welcomes You To Amundsen-Scott South Pole Station." We live beneath the 165-foot-wide, 55-foot-tall Dome year round. Biomed arch to the left and power plant/garage arch on the right, partially buried under the ice. (photo by John Penney)

Beneath the Dome and looking toward the front entrance arch: From left are the galley, the entrance arch, Building 60 (electrical gear switch room), the greenhouse on top of the annex berthing building. Next to the buildings are the recycling bins. The floor is ice, two miles thick. (photo by Chris Rock)

Big John Penney and John Wright ("Master Blaster") in front of Southern Belle in the Heavy Machine Shop. (photo by John Penney)

January 1, 1999. Donna and Roger Hooker's wedding at the Ceremonial Pole. From left Ken Lobe, Liza Lobe, Donna Aldrich, Roger Hooker, Bobby Dunn (summer crew), and Lisa Beal, with paper in back. (photo by Jerri Nielsen)

Andy Clarke preparing the site for winter by placing a flag line between the Dome and the NOAA building. The flag lines were used in the dark of winter to find the path between the living quarters and the work areas. (photo by Joel Michalski, NOAA)

Thom Miller ("Power Plant Thom"), Joel Michalski, Charlie Kaminski ("Choo Choo Charlie)", and Dar Gibson ("Weatherboy"),with Tom Carlson ("Comms Tom") in front, getting ready for the 300 Club. (photo by John Penney)

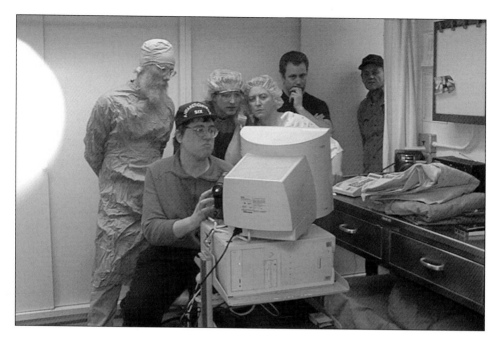

June 21, 1999. In Biomed, receiving instructions on real-time video from Denver before the biopsy. On camera from the U.S. were Dr. Katz and Dr. Sergi. From left: Bill Johnson, Lisa Beal, Walter Fischel, me, Mike Masterman, and Ken Lobe. (photo by John Penney)

June 21, 1999. I am inserting a needle in my breast while Walt is pulling up on the syringe for suction, during the first breast biopsy. From left: Walter Fischel, Lisa Lobe, me, and Bill Johnson. (photo by John Penney)

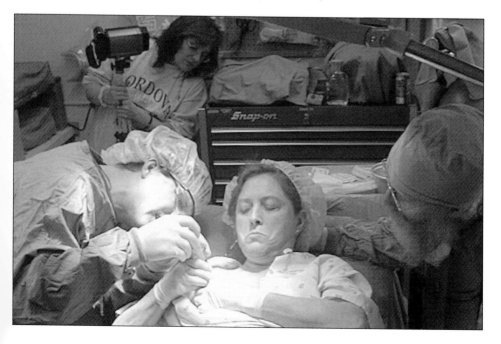

LC-130 Hercules aircraft receiving heat to the engines from portable gasoline heaters. This aircraft was grounded for the night at South Pole due to inclement weather in McMurdo. Fitted with skis for snow and ice landings, it is one of the few aircrafts that can reach the South Pole, and was the type of plane used in the rescue mission. (photo by John Penney)

Holding silk flowers that were included in the emergency airdrop of vital medical and tele-conferencing equipment, chemotherapy drugs and other supplies. (photo by John Penney)

In total darkness and temperatures as low as minus 92 F., the crew discovers the elusive sixth box from the emergency airdrop on July 10. Box 6 contained the ill-fated ultrasound machine. (photo by John Penney)

With James Evans ("Pic") in Biomed. (photo by John Penney)

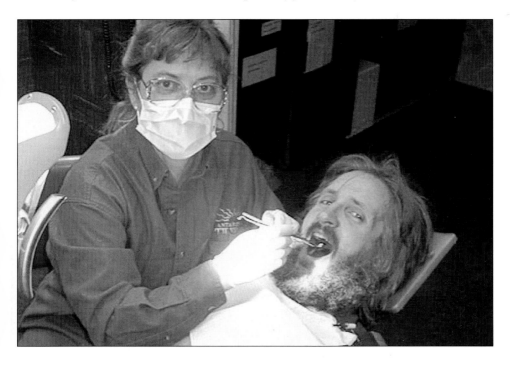

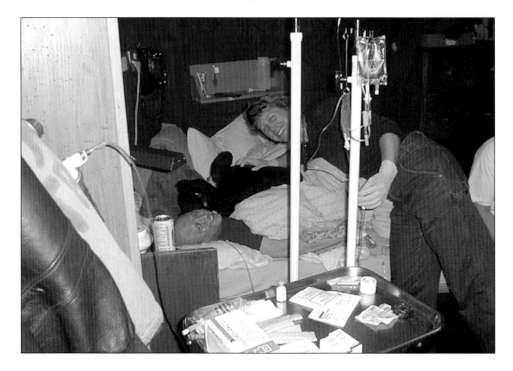

A chemo session in my bedroom/office with Heidi Schernthanner and Felix the Electric Dude in October, 1999. (photo by John Penney)

Off the ice, with Dr. Kathy Miller, in the oncology ward, Indiana University Hospital in Indianapolis, after I suffered a serious staph infection from breast cancer surgery in late October 1999. (photo by Lorine Cahill)

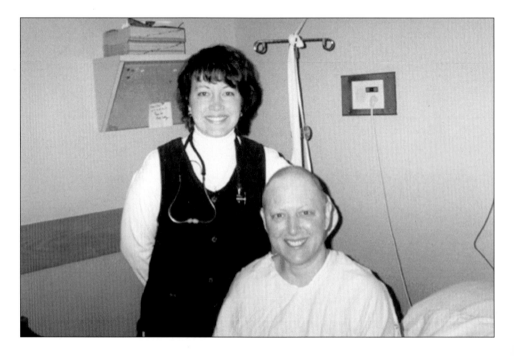

gaiter to keep your lungs from freezing. The hardcore run around the Ceremonial Pole, a three-hundred-yard round trip that takes three or four minutes.

Mike told everyone at the Saturday safety meeting that "doing" the 300 Club was not dangerous if you were careful. I begged to differ and went into my killjoy act. The doctors before me had treated severe frostbite of all twenty-one digits, hypothermia, cold-induced asthma, and recently, bad frostburn of the entire backside after a fellow slipped and slid down the hill on his butt.

My warnings were, of course, ignored. The 300 Club was a forty-year-old ritual and there was no stopping it. What was worse—I knew I had to join it if I wanted to call myself a true Polie. If I didn't freeze to death I might die of embarrassment. The guys were going to wear wool socks on their privates, but what would the ladies do?

It turned out that Loree was just as anxious about the event. She wanted the experience but didn't want anyone to see her naked. My feelings exactly. We discussed our options. A women-only club would invite catcalls and cameras. We thought about asking the men to be gentlemen, buying them a couple of cases of beer and locking them all in the pool hall with guards at the door. That might only breed more interest. No, our best option was to wait until three a.m. and run out alone. We made a pact to do our private 300 Club at the first opportunity.

Meanwhile, conditions outside the Dome were making our lives more dangerous. Our goggles fogged up in the freezing winds. The terrain changed daily due to the drifting snow. What was flat yesterday was often a gully or wall of ice today. One day Reza fell about twenty feet into the hole that surrounds the Dome. Another friend got disoriented walking back from slushies out at the Clean Air building. He took a wrong turn in the dark but by luck found his way to the garage arch, where he called for me to come get him. By the time I reached him he was so nearly frozen he could no longer move.

I now stood by in Biomed most working hours because the outside jobs had become so dangerous. Big and Power Plant Thom were often out in the boneyard, tearing the axles from the machinery in order to pull them into the shop for maintenance. It was a horrible job in the dark, at 95 below zero, often without gloves, and with slick frozen oil all over the ice.

Big John rarely complained. In fact, he loved visiting the bone-yard. He treated the machines like friends, and he had names for every one of them: the Wrench, Cassie Rose, the Drag Queen, and so on. He talked about each of them as distinct personalities in his letters. Everybody at Pole constantly emailed each other, or copied the ones we sent back home to each other. Sometimes we wrote to offer thanks or to complain, or just to entertain each other. You would think that forty-one people living together in a little hole would just talk, but I think the writing helped us express our feelings more precisely and more freely. This letter from Big John, sent to his family, and copied to me, perfectly captured his relationship with the machines in his charge.

From: John W. Penney
To: Cyprus/Nielsen
Date: Tue, 27 Apr. 1999 14:43:26 +1200
Subject: Winter

I have begun the winter maintenance on our machines. The machines are stored at the far end of the station in the bone-yard. We park them there at the end of the summer season, pull the batteries, and put duct tape on the exhaust stacks. The machines sleep under their blankets of snow until it is time to come into my shop for their winter massage. Some of the machines are quite recalcitrant. They are very happy where they are, nestled in amongst their comrades, away from the hustle and bustle of the station. They protest mightily with frozen tracks that skid on the snow until they begin to rotate, then squeal and scream when you drag them to the station.

Other machines are more social and seem to relish coming into my nice warm shop to shed their coating of ice and snow, and be around people again. Their glass gleams at you when you turn on the shop lights first thing in the morning, and they seem to enjoy it when you remove their valve covers and restore their racks to factory specs. All too soon the time comes for them to go back to bed. They sense this and ask you to at least take them for a little spin around Summer Camp instead of straight to bed. I oblige and we take a little run around the Jamesways and blast through a drift or two and straighten out some sastrugi . . .

Often, Big would drive himself out to the boneyard when the only source of light came from the stars and the auroras doing "their dance in the sky," as he once wrote. Sometimes he was a bit unnerved when he shut the machine down and all he could hear was "the distant drone of the power plant, the marker flags flapping in the wind, and the occasional soft ping from my snowmobile cooling off. I almost spooked myself, like when I was a kid, thinking that some Antarctic monster would awaken after sensing my presence and come grab me and have his horrible way with me . . ."

We had to keep reminding ourselves that there were no real monsters or demons under the ice at the South Pole. The worst ones were those that we made for ourselves, in our minds.

Since arriving at the Pole, I had been corresponding with Juergen Lehman, a radiologist whom I had met in an ER at the beginning of my career. He was one of my oldest and closest friends, and his wife, Sue, is my best girlfriend. We had known each other for twenty years. I had been thinking about writing to Juergen about the lump in my breast for some time. It had grown larger and harder, and although it had not changed in a few weeks, it was starting to hurt like hell.

Big was the only person I had told about the lump. He was my best friend on the Ice, and I trusted him to keep my secret. Since we depended on each other for our very survival, Polies tended to trust each other more than any outsider. At this point, I valued Big John's judgment most of all. He kept my confidence, but he was worried, and he encouraged me to mention my condition to another doctor. So I did. In the course of a few days, my level of hope lifted and plunged like a carnival ride.

From: Jerri Nielsen
To: Juergen Lehman
Date: Wed., 28 Apr. 1999 07:37:05 +1200
Subject: hello

Dear J.,

Nothing is happening here. Today I did 2 dental patients and 3 massages for fibromyositis, which is a lot of time spent.

I am having a great deal of trouble thinking due to my chronic hypoxia. Today my pulse ox was 86-87 all day. I also have a large hard breast mass which worries me. I had a mammogram in October. This thing is hard and irregular and not going away.

I have no doctor to reassure me, only myself to imagine things.

Love, Jerri
Doctor of Darkness

From: Juergen Lehman
To: Jerri Nielsen

Date: Thu., 29 Apr. 1999 01:29:41 -0400
Subject: breast mass

Dear Jerri,

Breast mass? What a horrible subject line! There are other possibilities, namely fat necrosis and, of course, fibrocystic disease, either of which may not show as a discrete mass on a mammogram, or, at least, not invite comment. You did have a mammogram before going down there, right? As regards the more grim possibility, I don't suppose South Pole Station Biomed carries tamoxifen, does it?

J.

From: Jerri Nielsen
To: Juergen Lehman
Date: Thursday, April 29, 1999 11:32 A.M.
Subject: Re: breast mass

Dear Juergen,

This damned thing is multiple and hard. It could be multiple cysts but it hasn't changed in over one month. This is scary. Maybe I should cut the mass out using a mirror?

I am going to bed. I have been feeling ill for weeks. I am never OK (physically—mentally I am great). The fatigue is getting terrible.

Hope this reaches you. We have problems with email due to satellite connections.

Love,
Doctor of Darkness

From: Juergen Lehman
To: Jerri Nielsen
Date: Mon., 03 May 1999 20:34:17 -0400
Subject: RE: breast masses

Dear Jerri,

I read your last email with joy. These being multiple, the likelihood of malignancy has suddenly taken a very far back seat. I checked this out today with a breast surgeon, just to be sure, and her response was, "that's a relief." She now says it's much more likely to be fibrocystic. I think you will live long and happily.

Love, Juergen

I was willing to take some comfort in Jeurgen's optimism, but in my heart I felt he was being unrealistic deriving so much hope from one piece of information. There was always the chance that my "multiple" lump could be two parts of the same growth. Or that this mass was the exception to the rule. Yet, for the time being, I was willing to accept his reassurance, and like everything else that might hinder my work—put it out of my mind.

On May 5 we were eating tacos for lunch, as part of a Cinco de Mayo observance, when the TV screen with our up-to-the-minute weather showed the temperature falling again. We called out each time the new digital display showed yet another drop. Finally, it hit the dreaded 100 below. As the crowd cheered, Loree, the meteorologist, flew to her instruments only to return with the news that the official temperature had not yet reached three digits. Everyone sighed dramatically, and we went on with life at Pole.

The Mexican theme continued all day, capped off by a viewing of Cheech Marin's movie *Born in East L.A.* After that, a few of us decided to watch another, non-Mexican, video, *Primary Colors.* Then Big John and I went to the galley for a cup of tea before calling it a night. We had been sitting in the galley for a while when Loree ran in and announced that the temperature was officially 101.8 below. She looked at me expectantly. I knew then the weighty pact I had made a week before while warm and in an impressionable mood would have to be honored. She had decided: Tonight, we go!

I was still worried about how easy it was to run into trouble while doing the 300 Club. I probably could not carry Loree if she fell in the dark at 100 below while everyone else was asleep. She certainly couldn't carry me. So Loree and I decided that we would enlist the help of our two best friends, Big John and Andy. They had always respected our privacy and had shown no perverted tendencies. They graciously accepted our invitation. The boys agreed to stand by the door to the Dome with their gaiters pulled over their eyes when we ran out. They would throw blankets on us as we came in, and promised not to look unless one of us was hurt and had to be rescued.

Andy and John had planned to run with the rest of the group during the big public show, probably tomorrow. To cinch up the parts he feared would freeze, John had specially purchased a bottle of Crown Royal just to get the cute blue velvet bag with yellow ties that it comes in. Andy planned to wear his South Pole baseball cap, just in case he needed protection.

Reza, who was hanging out in the galley because he never slept, got wind of what was happening and began to prepare the sauna. Loree and I wrapped ourselves in towels and hid in the meteorology department. Big John intercepted Reza and explained that "the ladies are bashful and don't want a crowd." That was the truth. Fortunately, Reza was a Muslim from Bangladesh and understood such things.

By now Andy decided that he wanted to go with us.

"Well, if Andy's going then I want to go too," said Big.

Loree and I looked at each other.

"What the hell," I said. "We're all in this together."

So now we were four. Andy talked Big John out of the Crown Royal bag and Big John talked Andy out of the baseball cap. We got in the sauna and started to bake. You have to dip the thermostat in cold water so that you can trick it into heating up to 200 degrees. After about ten minutes, when we couldn't stand it anymore, we put on our boots, ditched the towels, and started to run: down the hall, out the double doors, down the metal staircase, through the Dome, down the arch, out the door, up a steep icy ramp into the cold dark night.

We were as giddy as kids doing something naughty. The wind was blowing at about seven knots at the top of the hill, but, amazingly, I didn't feel cold. And there was no cause for embarrassment: Steam was billowing off our bodies, and everybody was coated with a dusting of white, frozen perspiration. Big John said we looked like yetis. I was too caught up in the strangeness of the event to register any physical discomfort. We didn't try to make it to the Ceremonial Pole. We took some quick, blurry photographs to document our feat, and within five or six minutes headed back to the Dome. Only once inside did I feel slightly cold and notice that my skin was numb.

We ran back to the sauna to warm up again, and promptly had asthma attacks. We had skipped wearing the neck gaiters and the cold air had chilled our lungs. Later, we met at my quarters for hot chocolate spiked with a splash of Bailey's. We recounted our run to each other like old soldiers telling war stories, while we coughed and laughed and sipped the warm drinks. Loree and I were so happy we made it into the Club. We were true Polies, and we never would have done it without each other.

"It's kind of sad, though," said Big John. "The 300 Club is a major milestone in our winter. Now we're past it. And I'm not ready for my first winter to be over yet."

We were now halfway through our polar adventure. The sun did not rise or set and my life had settled into a routine: I got up between seven thirty and eight every weekday morning. To get to work all I did was crawl out of bed and turn on my computer. The night before I always put the clothes I would wear the next day on my computer chair so that I could dress while I logged on. Then I read and answered my business mail. After making tea, I decided what work to do that day. I would choose one room in Biomed and start tearing it apart, cleaning, evaluating, and fixing things. I scrubbed the floors and counters in the morning and did the medical laundry, which entailed going out in the Dome and climbing two flights of stairs. I had to separate all my trash into different categories and tote it outside to the containers. There was always something that needed doing before noon, such as developing x-rays or doing lab tests or medical records. I had reams of spreadsheets and reports to send to Denver every week, such as accident reports and other medical business, which I usually tackled in the morning. Everything I used in Biomed had to be recorded in triplicate and entered into the Mapcon inventory system.

At nine thirty I joined the other Dome slugs in the galley for more tea. Our food service was the center of our social life. Mealtimes were when you got to see the other workers. After the morning break, I usually saw patients until lunch at eleven thirty. Sometimes I set up an informal clinic right in the galley at mealtimes, since some of the macho types wouldn't come in to Biomed to make an appointment. While eating, I would observe everyone to listen for coughs, watch for limps, and drum up work. It was the polar equivalent of ambulance chasing.

In the afternoon, I attacked major projects and saw the majority of my patients. We took another break at three thirty, but I tended to work through it. Supper was served at five thirty. Sometimes I would skip the meal to study Russian with Power Plant Thom, Big John, and Lisa from five thirty to six thirty, and eat from the refrigerator later.

On Monday and Thursday evenings I worked in the store from seven thirty to eight. Tuesday was still science-fiction night. On Wednesdays you could swing dance in the gym. Since we worked six

days a week, we generally only went out on Saturdays, although some
folks still observed slushies on Friday nights. The construction crew
drank beer together on Fridays after work on the job site. On Saturday
afternoons we had a safety meeting and then a science lecture. Saturday night was action-movie night, and there was live bluegrass in
the Communications Center. On Saturday evening I visited friends,
attended social events, or watched the movie. We usually stayed up until
2 or 3 a.m., and then everyone slept until noon. Russian-language
class, taught by Nuclear Nick, was at one o'clock on Sundays. I spent
the rest of Sunday reading or studying and visiting friends.

As with all true adventures, life at Pole was routine and monoto-
nous until interrupted by episodes of pure terror. Toward the end of
May, the glycol ghoul reappeared with a vengeance.

> From: Jerri Nielsen
> To: friends and family
> Date: 28 May 1999 22:12:42 +1200
> Subject: emergency
> Dears,
>
> I am trying to get word to you in case I soon lose the ability
> to do so. We have lost power. We are in a brownout. The
> only electricity that I am using here in Biomed are my refrig-
> erators and my computer screen. I shouldn't have the com-
> puter on but I wanted to get word to you in case I can't in
> the future. Flashlights and portable radios are all we have at
> the moment.
>
> The power plant is malfunctioning and we don't know why. I
> have faith that the boys can fix it. They can do anything. It's
> not time for the cyanide capsules yet, but I am concerned as
> they are unable to find the problem. I am glad that I man-
> aged to send my month-end store report to Denver before all
> this happened. (That's how crazy life is here. You really lose
> perspective on life and how precarious it is.)

We can easily survive anything down here with our human resources as they are. If we have to abandon ship, we will be fine, but I won't have the ability to make any contact with you. So, if you don't hear from me, it is because I have changed my address. Otherwise, I will make contact as soon as I know what is happening.

Love always, Duff

I was much more worried than I let on in my letter. The glycol loop was leaking again and an eerie, dense fog filled the inside of the Dome. The glycol in the lines was boiling hot, and nobody could figure out why it was overheating. Once again we were on emergency power, and the dim lights made the scene even more frightening.

I was standing by in Biomed, monitoring the radio, while Big John and Manager Mike were up on the roof of the power plant in SCBA (self-contained breathing apparatus) gear, trying to fix the problem. They worked for two hours at 90 below zero, in a scalding glycol spray, and bled the lines. This worked. The temperature in the glycol loop returned to normal. But nobody knew why.

When we were back on line, Power Plant Thom, Tool Man Tim, Floyd, Ken, and Dennis the Plumber went into the power plant and ran a series of diagnostic tests that didn't show anything wrong.

When Mike walked in the door to our home, he was covered with black soot and was what we called "frosty": a crust of ice coated his mustache and eyelashes. I ran over to give him a big hug.

"Thanks for freezing your butt off out there for us!" I said. When I squeezed him a terrible cold puffed out of his parka that made me shiver.

It was never easy to get Mike to accept advice, nor my attempts at mothering. He was the kind of guy who wouldn't see a doctor for a broken leg. Even though he sometimes seemed to forget it, I was supposed to be his second in command, his "Bones," the only one who would and, by position, should, tell the captain that he needed help, or sleep, or that perhaps he ought to consider another line of attack. At times this caused friction between us, but my affection for him never waned. Nor my efforts to help him. And the poor guy had to pass my door to get to his room, so he couldn't escape my nagging.

"Damn it, Jim," I said. (*Star Trek* he understood.) "You need to take care of yourself. I was worried about you on that roof. Let me get you an electric blanket."

"No, I'm fine," he'd answer on his way to his door.

I'd follow. "How about some nice hot tea?"

"No," he said, starting to tire of me.

"Some hot chocolate?"

"No, I'm all right!"

"You seem really cold."

"Yes . . ."

He gave me his handsome smile that was halfway between that of a boy and that of a man. Although only thirty years old, he had the weight of our world on his shoulders. When he smiled and hesitated, I knew I might be getting through to him.

"I'll go take a sauna, okay?"

"Okay, Michael, that sounds like a good idea." Perfect.

I saw Big John in the galley that night, eating cold cuts because supper had been canceled due to loss of power. He was acting extra casual, as if nothing serious had occurred today.

"Wow, Big, what happened? I left Biomed and the Dome was dark and full of smoke."

"You know not to leave Biomed, we wouldn't know where to find you!" He was nearly scolding me. "And you shouldn't be opening the hospital doors. Hold on to your precious heat."

"But there was no light for so long and I couldn't hear anything on the radio . . ."

"That's because we were on the roof in SCBA gear," Big answered.

I took a deep breath, trying to hide my anxiety, and my irritation. "So what caused it? Did you figure it out?"

"Whatever went wrong is still wrong, but there's nothing to do until the monster shows its ugly head again," said Big, wolfing down his ham sandwich. "Don't worry. We'll figure it out."

"Don't worry! Of course I'm going to worry!"

"Hey, it's no big deal," he chuckled. "The brothers are working on it . . ."

He thought it was funny! And he thought my serious reaction was amusing. I stewed about it that night and then sent him an email to explain my point of view:

From: Jerri Nielsen
To: John W. Penney
Date: Sat., 29 May 1999 14:59:02 +1200
Subject: defibrillation
Dear John,

I know that you think it is amusing how I get alarmed sitting in the dark, losing heat in Antarctica. Especially when I am told that there is a serious problem with the power plant and that we don't have any idea what is causing it. And by the way, supper has been canceled. And take a flashlight when you go out because the Dome is full of smoke.

For you it is no big deal because you know that YOU will figure out what is wrong (or die trying). I understand that, as I have no fear when I am in charge. Let me change the perspective.

Let's say that you are having shortness of breath and chest pain and your blood pressure is high. This is because your heart is fibrillating. You are brought to the hospital, lights and sirens, where you meet me. I have been doing this sort of thing all night, actually, for over 20 years. I look at you and tell you that your heart is fibrillating. You anxiously ask why.

I tell you that I have no idea and probably won't figure that out tonight. But I'm going to try and make it go away. "We will try some things."

So then I bring in all my residents and a cardiologist and we all stand outside your door and talk about you in a huddle. I look as calm as can be, in fact I am perfectly calm. I won't even start to truly be concerned until I have tried 2 drugs that don't work. And I have faith, from experience, that that won't be needed.

Meanwhile, the nurses ask you for your next-of-kin's phone number and they want to know if you have a living will.

Fondly, Doc

CHAPTER 9:

The Sea Change

The Navy psychologists who studied group behavior on polar expeditions recommended an event like a party or special dinner at least once a week, to give those in isolation something to look forward to. We, at the Pole, were happy to comply. Traditional holidays were even better excuses to party, and on the first weekend in June, we celebrated Memorial Day.

Tool Man Tim Briggs, the construction supervisor and a great social director, opened up the cavernous new garage construction site for an all-day barbecue. Mike had spent the past two months welding a huge metal grill for the event and christened the barbecue, which was big enough to hold a large human (we tested it with Giant Greg), by cooking up some ribs for the party. Roo provided vegetarian fare. Tool Man found a smoker, constructed by some forgotten winter crew from an empty fifty-five-gallon drum, and made delectable smoked trout and salmon. When Tim wasn't a contractor, he did commercial fishing on Lake Superior and in Alaska.

We had plenty of refreshments, music, and games. The multisection garage, enclosed under a new archway, had been transformed for the party. The electrician's shop, at the rear of the building, now featured a full-size Ping-Pong table. Food and drinks were offered in the carpenter's shop, at the center of the building. Horseshoe and blow-dart competitions were held in a large open area in the front of the garage. The guys had built a regulation horseshoe pit, complete with boxes filled with sand-blaster sand and horseshoes shipped to the Pole from Tool Man Tim's shed in Minnesota. The dart gun was made from a five-foot piece of electrical conduit and the darts were regular dartboard darts with the feathers replaced with paper cones. The blowgun was so well engineered that we could sink darts a quarter of an inch into the plywood backdrop behind the target from a distance of twenty feet.

The wonderful party seemed to reunite the community. It was good to see happy astronomers hugging happy ironworkers and looking very much like the brothers they had become.

I had to be ready to remove darts from people's eyes and treat concussions from misdirected horseshoes. Thankfully we had no significant injuries all day, although I did hold an impromptu clinic. I brought a pen and paper and medications to the celebration and set up a barrel under a construction light for an examination area. No one was willing to leave the fun to go to the hospital. I saw six cases of facial frostbite, one presumed fractured great toe from a sledgehammer, one case of moderately severe foot dermatitis, and one case of facial cellulitis—all without leaving the party.

For big events like this, some Polies wore their personal "colors"— Carhartt jackets decorated with slogans. Big John's was particularly flashy, with devil's horns drawn on the back with colored markers and the inscription EVIL SON OF A BITCH (a reference to my response to one of his clever, biting comments, which I no longer remember). Pakman's coat said INNOCENT SON OF A GUN, playing off Big John's. Mine was even more elaborate: On the back was a large caduceus— the staff-and-snake symbol of the medical profession—and the words HARD TRUTH MEDICAL CENTRE, SOUTH POLE STATION. One sleeve was decorated with the motto BORN TO RAISE HEALTH. The other sleeve had a replica of the best tattoo I'd ever seen on a patient: LOVE BITES, LOVE BLEEDS. Below the legend was a picture of a heart with a piece bitten out of it, dripping a pool of blood. I wore it as a memento for my children.

*   *   *

After I wrapped up the clinic I challenged some Polies at Ping-Pong. Suddenly Wendy ran into the electrician's shop, grabbing film from her coat that was hanging on the wall. "All I heard was something about William Tell," she said, "and I knew I'd better get my camera!" We stopped the game and ran to the front of the garage to check it out. Sure enough, we found Tool Man Tim wearing a welding helmet to cover his face, holding a homemade archery target in front of his body with a beer can balanced on his head. Nuclear Nick had the blowgun with a dart in it, leveled at our construction boss. Nick was a good shot and knocked the beer can off T.M.T.'s head in one try.

By now things were getting rowdy, with some folks playing King of the Mountain with large tar drums. By the end of the night, we had all stuck fake tattoos somewhere on our bodies. Mine was a gift from Power Plant Thom: A skull with a sword through it. I put it just above my right breast.

> From: Dar Gibson
> To: #winter
> Date: 6 Jun. 1999 03:54:39 +1200
> Subject: Hello?
>
> To Whoever Vomited in the Upper Berthing Bathroom:
>
> First of all I hope you feel better. And in case you don't remember, you missed. Badly. And as for clean-up, you're welcome. But really, I don't think that it was done by anyone here. I think the Clinton administration was behind it. What do you all think?
>
> Let's discuss it over email so we don't actually have to talk to each other.
>
> -Weatherboy-

From: Jerri Nielsen
To: #winter
Date: 6 Jun. 1999 08:31:42 +1200
Subject: vomit

Dear Brother and Sister Polies,

Anyone so sick that they miss the toilet should consider a stay with me in Biomed. I don't care why you lost your cookies. Illness or the inability to hold your liquor, it makes no difference to me. I am not here to judge, only to serve. There is a bathroom right beside the bed and a basin if you can't make it.

Remember in the future, I DEAL IN VOMIT. It is my job. Dar watches the weather, I am the pukemeister.

Fondly, Doc

A week earlier I had received an email from Norman Wolfe, ASA's manager of health services who had recruited me for this job, inquiring about the psychological status of the station's personnel. "I know that you have been providing some counseling support, formally or informally, and suspect it is well received," he wrote. "With the solstice approaching, this 'hump day' can be difficult for many." He was not asking for names or anything that would compromise confidentiality. He just wanted to hear my "overall impressions of the atmosphere of the community." I got right back to him with some suggestions.

From: Jerri Nielsen
To: Norman Wolfe
Date: 7 Jun. 1999 08:34:11 -0600
Subject: Station status

Dear Norman,

The station's mental health is excellent. I have done a lot of counseling and conflict resolution. I believe in preventive maintenance. No one was in serious trouble. I don't believe in using medication when time and energy spent working with people can heal better.

My suggestions for station health:

1. A five-day workweek. My concern is that there are quite a few who are so tired with these six-day workweeks, for one year straight, that all they do is sleep and read alone when they are off. People don't have time to get involved in creative projects when they only have one day off. Instead, they engage in mindless activities that could breed depression and boredom like drinking and watching endless bad movies.

2. More "without alcohol" activities. I know that that is difficult here. We need to continue to think about new forms of entertainment in limited space.

From the Pole
Fondly,
Jerri Lin

Norm wasn't the only one wondering about mental health issues at the South Pole. My mother, the psychologist, had recently written, asking me to describe my feelings now that winter had set in. I sent her this note:

From: Jerri Nielsen
To: Family and friends

Date: 7 Jun. 1999
Subject: Of the Ice

Mom asks, "What am I really feeling now?"

I can say that after living at the South Pole nothing can possibly terrify me, even looking at my own death. That is one
of the many things that this place does to you. Nothing after
this really matters. Those who become "of the Ice" cannot
imagine life on the outside. They say that the first time you
come for adventure, the second time for money, and the third
because you now fit nowhere else. I am already at the third
stage.

All that matters here are the things that really matter. I have
received such wonderful gifts: an old dried apple, a jar of
Skippy, a handmade corkscrew for my parties, a friend who
surprised me by bolting down my reading lamp that constantly fell over. Time spent in listening or helping is so
important and so appreciated, as it should be. And people are
loved for what they give and contribute, their honor, their
love and sacrifice. Not, as in the world where I was, for how
skinny they can force themselves to be and such nonsense.

The only thing that sustains me through these feelings is
that I have an extremely close and extraordinary family to
rejoin, and some wonderful friends. But is that enough to
deal with traffic jams and the horrible daily drivel that is life
in the United States? How can I go back to American medicine with its emphasis on "moving people through"? I had
serious problems with that before. Now I must compare that
to having a personal, interdependent, and truly loving relationship with each person whom I care for.

I am wondering: how will I ever leave the Ice? They will
make me leave. A doctor can't stay for two contracts in a row.

Where will I go? How will I ever readjust? I know, at this point, that I won't. Maybe I can find other Polies to live with. Maybe I can join the Peace Corps, as so many Polies do. Other Polies never work again, only travel and wait for the Ice to take them back. For the Ice to consume them, hold them, comfort them. This is home. It is as if I never had another.

So that is, tonight, what I am really thinking.

Love from the Ice,
Doc

This wasn't the answer Mom was hoping to hear. She wanted me to come back stronger, but essentially the same. What I was trying to tell her, and all my friends and family, was that a profound change had taken place inside me. Sailors who cross the oceans call it a "sea change." It happens days into a voyage, when you lose sight of land and stop feeling seasick. Time no longer exists; nothing matters except the path you're following, the sky, and the rolling water. It doesn't happen to everyone. But those who undergo the sea change are transformed forever, reborn in a new element. I suppose the phrase was coined by Shakespeare, who described the phenomenon metaphorically in *The Tempest,* when the nymph Ariel describes how the drowned king's body was remade from the sea: His bones turned to coral, and pearls became his eyes.

> *Nothing of him that doth fade,*
> *But doth suffer a sea-change*
> *Into something rich and strange.*

Like a sailor who could become "of the sea," I had become "of the Ice." Many people responded when they read my letter. Big John had forwarded it to his distribution list. His father, a professional forester in Oregon and California, wrote back that he understood what it meant to be of the Ice, because he was "of the Sierras." A Vietnam veteran wrote that he understood because he had come to love the heat and went to live in the isolation of the Arizona desert. I believe it can happen to anyone whose heart bonds with a landscape. It is like a love affair with a place. And of all places, Antarctica is the most demanding lover. The early explorers returned again and again until it took their lives. Scott froze to death on the Ice; Shackleton, sailing south for yet another expedition years later, died of an apparent heart attack. In the end, only the Ice held meaning for him; he was lost back in the world.

Some people in Antarctica already had eighty and ninety months of Ice time. They were hooked forever. And some first-timers in our winter crew had crossed over quickly. One was Comms Tom, who had traveled in seventy-five countries and worked on five continents. One night, sitting in the bar with Big John, he said, "Big, I'm scared."

"What are you scared about?"

"Man, I don't know what's gonna happen after this," said Comms Tom. "This is the best adventure of my entire life."

We all wondered if, like Scott and Shackleton, we would be compelled to return again and again, trying to relive the exhilaration of our first time on the Ice, and the rapture of being alive.

I suppose this was the greatest irony of my own life: now that I finally felt fully and completely alive, I had to face the possibility that I was dying.

The mass I had found in my breast in early March had not shrunk, as I had hoped. Now, three months later, I also had a painful swelling under my right arm. While I still held on to the remote chance of another explanation for these symptoms, all my medical training and personal experience told me this was breast cancer. For a while I thought I would simply hold on to my secret and die at the Pole, or shortly after redeploying. But now, with the possibility that the lymph glands under my arm were involved, it was likely that I would become too sick to carry out my duties as station physician.

It was time to inform my employers about my medical situation. I first told Mike Masterman, my immediate boss, in hopes that he would excuse some Polies from their regular duties for special medical training. If I became incapacitated someone's life might depend on it. I never imagined that it might be my own. We had all accepted and understood the consequences of this mission. There was no way out. As the medical officer, I knew better than anyone that in case of serious illness, we could depend only on our own scant resources. There was no way to evacuate the injured and no way to get more medication or equipment. I was not asking for help for myself, but for permission to prepare my people to survive without me.

When I knocked on his door, Mike was on the computer. "Michael, I need to talk with you," I began.

"Yes." He saved his work and moved his chair so that we were now face to face.

"There was a reason I held the airway course for the trauma team this week. We should probably step up their training. Pakman is good with the x-ray machine, when it is working. We have a number of people who can do excellent suturing. You've been with me on enough eye cases that I think you could deal with foreign bodies easily. I would like to have a casting clinic this week."

By now, most any Polie could read another, and he could read me. I could tell by the way he dropped his manager mask and pulled his body closer to me. His conservative, captain-of-the-ship demeanor shifted and he was once again my dear friend. Until now, I had made a tremendous effort to do "showtime" so that no one could detect what I was feeling inside. It was a relief to drop all the energy I had been harnessing to hide my condition.

"Mike, I have a large hard mass in my breast. It may be cancer. It's been there since March. I didn't tell you, since there wasn't anything we could do about it. But now I have a lump under my arm and I'm starting to fear the worst. I may not survive to open the station, or I could become too sick to do my job." He let me go on. "I'd like to pick individuals to teach to replace me. The ones with some of the best manual dexterity and deductive reasoning are on the construction team or in station operations. But they'll need so much training that I need your help to get them off their regular jobs."

"Jerri, we could cut the tumor out," Mike said, back in his manager mode. "There's got to be something that can be done. Have you contacted Denver yet?"

"No, Mike, you know I believe that we should always go through channels at Pole first."

We had a maxim: Things that happen on the Ice should stay on the Ice. This was different.

"I think you should contact Dr. Katz," he said. "I'll work on this from my end of things. There *has* to be something we can do, Doc."

That Thursday, June 10, I wrote to Gerry Katz, the doctor in charge of Antarctic medical stations, in Denver.

From: Jerri Nielsen
To: Gerry Katz
Date: 10 Jun. 1999 04:34:30 +1200
Subject: Medical problem with me

Dear Gerry,

I have a significant problem that I need your advice on. This is medical and confidential.

A month after station closing, I developed a breast mass. It was originally a nodule the size of a marble in the right upper quadrant of the right breast. I hoped that it was a cyst and would go away. It has not. It has become progressively larger. During the first two months it developed a large mass under it that now measures 4X5 cm. The nodule remains the same. It is relatively fixed and goes down to my nipple. The borders are ill defined. In the past month it seems to not have had any growth. I now have a possible tender node in the right axilla. My arm hurts. I have just hoped and wished that it would go away, but it has not. I have no skin changes and no nipple discharge. I have kept this secret from the rest of the station, confiding only in my best friend.

My mother's grandmother died from breast cancer but there is no other history in my family. My mother has had many biopsies for fibrocystic breast disease which were all negative. I have had very cystic breasts my entire life, but nothing like this. They have previously been very cyclical, but not this one. It is not changed by my period. I am 47 years old and have had no symptoms of menopause. My mother and female relatives all went through menopause in their mid-50s.

What I am asking you is tough. You know the Ice. Should I sit on this for five more months, or should I perform an operation on myself and remove it?

Fondly, Jerri

That same week I wrote to Will Silva and Hugh Cowan, the doctor at McMurdo who had also served at the Pole, to ask their advice.

Will Silva wrote back that he hoped the lump might be an inflammation. He suggested taking a powerful antibiotic and a course of Prednisone, an anti-inflammatory, before I started sharpening the scalpel. Hugh Cowan also advised against surgery. Assuming the worse case, breast cancer with involvement of the lymph nodes, there was no way to excise it all while operating on myself one-handed. In addition they both feared the overwhelming possibility of postoperative infection. Both doctors agreed that the one procedure I could and should perform was a fine-needle aspiration of the mass. If the fluid inside was clear, chances were good that the cyst was benign.

Gerry Katz contacted a surgeon to instruct me on how to aspirate the mass. Meanwhile, he was working behind the scenes, notifying officials of the ASA in Denver and the NSF in Washington, trying to come up with a course of action.

I didn't want any of the winterover crew to learn about my condition from secondhand rumors. On the same day I wrote to Gerry Katz we held an all-hands meeting to inform them and I tried to be as upbeat and positive as possible. After all, they had to face the terrifying fact that their only doctor might be gravely ill—and unable to care for them for the rest of the winter. Everyone listened quietly. Then in typical Polie fashion, they all used their expertise to suggest options I might not have considered.

My favorite suggestion came from Floyd Washington. He proposed that the government fly an aircraft over the Pole and hook me in a harness to catapult me into the moving plane. He'd seen it in a movie and promised that he could make the harness. He wasn't kidding. We all knew that Floyd could make anything, and since he was ex-Navy, he knew the military was capable of spectacular rescues.

Of course we never seriously considered the plan, but it sounded about as safe as performing a lumpectomy on myself. That option, I had heard, was being earnestly debated in Denver and Washington. Before deciding on such a drastic measure, however, we had to rule out the possibility that the growth in my breast was a harmless cyst.

We tried to draw fluid from the mass a couple of days later, on Saturday, June 12. I chose my friend Pakman, the rock 'n' roll electrician, to help me perform the aspiration because he had trained with the trauma team during the summer. I used an ice cube for local anesthesia and let Pak perform the procedure, as the site was hard for me to reach. Our instructions were to sink a fairly large needle into my upper breast until it entered the lump and then, using suction from the hypodermic, try to extract its contents. A cyst would produce a clear liquid; a cancerous tumor would not. Each time Pakman inserted the needle it hit a solid, gristly, immovable mass. After four tries, we gave up trying to withdraw fluid. I had to wonder if I would have found fluid if I had tried to aspirate the mass myself. Pak did a good job, but he wasn't a doctor or a trained nurse. At the same time I realized I was probably clinging to false hope. After twenty-five years in medicine, I had seen a lot of lesions and knew how to recognize cancer. Still, I wasn't a specialist, and we had to go through the motions of making a diagnosis. I reported the disappointing results of the aspiration to Gerry Katz, who in turn contacted Eric Jeurgen and Harry Mahar, his superiors at ASA and NSF:

> From: Gerald Katz
> To: Eric Jeurgen and Harry Mahar
> Cc: Jerri Nielsen
> Date: 14 Jun. 1999 07:53:28 -0700 (PDT)
> Subject: medical case
>
> Harry and Eric,
>
> Here is an update. Unfortunately, no fluid was aspirated from the mass after four attempts, suggesting that the lesion is solid. Although a benign fibroadenoma is the most likely diagnosis, there is concern that this lesion is a rapidly developing breast cancer.
>
> The individual is appropriately concerned and would like to leave the Ice ASAP, recognizing that this likely isn't feasible till late October. There are no therapeutic options for breast cancer available at the South Pole. Standard treatment is breast biopsy, and if positive for cancer, a lumpectomy and/or mastectomy. The latter two options exceed functional medical capabilities at the South Pole, and would be heroic and perhaps too risky, given the fact that this mass has a probability of being benign.
>
> The following steps have been taken.

1. The individual has initiated therapy with antibiotics and anti-inflammatory agents, on the
   off-chance that this an inflammatory/infectious
   growth.
2. I have notified an oncologist for further
   input.
3. I have notified a pathologist to see if there is
   any way to prepare a tissue sample for review
   via transmission over the Internet.
4. We need to entertain the possibility of a supply
   drop of materials necessary to diagnose and
   manage this condition.

At this point, we are gathering information. Whereas there
is a sense of urgency, this is not a medical emergency. We do
need a plan of action should this mass persist over the next
couple of weeks.

I'll keep you apprised of the situation.

Gerry

The only person I would allow to see my sorrow and fear was Big
John. After the attempted aspiration my breast was swollen and
painful. The mass seemed closer to the surface and my armpit ached,
which may have indicated cancer that had metastasized, or spread, to
the lymph nodes there. Or the swelling could have signaled an irritation or infection. Big did his best to keep my mind occupied. He
brought movies and books. We played poker with the boys on
Saturday night and had a good time. But by Sunday morning I was
crashing.

I was depressed and would have liked to spend Sunday in bed. I
needed time to adjust to the fact that I probably had cancer, to sort out
my emotions and get them under control, just as I had all my life. But

I was not allowed to "brood." Big John called my closest friends to my room. Big, Loree, Andy, Joel, and Lisa sat me up and combed my hair and marched me to the galley to have lunch. No one was going to let me worry alone. I don't think they could bear to see me drop my cheerful façade. Lisa, in particular, seemed to believe that a positive attitude was essential to recovery, as if you could will your illness away. I disagreed, since I had seen so much untreatable disease and death, and I thought it put unfair pressure on an ill person to "take responsibility" for a cure when none was possible. Still, there was nothing I could do to convince my dear, well-meaning friends that, just this once, I needed permission to be sad.

As the hours and days ticked by, many Polies were nervous about the reaction—or lack of reaction—from Denver and Washington. Although ASA and NSF staff were frantically working behind the scenes, we were too isolated to be aware of their efforts. This was my main complaint about the management of the South Pole station in general: Polies were literally kept in the dark about most decisions that affected them. It seemed as if the bosses back in the States felt we were too unstable or immature to hear the truth or to be consulted on major decisions. In hindsight, this paternalistic, authoritarian management style was probably just another holdover from the military, whose basis for sharing information was "need to know." Apparently, Polies did not need to know what was being done to help their doctor. This, unfortunately, contributed to an atmosphere of suspicion.

For instance, Gerry Katz's email said my condition wasn't a "medical emergency." Did this mean that Denver, adopting a wait-and-see attitude, had opted to do nothing? There was no way of knowing without further communication, and I was growing more concerned. Denver had not yet put me in touch with any breast cancer specialists, so I emailed my old friend Juergen, the radiologist, with a plea for assistance. I needed some answers, quick.

When I opened my email Monday evening, I saw an answer to my prayers:

From: Kathy Miller
To: Jerri Nielsen
Date: 14 Jun. 99 23:09:11 +1200
Subject: help

Hi Jerri,

I am a medical oncologist who specializes in breast cancer at Indiana University. Your friend Dr. Lehman [Juergen] contacted me about your current situation. Of course I am concerned that this represents a primary breast cancer—as I am sure you are as well. I will speak with my breast surgeon and local anesthesiologists at our breast conference Thursday morning. Before then it would help if I could have some additional information about your situation and conditions.

1. What is your practice and training? Unless you have surgical training I'm not sure any surgical approach would be feasible.

2. Is it absolutely impossible to get you out of the South Pole station (or merely very difficult)? I realize it is the middle of polar winter and the station is closed. I actually reviewed the posting for the station medical officer during a visit to Christchurch about 3 years ago so I am at least a little familiar with the station.

3. I won't even ask if there is any available chemotherapy, but what about any options for hormonal treatment. At your age about 45% of tumors would be ER+ and might respond to hormonal treatment.

Overall I am not enthusiastic about the possibility of a local resection. I am not concerned that surgery at the station would cause further spread. I am more concerned about complications from the procedure. Also unless we could do a mastectomy and axillary node dissection I don't know that the surgery would be beneficial (in other words, removing only a portion of the tumor doesn't help us).

You are describing an aggressive, large tumor that we would not treat initially with surgery if I were seeing you here. After a needle biopsy confirmed the diagnosis we would proceed directly with chemotherapy to decrease the tumor size before surgery. I am worried about the pain in your arm and the emerging axillary adenopathy—this could become a much more significant problem before spring.

I look forward to hearing from you soon. I will discuss with my surgeon as soon as possible.

Kathy Miller

From: Jerri Nielsen
To: Miller, Kathy D.
Date: Tuesday, June 15, 1999 2:20 A.M.
Subject: Re: help

Dear Kathy,

Thank you for your kind letter and help! You can just imagine the logistics here.

To answer your questions:

1. I am an ER Doc. I had two years of Family Practice Residency and then an ER residency. I practice big-city ER. Due to being in a teaching center where there are trauma teams, I don't do many procedures by myself. I am practiced in all ER procedures, though. In the past, I have been at a number of level 2 centers where I did everything.

I have had training in neurosurgery, thoracic surgery, plastics, orthopedics, general surgery (back in the days when they did everything), OB-Gyn, outpatient surgery, ENT [ear, nose and throat], and ophthalmology. I am certainly not a surgeon, but it was always what I liked the most. Women were not surgeons in the '70s, when I trained.

It is my opinion that I could take out my appendix if it would save my life. I don't think that I should attempt a partial procedure on a possibly benign lesion at the South Pole. We have no one here trained to help me. We have taught a few individuals how to start IVs and do some suturing. It took five tries and 2 hours for 2 of these individuals to start an IV on me for antibiotics.

This place is a one-room Emergency Department with a door that opens to the outside. Much of our equipment was left by the Navy many years ago. We have a good pharmacy, an autoclave, and a small lab. I do my CBCs [Complete Blood Count] by hand, I can do an HCT [Hematocrit-red blood cell volume] by centrifuging a capillary tube and putting it on a wheel that reminds me of a slide rule. You get the picture. I thought that this digression might be of historical interest to you, as you are a hemo person, and it well explains the level of my facility as seen by your specialty. I have some major surgery equipment left by the military. There is a monitor/defib and a portable suction machine. The coagulator doesn't work. The x-ray machine rarely works (it seems that the tube is blown).

We have the ability to use a videocamera connected to the microscope to send photos of slides. (We have very limited email and satellite phone connections for some short hours in the middle of the night.) I have Wright

stain and Gram stain for slide preparation. I also
have path specimen bottles with an unknown fluid
inside of them, left by the Navy.

2. There may be a way to airdrop supplies to me. They
have done it before. If I could have anything that I
want, I would like to have them airdrop a surgeon.
But there seems to be a macho attitude here that we
should remove it ourselves. I think that they might
be able to get me out if it got very warm for a long
time. Now, the belief is that mid-Oct would be the
earliest. The jet fuel turns to Jell-O at these temperatures. (It was 94 below zero today.)

3. I have Methotrexate. The only hormone treatments
we have are Premarin, Provera, and birth control
pills that have been expired for some time. I may be
able to get anything by airdrop that I need. I don't
think it wise to take chemotherapy without a diagnosis.

At this time, I can't find any nodes, only tenderness in my
axilla (but it could be inflammatory from a benign lesion).

Thank you so very much for all your expert help!

Fondly, Jerri

Kathy wrote back right away. She agreed that it was not a good
idea to try to cut out the mass or to start chemotherapy before we had
a confirmed diagnosis of cancer. She wanted to explore the possibility
of a biopsy and sending the images by video microscope. If an airdrop
was feasible, she wanted to include drugs that would stop my estrogen
production. As she wrote, forty to fifty percent of breast cancers in
women my age were ER+ (estrogen positive), meaning their growth

was fueled by estrogen. Hormonal therapy could help stop the spread of cancer but would also put me into premature menopause. With the sudden drop in estrogen, I could expect the hot flashes, loss of libido, dry skin, and mood swings sometimes associated with natural menopause. Only worse.

With that happy thought in mind, I wrote to my family and friends to break the awful news. I had held off telling them anything about my condition until it was absolutely necessary, since I knew it would upset them. At the same time, Big John had written to his U.S. congressman and senators in California, urging them to support an airdrop of medical equipment and a flight surgeon to the South Pole to help me. He encouraged everyone on his extensive email list to do the same.

Now that congressional staffers were hearing that there was "a woman with a breast lump" stranded at the South Pole, I didn't doubt that the press would be reporting this story very soon, and I had to get word to my loved ones first.

From: Jerri Nielsen
To: Family and friends
Date: Monday 15 Jun. 1999
Subject: Serious Medical Problem at Pole

Dear Family and Close Friends,

I have some very bad news. I have been holding off telling you, as you couldn't do anything to help me. At this point, I must let you know, as Congressmen and Senators, the Air National Guard, and who knows who else, is involved. As it could now become a media event, I need to let you know before you read about it in the newspaper.

After the station closed, I developed a lump in my right breast. At first it was small and like other cystic changes I have had intermittently throughout my life. During the third month, it grew very quickly. It is now 4X5 cm or larger and is hard to define. I told Mike Masterman at that point. We have been looking at options for evaluation and treatment at Pole. They say that there is no way to get me out. I knew that this was the chance that all of us took when we signed up for this mission. For the Doc it is worse, as there is no one but me to take care of it.

I have been on IV antibiotics without improvement. This week, we attempted a needle aspiration but there was no fluid on four tries. Although it still could be benign, we still must prepare for the worst. Through Juergen Lehman, I have been put in touch with some fine doctors in Ohio and Indiana who have been providing a plan of action. Tomorrow at midnight, I will be in touch with Denver through a video satellite connection, if all goes as planned. They will talk with me about our next actions. They seem to be in favor of me operating on myself. I have no one to help me. There is no one trained enough to do it. We don't have the facilities, and from what I have read, it is a bad idea. I may have no choice.

There is definite talk about making a military airdrop with any needed supplies and medications. They used to make airdrops, midwinter, for military training and for midwinter supplies. This was abandoned some years ago but we have people on station who have been through airdrops before and can prepare for it.

Today Big John went out to the boneyard and talked with all the machines to get them mentally prepared to handle the air-drop. He believes that they listen to him. (From what I can tell, they do.) Everyone has been very supportive and helpful to me, as you can imagine.

Many people, including me, are in favor of air-dropping a military surgeon and medic. I wrote to the National Science

Foundation today asking for precisely that, but I fear there is not much chance.

The plan now is to do a biopsy and make slides. The slides will then be sent to a pathologist over the computer. Lisa has been working on this technology all week. She now is able to transmit 100X power through a microscope. She has also set up a fiber-optic scope for surgeons to look through in the USA, and a videocam set up so that they can be watching if anything goes wrong. She is truly amazing! From those, they will determine what kind of medication to air-drop. I will know more, but not much more, after tomorrow.

So that is the State of the Union. I am afraid. But I would not have missed this life, at my beloved Pole, for anything. When it gets tough and I still have to work each day, I look at the pictures on my wall of the two men who, in the past few months, have even more become my colleagues. Dr. Frederick Cook, who was the first doctor to winter in Antarctica, and Dr. Edward Wilson, the first doc to the Pole, who froze to death in the tent with his best friend, Scott. These men came here before me. What I have learned from their lives is that they truly lived. More and more as I am here and see what life really is, I understand that it is not when or how you die but how and if you truly were ever alive.

I love you all. I promise to send more word when it is available.

Wilson

I worried about how my family would react. Mom assured me that she wasn't too upset. She chose to believe the mass might be benign, and if not, she wrote, "You are very strong and smart and will know what to do."

For the first time, I removed my children's email addresses from my "family and friends" list. I did not want them to learn that their mother might have cancer in an email, assuming my ex-husband was allowing them to read any of their letters from me. I asked my mother to phone them, so she could break the news more personally. No one picked up the phone when she rang, so she left a message on their answering machine. No one called back. Next, my sister-in-law Dee Dee tried to reach them. Again, no one answered the phone (my ex-husband always used caller ID), and so she, too, left a message about my predicament and asked them to please get in touch. None of us heard a word in response.

A few days after my "bad news" email, I received a message from my brother Scott. It was a classic example of Cahill stoicism, written by a man who, like me, had been taught to charge up every hill. He was not going to waste time giving me false words of reassurance.

From: Scott Cahill
To: Jerri Nielsen
Date: June 18, 1999 9:37 A.M.
Subject: lump

Hi Duffy

I am sorry to hear about the lump. You already know what you must do. You mustn't allow anyone to risk their lives trying to get in there in the dead of winter.

This is your opportunity to work valiantly and with honor. Be strong, Sis. It is probably nothing. If it is bad, then you will deal with it as a professional, competent doctor and do what you must do. You can only control your response and your professionalism along the way. The outcome is predetermined.

I know that you are alarmed and frightened. That is normal.
Please keep in touch. I have no doubts about your abilities to
manage this situation.

I love you so much. Be strong.

Love always, Scotty

I found the letter comforting. Scott was evoking the family spirit
that had sustained me during many difficult periods of my life. Now it
would see me through the hardest test of all.

I was getting letters from all levels at both the ASA and NSF,
wishing me well and assuring me that everything possible was being
done. But I was most concerned about my fellow Polies. I wanted to
keep those who were interested up to date and to keep the avenues
open for them to express their worries or to offer suggestions.

It was incredible to watch these talented, resourceful people pull
together to help me. The biopsy was scheduled for Monday, June 22,
which happened to coincide with the winter solstice. We had only a
few days to come up with a plan to do something that had never been
done before: set up a live video hookup with doctors in Denver, draw
tissue from the mass, transfer the tissue to slides, stain them to see the
cells, and then transmit images of the slides to the States via a special
video-microscope.

The easiest part would be performing the actual biopsy, which was
similar to an aspiration but required a larger needle and a more
aggressive technique, because its goal was to extract a tissue sample.
As I had told Mike, I had been training certain Polies to operate the
equipment in Biomed and to perform simple medical procedures such
as suturing and starting IV lines. These guys had already gone
through basic EMT training during the summer, so they knew the
basics. Out of this group I chose Welder Walt to assist me with the
biopsy. Twelve years before, he had been trained as an army medic.

Bill Johnson, the carpentry foreman, would assist, as he had had experience suturing his own horses. We had detailed instructions from the inventor of the procedure, who called me on the satellite phone connection to tell me how to do it. She was very nice and friendly with a great sense of humor: She asked if I had any ice cubes for anesthesia of the skin! I assured her we had no shortage of ice around here. I couldn't give myself any tranquilizers or painkillers, as it is illegal to prescribe controlled substances to yourself. So I would rely on ice and lidocaine to cope with the pain.

Meanwhile, Walt and I needed to practice our technique. Wendy managed to skua some vegetables from our food supply, and a day or two before the biopsy, we sat at a table in Biomed practicing sticking needles into an apple, a shriveled yam, and a dried-up potato. It was so absurd we ended up laughing like clowns while Big videotaped us. Halfway through the session Walt turned and asked if we were working on a peach or an apple.

"It's an apple," I said, looking at him.

Walt shook his head. "I've been out of society so long that I don't remember my fruits and vegetables."

Although our supply of syringes left much to be desired since they had frozen and lost their seal, we were soon reasonably certain that we could obtain enough tissue cells from the mass to be able to analyze them.

I enlisted Ken Lobe, who had been a lab tech during Vietnam, to stain the slides. We were a bit worried about this procedure because the only stain we had was badly out of date. The replacement stains had been on the last flight of the season that boomeranged back to McMurdo.

As for video transmissions and satellite linkups, luckily we had a bunch of resident geniuses who were eager for a challenge. Comms Tom had to coordinate our session to fall within the short window of opportunity when satellites briefly peeked over the horizon and connected us with the world. Choo Choo Charlie Kaminski, the astronomer and telescope wizard, fine-tuned Lisa's video-microscope that could magnify the slides' images and transmit them to the States. ASA had brought in Karim Sergi, M.D., a cell cytologist, to stand by in Denver to help direct the biopsy and interpret the results.

In the midst of all this commotion, life went on. The construction workers worked their shifts, Denver still expected weekly sitreps and accounting reports from the store, and I saw patients every day.

President Clinton wrote a letter to the station to commemorate the coming winter solstice and to congratulate us on our fine work and brave sacrifice, as if we were polar explorers or something noble. In fact, we were starting to feel like charlatans. Maybe it was just our oxygen-starved brains, but by now we no longer considered our lives particularly unusual or dangerous.

On Saturday night before the biopsy I played cards with Carpenter Larry, Power Plant Thom, and Tool Man Tim. Tim, who is from Minnesota, was now known as Minnesota Mayonnaise. He confided to us all that nothing below his waist had seen the sun more than twice in the past ten years, giving him a "Minnesota mayonnaise tan." Bad move. A new nickname was born.

The game ended at midnight, and I went to the galley to chat with Andy, Loree, and Larry. When Larry announced he was heading out to the El Dorm in the suburbs to hit the sack, I reminded him to be careful walking along the flag lines in the dark.

"It's only a three-minute walk," he said.

"Yes, but it's three minutes on the edge."

Then we started telling stories about how boring our correspondence had become. We were so used to the place that walking outside in the dark, alone in a whiteout storm at 80 degrees below zero with a large aurora across the sky, hardly seemed worth mentioning. We were more interested in describing the six-foot icicles that had formed inside the roof of the Dome, making our home look like the Carlsbad Caverns. And we worried more about what was for supper than the fact that we had almost lost power again this week. We had lost all conception of what was dangerous and what wasn't. Then something would happen to break the monotony of this sleepy little life of ours, and we would realize how quickly three minutes on the edge can become an eternity.

From: John W. Penney
To: Mr. and Mrs. Cahill
Date: 23 June 1999 02:39:39 +1200
Subject: Doc's Surgery

Hello Mr. & Mrs. Cahill:

I asked the Doc if it was okay with her if I wrote to you. I wanted to give you the perspective of a bystander about her surgery last night.

We had a very nice Winter Solstice Dinner last evening. We had appetizers from 5 to 6 and dinner from 6 to 7. The appetizers and dinner were very tasty and well presented. Some of the people on the crew were a little difficult to recognize, as they were disguised with shirts with buttons and collars on them and a few even wore ties. All the ladies, with one exception, wore dresses or skirts. A rare sight, and quite welcome. We had linen tablecloths and napkins and candles on the tables. Wine was provided as well, but those of us scheduled for surgery later in the evening abstained.

Near the end of dinner, Heidi proposed a toast of good luck to the Doc. We all joined in and the toast ended with a round of applause.

After dinner the Doc and I retired to her surgery where we prepped for the action to come. We laid out all the surgical gowns, hats, and gloves for the team. We draped the operating table and prepared the syringes and needles for the biopsy. I threw away two out of three syringes, as they did not hold suction when testing them. The 10cc syringes are made in Malaysia and have been frozen. I wanted to make sure they would function when their time came. I remembered the time when the Doc was attempting to give me some local anesthesia before sewing up my finger, and she went through three syringes before finding one that would work. I wanted to remove as many variables as possible.

The Doc is amazing. You would have thought we were setting up the surgery for an operation on someone's sled dog. Anyone looking on would have had no idea that she was preparing her surgery to perform surgery on herself. We completed the preparations and she said she was going to attempt to take a nap. I returned to Biomed an hour and a half later to find that it had been transformed into a high-tech communications center. The ever-amazing Lisa (we believe her to be an alien) had all her computer gear for real-time video communications with Denver set up along with an Internet phone for real-time audio as well. The linkup with Denver was made, Doc was dressed in one of those always alluring hospital gowns, and we were ready to begin. The Doc did the initial procedures herself. We elevated the head of the operating table, so she could see better, and she went to town. Again, you would have thought she was operating on someone else. After performing multiple tissue extractions, and turning the syringes over to Ken (the man who prepared the slides), she took a moment out and placed some ice on herself and had a drink of club soda. Then it was Welder Walt's turn. The Doc just lay back and let Walt do his thing. She was quite comfortable with Walt performing the procedure. She and Walt had practiced the day before on various fruits and vegetables. Walt said that the lump he was working on most closely resembled the yam they had worked with the day prior. When Walt's turn was over, more ice for a couple of minutes, then the Doc went at it again herself. Lisa was taking video of the slides as Ken prepared them, and none too soon the specialist in Denver said that we had enough slides.

The Doc got up off the table, retired to her room (right next door), and lay down with an ice pack. After doing this for half an hour, she said she wanted to go help Lisa and Liza prepare the slides. I told her that Lisa and Liza were very capable of preparing the slides without her assistance and I thought it a good idea for her to just chill out. I was surprised when she took my advice and just lay back. We made pleasant conversation. We spoke of world travel and the places she wants to go. We spoke of flying and sailing, and how she is looking forward to getting her flying license, and doing some sailing with her brother. We also spoke of her family and her folks' beloved spot in the woods.

She finally decided that she could go to sleep around 3 a.m., so I tucked her in and bade her sweet dreams.

We are in waiting mode now. The pictures are on their way to the world. We may hear something in a few days.

I just wanted to give you a glimpse of how your beautiful daughter is handling the current situation. She is the consummate professional. To see her in the galley, interacting with the crew, you would never guess what she is going through. She is truly a brave woman. We all love her very much.

Regards,
Big John

CHAPTER 10:

The Other Side
of Winter

From: Jerri Nielsen
To: Family and friends
Date: Sun, Jun. 27, 1999, 7:51 p.m.
Subject: Winter

Here we are looking down the hill at the other side of winter. Our astronomer is sending us emails explaining what to expect at dawn. Dawn . . . What a concept. I am so comforted by the dark and by the depth of winter, that I do not look forward to the sun. The new dawn, what will it hold for me? Will I receive some of the best news in my life, or the worst?

Although we are halfway through the winter, we have not yet seen the worst of the worst place on earth. The coldest months are yet to come. And then, just as the sun peeks over our horizon, we are hit by the terrible Antarctic storms of spring.

Today was cold. It surprises me, as I walk out of my dear little hospital and my hands freeze and my washed hair turns to ice. It really shouldn't surprise me, at this point, but it does.

At other times, it seems so normal that it is so cold, and that my home has a floor of ice 9,300 feet thick. Then I wonder what would possess forty-one people to sign up for a mission to the bottom of the earth, to live in small orange refrigerators that keep out the cold.

Deep down, I always know the reason: "We" are why we are here. We are here for each other. The longer that we live together, the more love and respect I have for everyone. People I wouldn't talk to in the world, I relish seeing in this place. We come to understand and rely on each other in a way that is not of this century, not of this time. This is how human beings were meant to live, in tribes.

The tribe is all that we have here and it makes its own laws, customs, rules of interaction, and concept of duty. Here, duty is everything. How beautiful and simple that is. It is my duty to love and accept and care for everyone, and worry about their mental, physical, and spiritual health, all the time—just like those who have done my job since the beginning of time.

And now, in my unique situation of being the most sick and the only healer, it is my duty to never let the fear or concern for my condition become real. And in doing so, I heal myself.

Love from the Ice,
Doc

In the days following the biopsy, the NSF and ASA began organizing an airdrop of medical supplies to the South Pole for sometime in early July. While we all knew the best solution would be to land a plane and get me off of the continent, this was not a feasible option. The Air National Guard had considered a rescue operation but decided it was too risky. Their aircraft could operate safely only at temperatures warmer than minus 58 F.; our current temperatures were hovering in the minus 70 F. to minus 90 F. range. If a plane did manage to land at Pole in such weather, it was unlikely that it could take off again, or be able to retract its landing gear and fly safely back to New Zealand. I knew the danger, so did my family. My brothers had actually mapped out a plan to extract me from the South Pole—my pilot brother Scotty was ready to fly down and get me—but they, too, quickly realized it was impossible.

The airdrop was a more realistic option. In fact, midwinter airdrops of mail and fresh food had been an annual, morale-boosting tradition when the Navy ran the Antarctic Program. Government budget cuts had doomed the airdrops, which had stopped running in the mid-1990s. Now we had to make do with email and frozen food, and I supposed they figured we'd find our own ways to boost our morale. Luckily Mike, Ken, Liza, and Tim had been on station during the good old days and remembered the proper procedures.

I was increasingly grateful as I learned about the effort and expense that these agencies were willing to incur on my behalf—but I was plagued with doubts about the drop. Previous airdrops had been conducted only in June, on clear nights with a full moon. The next full moon wouldn't occur until the end of July, which might be too late to help me. Even under the best conditions, the operation would be risky for the aircraft crew as well as for those on the ground who had to retrieve the packages in punishing temperatures. The plane's cargo doors could freeze open, or the parcels could miss their mark and kill someone on the ice. I did not want to put anyone in danger unless I was sure that an airdrop of drugs and equipment would increase my chances of survival. Such a risk would not be worth taking if my breast disease was benign, or if I had cancer so advanced that I would die anyway.

Unfortunately, we just didn't know. After many agonizing attempts, Lisa could not enhance the cell images on the slides to make them sufficiently clear for the teams of pathologists in Denver and Washington to interpret. It would take fresh stains and a more powerful video microscope setup for the biopsy to be conclusive. With so much at stake, the uncertainty was difficult.

While there was still a faint hope that the mass was not malignant, I chose to assume that it was what it appeared to be: an aggressive cancer. With that assumption, I wanted to know my odds of surviving without immediate surgery.

From: Jerri Nielsen
To: Kathy D. Miller
Date: June 23, 1999 6:37 A.M.
Subject: Questions

Dear Kathy,

I have no new information about breast cancer, only what I read in the surgical texts here and in the emails that I have gotten from the consulting docs. So I have a few questions. I need to know my chances, as I don't want people risking their lives to airdrop things to me if it doesn't matter and won't save my life.

If it doesn't really matter if a cancer stays in the breast for four more months and won't change anything, why do we try to remove the mass as soon as possible? Or have things really changed recently in the management of this disease?

Isn't it true that if you have breast cancer, there is no cure (unless it was totally removed initially) and that you will always die from breast cancer unless something else kills you first?

Thank you for answering these questions.

Fondly,
Jerri

From: Kathy D. Miller
To: Jerri Nielsen
Date: 24 Jun. 1999 08:41:51 -0500
Subject: RE: Questions

Hi Jerri,

You ask some important questions that are difficult to answer via email (mainly because my typing skills are nonexistent) but I'll try. I haven't seen the slides yet so I don't know how they turned out.

I generally like my patients to read as much as possible about breast cancer so we can best work as a team. I suspect in your case that may be limited by the material at hand. Surgical texts tend to be very nihilistic about the treatment of breast cancer—especially if they are out of date, as I suspect the ones you have are.

The treatment of breast cancer has changed substantially in the last five years:

1. About 20% of my patients (percent increased by the local referral pattern—young patients with bad disease are more likely to be sent to me) receive all or a portion of their chemotherapy before surgical removal of the tumor.

    This has been tested in several randomized trials comparing surgery followed by chemo to the same chemo followed by surgery to remove any remaining tumor. About 75-80% of pts. have a decrease of at least 50% in the size of the tumor with chemo first. Overall survival is the same between both groups but about 1/3 of pts. who would have required mastectomy can have breast-conserving surgery after chemo.

So, leaving the tumor in the breast for 3-4 months for active treatment (the time usual required to give chemo first) is not harmful as many surgeons had feared. This is not the same as leaving the tumor in for 3-4 months and doing nothing—which is our only option without the airdrop to get you the necessary drugs and supplies. We know from several epidemiologic studies that a delay in treatment of more than 3 months does adversely impact survival.

Assuming I were seeing you in my clinic here in balmy Indy I would recommend chemo first. We can come close to duplicating that at the station with some modifications to the chemo to limit toxicity and ensure safety.

2. Whether or not I ever cure breast cancer depends on what you mean by cure. I have the same goals of any other specialist—women should die of someone else's disease rather than mine. I.e.: if you die of a heart attack before a recurrence of your breast cancer we cured you and no one can prove otherwise. If on the other hand you look at population survival curves for women with and without breast cancer, they never become parallel. I.e.: there are an excess of deaths in the breast cancer group even 25 years after diagnosis. Bottom line: I have not yet made a woman immortal but if I can help it they won't die of breast cancer!

From everything I know about your situation it is not hopeless and there is a real chance for long-term survival.

I applaud your concern for those around you and I agree that if starting treatment four months sooner would not change anything the airdrop is not worth the risk. I think it does make a difference and you deserve that chance. I know we've never met so I have to ask you to trust that if I thought your situation was hopeless I would tell you. I always tell my patients the blunt truth—they make important decisions based on that information so they have to know what they are up against (even if they don't want to).

I'm not sure if I have answered your questions but I have rambled enough for now.

Stay well,
Kathy

I liked Kathy's style, but I still wasn't convinced I had much of a chance. I believed that my fate was predetermined—if I had cancer, I had cancer, and it would kill me or it wouldn't. After all, if I had breast cancer it had already gone untreated for three months, and that, as she noted, would "adversely impact" my survival. Still, she was telling me there was hope to extend my life with an airdrop, and none without it. I put my reservations aside, agreed to go along with the program, and tried to get on with my life and my work.

Three Polies had birthdays in the last week of June, and, during breaks in my office hours, I went shopping on the rooftops to find presents. For Roo I found a board game based on interplanetary travel, and for a woman who enjoyed Scrabble, a game resembling the old sixties party game called Twister that used words instead of colored squares. Middle John got a special Hank Williams tape.

While I was skua-ing gifts I stumbled on a real treasure: a set of bingo cards. I organized a bingo game Saturday night, right before poker. People bought cards for fifty cents each, or three for a dollar. The jackpot for the overall winner was $108—a fortune at Pole, so the stakes were high. We had to recycle the cards for future games, so instead of writing on them, we used Froot Loops to mark the numbers.

Halfway through the game we took a break for a John Davis dance-alike contest. Middle John Davis, who turned sixty-two on the Ice, was well known among the astronomers for his awful taste in music and his inclination to break into song and dance around the telescope. We made Middle John demonstrate his technique, then offered a pound of good coffee and a fifth of Amaretto to the person who danced most like John Davis to the strains of "Sweet Caroline." Giant Greg won hands down, but he had the advantage of working with Middle John every day.

"All these months of practice and tutoring paid off," said Greg as he accepted his prizes. We gave Joel a prize for the best style, since he was such a fabulous dancer and we thought that we should give him something. I made a good showing, too. It was truly a hoot. Anyone watching me laughing, clapping, and dancing to Neil Diamond would never guess that I was waiting to find out if I might be dying. And that was the way I wanted it to be.

There was still no word from my children, no indication that they knew about my problem, or that they even remembered me. Mother's Day had come and gone. My daughter had turned eighteen, but she never acknowledged the letter I'd sent through a friend in the States, hoping to slip it past her father. I heard, secondhand, that she had been accepted at a good university and would be studying linguistics, which was one of my favorite subjects. It tore me apart that I couldn't experience any of this with her, but there was simply nothing I could do about it.

Now I was hearing from my mother constantly, sometimes several times a day.

From: Mom
To: Jerri Nielsen

Date: 30 Jun. 1999 07:56:05 EDT
Subject: Hi dear,

I worry so much about you. I know you don't want me to
but I can't help it. I wish to hell they would get some definition from the slides. Not knowing is almost as bad as knowing the bad news. I just hate the thought of you being sick.
Dare I to hope there is still a good chance it is not malignant? This week should bring some idea if the pathologists
are ever able to see the slides, right?

Sometimes I dare to think that everything is going to be all
right and you will come home and begin your life over and it
will be a good life. And if that is the case, I don't want you
to come home sorry for cutting all ties to this world only to
find that this is the real world and the Ice was a temporary
experience which will fade away into memory. I know that is
hard to realize right now. But it is probably the truth. People and things look different once one is away from such a
close group. The dynamics are similar to being in an army
unit or a cult compound. Ways of thinking down there are
stifled by a lack of external input. Be careful that you don't
try to build a life from something which is really fun but has
little permanence.

Right now you are under terrible stress waiting for a diagnosis and expecting the worst. It must be horrible for you to
keep reading all that mail. Every time I see the word "malignant" a chill goes in my guts and I feel sort of sick. I can
only imagine the flood of thoughts you endure every "morning" when you awaken.

I long to hug you. I wish you were here to be in the sunshine
and to go out to dinner with Daddy and me.

I love you so much.

MOMMA

It was astonishing to read the messages now shooting back and forth between the NSF, the logistics experts at ASA, and Pole. The "medical emergency," as my predicament was now being called, had suddenly transformed our sleepy, half-forgotten outpost into the object of an intensive military mobilization. The plan called for a C-141 Starlifter cargo plane, a larger version of the Hercules model, to leave from McChord Air Force Base near Tacoma, Washington, on July 7. It would fly the entire breadth of the Pacific Ocean, refueling over Hawaii from a KC-10 tanker plane, crossing the international date line, and landing in New Zealand on July 9. After the crew had rested and the remainder of the cargo was loaded, the aircraft was expected to launch from Christchurch on July 10 (which was July 11 back in the States—a situation that made tracking the operation in Denver and Cheech very confusing).

Sam Feola, the logistics director at ASA, sent us updates on the purchase and shipment of medical and teleconferencing equipment and an ultrasound machine to the staging area at McChord. The Starlifter could take a maximum of six parcels, each weighing no more than five hundred pounds. Essential goods would be duplicated in different parcels in case one was lost or damaged. Medical supplies would get first priority; if any room was left, freshies would be added in New Zealand, along with mail for the crew.

The scale of the operation was awesome and humbling. All I could do was to hold on and watch it happen, and to try to keep my people as informed and reassured as possible.

From: Jerri Nielsen
To: #winter
Date: Thu., 1 Jul. 1999 02:05:21 +1200
Subject: medical plans

Dear Fellow Polies,

Someone shared with me that they did not understand the plans for my treatment and were hoping to be told at the noon meeting.

The basic story is this:

No one knows if I have cancer or not. From what I can read between the lines, the specialists on my case feel that there is a very good chance that it is cancer but cannot know without a positive aspiration or biopsy.

The slides that we sent from the biopsy showed good tissue and Lisa, Liza and Charlie, and Ken, with phenomenal work on the project, have been able to send very good pictures to the pathologist. The problem is that we don't have the correct tissue stains here, and those stains that we have are . . . would you believe? . . . out of date.

The plan now is to send us better equipment. (In duplicate in case of loss or breakage, the extra to be used to upgrade McMurdo's telemedicine capabilities next year.) This includes cameras, microscopes, and special stains.

If I am found to have cancer, they will start treatment. This will be a chemotherapy agent chosen for effectiveness, lack of side effects, and ease of administration. They hope to not give me something that would decrease my ability to perform my duties here. Or that would greatly decrease my ability to fight infection.

If we don't definitely find cancer, I will still be given anti-estrogen therapy as a precaution. (We can't be sure that I don't have cancer without totally removing the tumor and evaluating it. Which can't be done here.) This will cause premature menopause, basically shutting down my ovaries.

This is done as 50% of breast cancers in women my age are affected by estrogen. They may be able to slow the growth of the cancer by depriving it of estrogen. We may also learn something about the tumor by this therapy. If it decreases in size, this could be meaningful for diagnosis.

Thank you for all of your wonderful support and understanding through this interesting adventure in my life. I know that you will all be asked to do things in excess of your usual tasking to make this happen. Thank you for that. I hope that it will be fun and exciting for us all, to have an airdrop. Let's hope for freshies!

If you have any detailed questions for me that I have not addressed, please feel free to ask me. I will be happy to explain anything regarding my health to any of you. We are all in this together.

Fondly, Jerri Lin

The whole South Pole station mobilized to get ready for the drop. Everyone found a way to contribute: Loree and Dar, the meteorologists, were monitoring weather conditions to help guide the pilots to our base. Comms Tom checked and double-checked radio and computer systems that would keep us in contact with the aircraft. Materials people and carpenters were helping construct the smudge pots that would light the drop zone. Roo reported to the ASA that the moon would drop below the horizon on July 6 and not rise again until July 18: There would be no ambient light at the South Pole on July 10. For the first time, a midwinter airdrop would take place in total darkness.

Big John had been working on his vehicles all week, tuning them up and talking to them, preparing the big tractors and snowmobiles for hard hours of hauling in temperatures far below their lowest performance specs. He gave Cassie Rose and Cosmo their two-thousand-hour maintenance and changed their hydraulic lines. Mike assigned everyone a job for the day of the airdrop, from retrieving parcels to photographing the event to processing the contents in the new garage.

Naturally all this activity did not interfere with the South Pole social calendar, which was loaded with big events this month.

Tuesday, June 29, was Comms Tom Carlson's birthday, and to celebrate we threw the South Pole's first Old-Time Square Dance in the gym. The string band, Scott's Revenge, made its debut with Comms Tom on the fiddle, Dar and Joel on claw-hammer banjo, and Choo Choo Charlie and Giant Greg on guitar. Big John was the caller, which may go down in history as the first time a guy in a Mohawk and a leather jacket called the steps at a square dance.

From: Tim Briggs
To: #winter
Date: 1 July 1999 23:40:14 +1200
Subject: THE PIG

Hello South Pole folks,

We need some volunteers to help prepare for the upcoming festivities. We will be having a pig roast on the third of July in the new garage shop. Entertainment will be much the same as the last party, as long as we can find people willing to have darts shot at them!

We need volunteers to do pig watches. We have to cook this guy (we named him Wilbur) for about a day and a half. During the time we are barbecuing him we would like to have someone watch to make sure the barbecue doesn't burn the new garage down. A sign-up list will be posted in the galley.

Thanks
Tim

Later that week we geared up for the "Fourth of July Pig Roast and TV Killing" celebration. It took several days in the freshies shack to thaw out Wilbur, a suckling pig that had been shipped to Pole for just such an event. Wilbur must have weighed 140 pounds, but Mike's barbecue in the new garage was big enough to accommodate him. Since the pig required a full day and a half of slow roasting, we divided the work into watches and everyone took turns making sure the pig didn't burn.

The first watch fell to Bai Xinhua, the nuclear physicist from China who worked on the AMANDA neutrino project. Bai was, of course, a brilliant scientist, but he seemed shy and reclusive during his initial months at Pole. We soon learned that Bai was not shy at all, but his English skills had been limited when he first arrived. In fact, we were not sure that Bai had fully understood that there was no way out of the South Pole for more than eight months once the station closed.

He was a kind, good-natured person, and I liked him immensely. I hoarded all the ramen noodles I could find for him, because that was all he liked to eat at Pole. And we all went out of our way to help him learn English and become more a part of the community.

Earlier in the year I ran into him in the galley and said, "What's up, Bai?"

He looked at the ceiling.

When I explained what "What's up?" means, he laughed and said, "You talk so funny, Doc."

With a bunch of Polies as his only role models, Bai's accent and English vocabulary became quite colorful. He worked with Nuclear Nick, the Ukrainian with a French-speaking wife and child in Montreal. Nick also coached Bai in English, particularly English expletives such as "Oh, shit!" Soon Bai was cussing like an old pro but was less well versed in the subtleties of friendly conversation. We would be sitting together at dinner and he'd suddenly say something like "Well, I don't give a shit about that."

One of the guys would then take him aside. "You know, Bai, it's okay to say that if you're, like, hanging out with the boys and spittin' yore tobacca, but it's not something you really bring up in mixed company at dinner."

"Oh, okay."

On Thursday afternoon, Manager Mike and Tim built a charcoal fire in the grill. They hoisted Wilbur into place on his spit and left Bai in the garage to keep an eye on the barbecue.

An hour later we all heard Bai's voice on the All-Call shouting, "Help, help! The pig is burning! The pig is on fire!"

I was one of those nearest to the site, so I sprinted out of Biomed and was nearly run down by Pakman, who was toting an opened beer at high speed. The garage was pandemonium. Tim, Mike, Power Plant Thom, and Bai were staring at Wilbur, engulfed in twenty-foot flames caused by dripping fat. His little hide was charred, oozing pig juice. They lifted him off the flames onto a piece of plastic and started adjusting the coals. I felt superfluous, as do all women when men are cooking over fire, so I went home to check my laundry.

The incident was soon known as the "All-Call of the Century." As with the day that JFK was shot, everyone knew where they were and what they were doing when they heard that the pig was on fire.

The burning pig problem was soon solved, and the watches continued all day and night. Celebrations began the following afternoon with "the main event": Cosmo the Crusher vs. Son of Sony. Comms Tom had donated three broken television sets that were going to be retro-ed back to the States for a "Kill Your TV" contest. We all ran outside into the minus 84 F. weather and cheered as Big John drove Cosmo, the twenty-four-ton loader, into view, its big lights flashing against the dark polar sky, its engine growling like a prime-time wrestler as it rolled up to its quarry. The TV put up a good fight and refused to be flattened. Cosmo had to turn and storm again and again before it finally vanquished its opponent. At the end, it danced a victory shuffle with its tracks going up and down and back and forth.

The next event was the "TV Toss" from the second story of the new garage. Again the TV fought valiantly. We had to finish it off with sledgehammers. My excitement was tempered by the fact that I still had no slit lamp to remove shards of glass from injured eyes.

The last planned entertainment was "Bowling for TVs." We drew names from a hat and the winners went to the end of a long hallway with a bowling ball that had been found on a roof. The final TV was positioned at the other end of the hall beneath a large sign that said KILL YOUR TV! Lisa gave her best effort, with no luck. But Dar hit it straight on, and the ball lodged inside the tube with a satisfying explosion. A perfect strike!

After that, we hefted the slightly well-done Wilbur out of the grill and Mike carved him. Tool Man Tim provided another delicious batch of smoked salmon and trout.

I wrote to Kathy Miller about the Fourth of July bash and sent her some pictures. I was starting to like her a great deal—we had so much in common and would have instantly been friends under different circumstances. Although she was ten years younger than I, she had also been born and raised in Ohio. She had gone to medical school at Johns Hopkins in Baltimore and had taken a year off to go to Botswana on a 4H exchange program .

Her good humor and humanity shone through her messages to me, but I had to be sure she was being perfectly straight with me about my prognosis before I could trust her completely. We emailed back and forth, tacking on comments in a time-delayed conversation. Our electronic banter sometimes resembled a ballet, or a Golden Gloves bout, with both of us dancing around the awful reality of my situation. These exchanges with Kathy were like holding a conversation with myself—the emotional versus the rational self. One was always playing the Devil's Advocate with the other. We would banter, and change sides. I needed to hash out the issues, pick the scenario down to its bones, and then reinvent it in a way that I could live with it.

From: Jerri Nielsen
To: Kathy D. Miller
Date: Tuesday, July 6, 1999 6:15 AM
Subject: 4th of July at Pole

Dear Kathy,

We have not had email for two days so I couldn't communicate with the outside world. Which pictures did you get? A bunch returned again, but some made it. The whims of the airway gods . . .

KM: I got lots of photos—all the several TVs in various states of destruction, a burning pig, Lisa with a pig head where her face ought to be, great shots of the Dome and some mountains. By the way, why is there a bowling ball at the Pole?

JN: Why are there bowling balls in the first place? . . .

KM: Good point.

JN: So, if I have cancer, will the mass get smaller with hormone treatment? Why wouldn't a fibroadenoma do the same thing? They change with menses. I may have already changed some. It may be smaller, harder, and deeper. I can't tell, I've felt it to death. I need to Magic Marker myself. No one will know or care. I haven't shaved my underarms or legs for 8 months, so what is a little marker track?

KM: All right, measure the damn thing today, then you go on the once-a-week rule—only measuring the mass on Thursdays. If this turns out to be benign I'll be overjoyed! (And not too troubled by having given you hormonal therapy.)

A fibroadenoma should definitely get smaller with hormonal therapy—without estrogen you can't make fibroadenomas.

Some breast cancers are sensitive to estrogen, some are not—those that are have a ~40% chance of shrinking with hormonal therapy. If it is not sensitive to estrogen the hormonal therapy won't work.

An immunohistochemistry kit for testing the cells will be included in the airdrop. I'll keep my fingers crossed that everything lands on target and safely.

Stay warm,
Kathy

After the Fourth of July we had serious problems with our communications systems, including a total email blackout. When our computer wizards restored contact with the outside world two days later, a flood of messages poured in. One brought terrible news for my friend Mosaddeque Reza.

From: Jerri Nielsen
To: Mom and Dad
Date: 6 Jul. 1999 18:16:45 +1200
Subject: Reza's Dad

Dears,

Reza learned last night that his Dad had been dead for four days before they got word to him. How terrible to lose someone you love in the world when you are on the Ice.

Reza grew up in Bangladesh, one of six children in a remote Muslim village. There is no dependable water or electric. The people live in shacks and do everything by hand. It is miles and miles to the nearest doctor or nurse. The roads are terrible and unpaved and there aren't many cars.

I had gotten to know him well as he had come to me when I asked for volunteers to learn my job. I have taught him to start IVs, suture, splint, do lab and x-rays, and a number of other things. Some day he will go back to his village and be the most qualified medical person. That is why he wanted to learn. He is one of the first persons to finish high school in his hometown (let alone college).

It is impossible for him to contact his mother. There are no phones, no computers, nothing. He emailed Roo's (an astronomer here) family who live 300 miles away. They will have the letter sent by post to his village and then to his Mom.

He is a very sensitive person who writes beautiful poetry about his love for his mother and about world peace and such. He is being extremely brave. He got up early this morning to do his experiments even though we had set up for another scientist to cover him today.

What a thing to happen.

STAY HEALTHY, DAMN IT . . . ALL OF YOU!
Love, Duffy

Now that the airdrop was a certainty, the NSF issued a press release detailing the operation. I had been in contact by email with Rita Colwell, director of NSF, and Karl Erb, who was in charge of Polar Programs, requesting that every effort be made to protect my privacy. I did not want my name released to the public. Since my problem was medical, I simply assumed that the media would respect my wishes. In fact, the NSF soon issued a press release that, while not naming me, gave my age. It was only a matter of time before a reporter would do the math, and my identity would be exposed.

Statement by

DR. KARL A. ERB, DIRECTOR,
OFFICE OF POLAR PROGRAMS
NATIONAL SCIENCE FOUNDATION

On Medical Status of South Pole Personnel

July 6, 1999. After consulting several medical experts in the United States, officials of the National Science Foundation (NSF) have determined that an airdrop of medical supplies is the best option immediately available to treat a woman "wintering over" at Amundsen-Scott South Pole Station. The woman recently discovered a lump in her breast.

Officials at NSF headquarters in Arlington, Va., were recently notified about the condition of the 47-year-old woman, a U.S. citizen employed by Antarctic Support Associates (ASA) in Englewood, Colo. Medical experts were contacted immediately and were provided information about the patient through a satellite communications link, so they could assess the threat to her health. After a thorough review of the information, the patient and her physicians decided on a course of drug treatment that they consider appropriate to maintain her health and safety. NSF, in consultation with the U.S. Air Force, determined that it would be possible to fly an aircraft to the South Pole station to deliver the necessary medical supplies. The 62nd Airlift Wing at McChord Air Force Base in Tacoma, Wash., is preparing for the mission, which is expected to take place within a week . . .

From: Mom
To: Jerri Nielsen
Date: 8 Jul. 1999 19:30:39 EDT
Subject: So much for privacy

Dan Rather's lead story was your lump. I think you should know that they identified you as a 47-year-old "mystery woman." Maybe you should email your kids or should I? They are bound to have heard it from somewhere. Eric said he got it on tape. Said he can't get his work done, he is getting so many calls and emails about his sister. His boss called him from Cleveland to tell him he saw "it" on the TV news. They talked about it being pitch black and the most forbidding place on earth. Talked about how you cannot get out until October because no planes can get in or out. They also said it is a million-dollar mission. (If this turns out to be benign maybe you'd better lie about it and tell everyone you got a cure.) I hope the crew of the plane takes some pictures of the Dome lit up in the darkness and the fire pots. That would be a dramatic picture.

Bye dear. Good luck to you. We all love you so much.
MOMMA

Over the next few days friends and relatives sent us all copies of the myriad of newspaper articles on the airdrop, from the *Washington Post* to the *Sydney Herald*. With each new clipping I grew more terrified that my name would be revealed.

On Friday, July 9, we learned that the Air Force C-141 had landed at Christchurch. Father Coleman, my friend from the summer, was in Cheech and wrote to me that he had blessed the plane with holy water. He planned to hold a Mass for the flight crew before they took off the next morning.

By now we were all like children waiting for Christmas morning; exhausted from anticipation but too excited to sleep. We hung out in the galley, drinking coffee and exchanging news. Pakman ran in saying his father had sent a message saying he had watched the TV news and had seen the plane being packed with melons! That started us dancing around the galley singing banana and watermelon songs.

Finally I called it a night and returned to Biomed. I sat nestled in my bed, wrapped in my down comforter, with an array of colored markers spread out on a lap desk, actually trying to study my medical books. A few feet away, Big John sat at my desk, borrowing my computer to tap out an email to his brother in California. Just down the hall, the two beds in my small hospital were empty. My three housemates in the Biomed building were in their rooms, hopefully getting some rest before the big day.

Suddenly the lights went out.

"Ah, *shit!*" said Big. (He later reminded me that this is usually the last thing you hear on the voice recorder as the pilot goes down with the plane.)

For a heartbeat we sat in total darkness, then the eerie white emergency lights snapped on. I was so absorbed in my books that it took a moment to register what had happened. Big was already running for the exit, wearing only his leather jacket, a T-shirt, shorts, and Pac boots, shouting, "Stay here! I'm going to the power plant."

I fumbled around, grabbing for my warmest clothes. I was still pulling on my heavy boots when Big slammed back through the door.

"I need a flashlight," he gasped, snatching one off a shelf. "There's smoke everywhere. The generator control panel was on fire, but the fire's out."

He looked at me, knowing what was going through my mind.

"Nobody's hurt," he said. "So stay put, and don't open the doors and let any heat out. If the shit hits the fan, I'll come back and get you."

He was out of breath, and worried. Ironically, in this world of cold and ice, our greatest fear was fire. Now, for the first time since I came to the South Pole, I was truly afraid.

CHAPTER 11:

From Hell on Earth

There is never a good time for a power failure at the South Pole. The timing of this one could hardly have been worse, with the emergency airdrop less than twenty-two hours away.

I switched on my handheld radio and started pacing the hospital floor. Liza Lobe took her position in the office, ready to help triage in the case of a medical emergency. Ken had already rushed to his job at the rodwell. Mike, the I-C or incident control, was in the power plant working with Power Plant Thom.

To conserve every stitch of power in the station, Liza and I turned off all electrical equipment and sat in the dark, waiting. With the electricity off, the hospital was unearthly quiet. The only sound was the crackling radio traffic, and I listened to the voices of my friends as they checked in with Mike.

"I-C, I-C, do you read?" It was one of the science techs, calling from the emergency power plant, more than a quarter mile beyond the Dome.

"I-C, go ahead."

"Emergency power, fired up and standing by."

"Okay. Roger that," said Mike, in his best Chuck Yeager voice. "Stand by."

When I thought of Mike and Power Plant Thom and Big John and the others out there in the dark, my heart swelled with an almost

237

unbearable tenderness. The history books call the times of Scott and Amundsen and Shackleton the Age of Heroes—an age that ended with Shackleton's fatal heart attack in 1922. But there were still heroes on the Ice: They were here, battling fire and deadly cold to keep us all safe, or for that matter, flying into the deep Antarctic night to drop a precious cargo into a small crescent of burning barrels.

I strained to keep track of every voice on the radio. If they were talking, they were alive. It worried me not to hear Big's voice, or Power Plant Thom's. I suppressed every instinct that told me to run outside and help them. My job was to stay at my post, I couldn't leave. Instead I paced in the dark, sometimes calling out to Liza in frustration. "I can't pick up their voices!"

Liza, who was also an Alaskan bush pilot and flight controller, was accustomed to knowing Ken was in danger and not being able to do a damn thing about it.

"Quit listening!" she yelled from the next room. "Haven't you learned yet not to listen to the radio?"

After another hour without word, I decided to switch on my computer and email my family in Ohio. If we had to evacuate the Dome and move to the emergency station, I wanted them to know what had happened. I told them about the fire and the power failure, and that Big had gone off to help get us back online.

Dear Sweet Mom and Dad,

. . . It has been 2 hours and I haven't seen him. I haven't heard his voice on the radio. He ran out of here in a pair of shorts. I am sure that he is deep in the middle of it. I guess they are okay or someone would have brought them in to me. We are not allowed to leave. We can't let the heat leave through open doors. I have to stand by in Biomed in case anyone is hurt.

I am sort of scared this time (the first time). Big looked very concerned when he returned here for a flashlight. No radio communication for quite some time. Many people I care about are out there. I have not heard any voices from the power plant. I hate to think. If anyone is hurt I will be the first to know. I wait in the dark for them.

I must leave the computer. I am using such precious power but I haven't used any light or flushed my toilet to make up for it. I just can't bear to think that my family might not know why I stopped communicating if we lose all but emergency life support. Don't worry, we will move to the El Dorm if anything happens.

Sorry for the disjointed nature of this report.

No time for thought . . .

Finally the phone rang. It was Big John, sounding tired but not as worried as before. He said it would take hours to fix the control panel, but everything was all right. I could hear the boys over the radio again, kidding about what color of wire to use, puce or mauve, mauve or sky blue . . . Their easy laughter comforted me and I decided to go to bed.

The next morning Big told me how close we had come to abandoning the Dome. When he had first reached the power plant and opened the control room door, he was slapped in the face by the acrid smell of fried wiring and burned electronic components. The emergency lights had failed, and all he could see were a few flames licking the control panels. Big took a deep breath and blew out the fire, then ran to the door on the far side, clearing the smoke by ventilating the room.

Then he ran for the flashlight. There were only three generators in the power plant. Gen number two had been on line at the time of the blackout and its control panel was still smoking. The paint on gen number one's controller was bubbling, because it was located directly above the controller for gen number two and the flames had begun melting it. They tried to start gen number one. It would crank, but wouldn't start. That left gen number three—the last line of defense between the South Pole station and the Antarctic winter. Big went back to the control room and hurriedly set up the sequence to start gen number three. It fired right off. The men put it back on line. The total blackout time: Eight minutes. Big and Thom stayed up until almost five in the morning repairing the damage caused by the fire. But there was much more work to be done. And they still didn't know what had caused the fire.

On top of this, one of the station's key workers had been badly injured during the blackout. Boston Bob, the electrical foreman, had climbed up on an oil drum to fix the emergency lighting and slipped off. Big and the others heard the thump as he hit the deck.

They raced over to find him lying on the floor, grasping his side. But since he got up and walked to the galley on his own steam, the others went back to work.

Bob didn't come to see me until the next day, when the pain got too bad. I found he had two broken ribs, a punctured lung, and a con-tused liver. This man had a reputation as the toughest guy at the Pole, and he earned it that night. But these injuries would put him out of commission for quite some time.

The airdrop seemed more dangerous now that we had lost a key person and so many others had been up all night dealing with the power failure. In the end, four people were injured preparing for the airdrop.

I was running around playing Sandman, trying to get people to sleep. Mike Masterman, who was organizing the drop, was a lost cause: He was so pumped he'd need a straitjacket and a darkroom to sleep right now. Power Plant Thom had tried but couldn't. He was hanging around the galley, chugging coffee and obsessing about the generators. He was sure the power plant would go down again that night, and he had contacted Christchurch this morning to ask that generator components be included in the airdrop. He reported that every power plant mechanic in New Zealand was looking for parts for us. Big John was old enough and smart enough to get his priorities straight: He was sound asleep. We would need him and Thom that night to fix the big machines during the airdrop, if they should go down, and to bring us up to power if we lost our jury-rigged generator.

At 4 p.m., all personnel met in the galley for a final briefing on the airdrop.

Mike stood in front of the group, reading from a sheaf of papers, assigning last-minute positions, going over safety procedures. He informed us that the Air Force C-141 Starlifter was in the air and would be refueled over McMurdo on its six-thousand-mile round trip to the South Pole. ETA was 10 p.m. "The plane will fly by, drop two packages, circle, and drop four more," said Mike. "Nobody goes into the drop zone until the sixth package is down . . ."

I had my videocamera out, recording the moment for posterity, for my family, for my own sense of history, I suppose. My people looked exhausted but alert. There was apprehension in their eyes, along with excitement. I lingered on their faces: Loree, Andy, Dar, Joel, Big, and Power Plant Thom, their heads together in a deep conference, Comms Tom, Nuclear Nick, Heidi—all of them dear friends. I held them in focus, as if to memorize them all, just as they were on this day, and keep them with me forever. And I turned the camera on myself for a moment, to place me with them, to show that I was here.

Mike was now talking about another extraordinary problem at the station: the media's appetite for news about the "mystery woman" with the lump in her breast had become insatiable. I was still hoping that I could remain anonymous, that the drop would take place, and everyone would forget me and move on to the next story. After all that I had gone through in my life, all that I had achieved and still hoped to achieve, the last thing I wanted was to be remembered as the "woman with the lump." Despite the loyalty of my friends, family, and colleagues in keeping my identity private, the press was relentless. Now reporters were contacting everyone they could find with a connection to Pole to try to get more information about me. It was becoming a terrible strain, draining our energy from the dangerous work at hand.

"Let me know if the press is harassing you or your family," Mike was saying. "If they're sending email to you, we've set up an email account for the press." Then he turned the floor over to Comms Tom.

Tom adjusted his wire-rimmed glasses, set the peak of his baseball cap, and took a long breath. "There've been a lot of rumors bouncing around, and I just want to fill everybody in on what's happening with the computer system," he said. "Basically, we got hacked. The network is pretty much controlled by somebody else."

Nobody moved or said a word. We had all heard the buzz that someone had been trying to get into the email system, and we'd wondered if it was a tabloid reporter looking for dirt. But now we learned it might have been part of a July Fourth hacker attack on U.S. government computers—and any site with a ".gov" address. Apparently spole.gov was not exempt from the barrage. In fact, the South Pole computers were a hacker's Everest because, like everything else about the place, they were so hard to reach. But unlike the FBI public relations site or other less significant targets, if the South Pole lost its computers, much more was at stake: years of priceless research data, our communications lifeline to the outside world. And possibly our life-support systems.

"Keep a low profile, everybody," Comms Tom said. "We've been encrypting messages to Denver because they could be intercepting anything we send out. Right now we want to keep the network up till after the airdrop. As long as we don't give them an indication that we know they're there, they won't shut us down. If we tip our hand and they think they could be caught, they could reformat every disk drive on station . . ."

Lisa Beal, who was sitting in the galley, added that the July Fourth hackers had temporarily disabled the Severe Weather Forecasting computer system, putting countless lives at risk. "These guys have no regard for human life," said Lisa. "They're pissing on anything that has to do with the government."

Everyone in the galley looked momentarily stunned. Then Mike took the floor again and reminded everyone to listen for the All-Call this evening to report to their stations for the airdrop. I was the only one without a real role in the operation. Feeling fairly useless, I busied myself by laying out extra hand warmers and ChapStick that I had brought from Biomed for people to pick up on their way out the door.

Before I left, Loree came in with a weather update: The visibility was good at five miles. The wind was 11.8 knots, still well below the cutoff for the drop, which was 20 knots. The temperature was minus 86 F.

I went home and tried to rest, but I ended up at the computer answering mail and writing some more of my own.

From: Jerri Nielsen
To: Kathy D. Miller
Date: July 10, 1999
Subject: In the drop zone

Dear Kathy,

When do I start on the medication? What do I start? How do I take it? How much? Are the instructions included in the drop?

Getting ready for the drop. Less than 3 hours to go. I am going to make hot chocolate and take blankets like it's a football game or something. My girlfriend is bringing a flask of Crown Royal.

Watch us tonight on CBS. "From Hell on Earth" (the title of a recent newspaper article) . . . What? This is a lovely place!

Fondly, Jerri

At 8:30 p.m. Comms Tom, who was in radio contact with the Starlifter flight crew, got on the All-Call and told us that the aircraft had refueled over McMurdo and was on its way to Pole.

At 9 p.m. Mike Masterman called for the smudge-pot crew to light the fires. The smudge pots—fifty-five-gallon oil drums cut in half and filled with wood, jet fuel, and gasoline—were placed every 110 feet in a three-thousand-foot-long C shape out on the skiway. Once they were lit, the flight crew had requested that the rest of the station's lights be blacked out to help them pinpoint the drop site.

Soon Comms Tom started the countdown, calling the approach every fifteen minutes. I walked over to the galley to make hot chocolate before going to the drop zone. Wendy and Lisa had already started turning out the lights in the Dome, which gave the corridors an eerie feeling of doom. Quite a few team members had gathered in the galley, getting a last bit of warmth and nourishment before the long night.

I went down to the Heavy Shop forty-five minutes ahead of time. Big John had Cassie Rose and the Wrench tuned up, warmed up, and ready to go. Cosmo and two snowmobiles were already out working on smudge-pot duty. I planned to ride shotgun with Big and Power Plant Thom in the Wrench, an 1800 Arctic Cat that would ferry searchers around the drop site and deliver the mechanics to any on-site vehicle problems. When the flight was fifteen minutes out, Big John fired up the Wrench and was ready to go when he got word that Pic was driving Cosmo back to the shop with a shattered hydraulic hose and a broken snowmobile in its bucket. The drive belt had broken on the snowmobile after the operator left it idling too long. The track had frozen to the ice and the belt had burned up while the driver tried to gun it loose.

For the next ten minutes the Heavy Shop looked like the pit at the Indy 500 as Big John and Power Plant Thom replaced the damaged parts and got the machines running again. There were just minutes to spare.

I almost missed my own airdrop when I received a call that someone was on his way in with a case of frostbite. I went back to Biomed and waited anxiously, but my patient never showed up. The call turned out to be a misunderstanding. Luckily Big John came by at the last minute and literally dragged me out to the Wrench.

We rode out to the zone where groups of cold Polies were standing around near Cosmo, who was back up and poised for action. The only light on the plateau came from the arc of smudge pots on the skiway, spewing yellow flames and thick black smoke. The smoke froze in the air and settled to the ice in an eerie haze. We busied ourselves checking our cameras but most of them seized up in the cold. We had to jump up and down to keep warm, and this lent the scene the feeling of a child's party, an Easter egg hunt. We were waiting for the signal to take off and find the hidden treasures in the polar darkness.

As the guys liked to say, the night was as dark as a miner's lunch bucket, and by now it was minus 92 F., the lowest temperature that any vehicle had been operated at the South Pole as far as we knew. While Comms Tom called the aircraft's arrival, we all drew a sharp breath together, like one connected creature.

We saw the plane before we heard it. The huge Starlifter, which is the size of half a football field, came in at seven hundred feet with its red and green running lights on and its white taillight blazing against the black sky. The cockpit lights were blacked out, but the cargo door was open, and you could clearly see the loadmaster, backlit from the cabin light, bracing himself with his arms and legs outstretched in the doorway, looking down to us as we looked up at him. I felt excited but also shocked to see another human being in our world. It was like watching a friendly visitor from another planet hovering in his spacecraft. We were all feeling it, I later learned, but now there was no time to reflect.

On the first pass, the drop team kicked out two parcels. Strobe lights and chemical flares were attached to each, but the fierce cold extinguished them before they hit the ice. We had spotters on the highest buildings on each side of the drop zone, and they were able to watch them land. Ten minutes later, the Starlifter came by for a second pass, kicked out four more packages, and its job was over. We heard its engines fade as the pilot banked and headed back to New Zealand, but there was no time to watch its taillights disappear. There were perishable items out on the ice, along with medical supplies that should not be allowed to freeze. We were poised like trotters at the gate to race for the prize.

As soon as we heard the "All Clear," the snowmobile drivers, with radio guidance from the spotters, fanned out over the skiway and found the first five packages. They signaled the loader operators with flashlights, and in no time we had them captured in the buckets and off-loaded in the new garage building, scene of the recent pig fire. Then everyone went out again to search for the sixth package.

While all the essential medical equipment was sent in duplicate, parcel number six contained an ultrasound machine, the most expensive and delicate item, which was not deemed essential and was not duplicated. Big, Power Plant Thom, and I were tooling around in the Wrench, searching for the package and listening for reports of equipment failure (there weren't any). It was easy to get off course in the pitch dark with a fog of frozen black smoke from the smudge pots hovering over the ice. Once we got lost but a spotter called us on the radio to say we were over Old Pole. This was not a good thing, since it was known to cave in with the weight of a human foot. We did an immediate 180-degree turn and shot out of there. To make things worse, the cab of the Wrench was built of floor-to-ceiling windows that soon frosted over, making it almost impossible to see where we were going. I was futilely trying to scrape at the frost with my mittened hand when Power Plant Thom said, "Wait a minute, try my credit card."

Big and I stared in disbelief as he pulled out his wallet and handed me a Visa card. "Don't worry," he said. "It's expired."

I never did find out what young Power Plant was doing with a credit card at the South Pole, but it worked great as an ice scraper. Before long we were back on the trail of the vanished parcel.

An hour and half later, Choo Choo Charlie called over the radio that he had found the package. A loader was dispatched to collect number six, which had fallen almost two hundred yards out of the drop zone. Its parachute had deployed improperly, and it had landed on the wrong side. The box was crushed on one end and some of its contents spilled on the ice. We could see x-ray film, freshies, coffee filters, Copenhagen tobacco, and Dutch Masters cigars scattered around.

We scooped it all into the bucket and delivered it back to the garage, where we found a party atmosphere. Music was playing and people were dancing around the tables while they unpacked and sorted all the incoming supplies.

By now we were conceding that the airdrop had been a great success: The flight crew was safe, none of the Polies was seriously hurt during the operation (just some frostbite, which was almost routine by now), the power plant was humming, the glycol ghoul was nowhere in sight, and the evil hackers had called it a day. You could feel the relief washing over us all.

When parcel six was unpacked we quickly discovered that the ultrasound machine had been smashed beyond repair. But that didn't dampen anyone's spirits. The rest of the parcels had survived the drop. The microscopes, the medicines, and the stains had arrived intact. There was mail for many of us. And best of all—there were freshies! Some of the fruits and vegetables had been damaged in the drop, but nobody cared. We were all picking the squashed kiwi fruits and oranges off the tables and stuffing them in our mouths, laughing like kids at a carnival. I ate a nectarine that tasted like sunshine.

The materials people at McChord and Cheech had included all kinds of special gifts for me. There were armfuls of colorful silk flowers (real ones wouldn't have made it), military medallions, and stacks of cards and letters. The airdrop teams had written me lovely messages on one of the cardboard packing boxes. I saved half of the box for myself, and the other for the museum in Christchurch.

We weren't allowed to stay in the garage, where we'd be in the way of the people assigned to inventory. I headed for the galley, which was full of people high on freshies. Much of it was bruised or frozen so we had to eat it quickly. Bananas were the most popular item, but they didn't interest me. I had a previously frozen, crushed green pepper which was the best I'd ever tasted. It was about this time that Comms Tom temporarily signed off with the crew aboard the Starlifter, saying, "I'll be back in a few minutes. They're eating all the pears!"

Many of us suffered gastrointestinal disturbances after going so long without fresh food then BoBoing on fruit, but it was worth it. The next day we had a huge salad with the first lettuce anyone had seen in five months.

From: Kathy D. Miller
To: Jerri Nielsen
Date: Sat, 10 Jul. 1999 21:18:10 -0500
Subject: RE: in the drop zone

Hi Jerri,

If the reports on NPR are correct you should be stuffed full of fresh fruits and veggies by now (anything particularly good?).

Here's the plan: We (okay, you) start with combined hormonal therapy.

This will stop you from producing estrogen and block the effects of estrogen on breast tissue. Nearly all benign breast cysts and about 2/3 of breast cancers need estrogen to continue growing. Since you are a premenopausal woman this requires a combination of 2 medications. Start both at the same time.

1. Lupron—this comes as a injection given IM [intramuscular] just once every 3 months. There is a special technique for the injection. Lupron stops your ovaries from working.

2. Tamoxifen—the dose is 20 mg daily. Tamoxifen blocks the estrogen receptor so the remaining estrogen you make (from peripheral conversion of adrenal androgens) doesn't have any effect.

Side effects are all related to the lack of estrogen: no more menstrual periods (perhaps a bonus), hot flashes, mood swings. Small increase in the risk of blood clots. The hot flashes are likely to be the worst—they can be bad in young women who get to menopause suddenly. Then again hot flashes may be a bonus in the middle of polar winter.

Measure the (mass) area before starting. I'll have you measure it again in about 6 weeks. Even when the hormonal therapy works it isn't quick. It is unusual to see a response before 6 weeks. As long as the area stays the same or gets smaller we'll just stick with the hormonal therapy. If it gets bigger we'll need to proceed with chemotherapy. I had them send 2 options for chemo but for now let's assume we won't need them.

They also sent new stains and immunhistochemistry kits for ER and HER-2 (a protein expressed in about 25% of breast cancers). The instructions are probably included and have been sent via email by Dr. Sergi. I'll look for the pictures. The camera setup looked good on the last attempt.

I think they were also sending some videoconferencing equipment so that if we do need to move to more aggressive treatment we can do that "together."

Kathy

As the excitement of the airdrop wore off, I had time to focus once more on my medical situation. I taught Choo Choo Charlie to give me the shots that would thrust me into menopause while I tried not to worry about the future. Now I wanted to thank everybody who had done so much to help me:

From: Jerri Nielsen
To: KogerRo@asa.org; chambeja@asa.org
Date: Jul. 12, 1999 6:34 AM
Subject: Letter to all at ASA

Dear Antarctic Support Associates,

I would like to thank everyone involved in the airdrop to the South Pole. It is so amazing to me that so much would be done for one person. I signed on this mission knowing the inherent danger, especially as the only medical person in such a remote area. I never expected to receive help and support on this level, or anything close to it. You can never imagine how grateful I am, or how very much I appreciate everything. So many people at ASA have reached out to give me support and help.

Things are going well at the South Pole. The airdrop was a complete success. We loved all the extra goodies provided in the packages. The fresh food was definitely the most popular. We had our first salad since February, today. We all loved the flowers. They are brightening this sometimes bleak, yet beautiful place. The Pole is a good place to face adversity. That might seem amazing, but it is true. In such a small, isolated society, there is a great deal of camaraderie and so many good friends that one never feels alone. So although I was concerned about getting treatment, my spirits are high and I continue to do my work.

Please send my sincere thanks to all those involved in this mission.

Fondly,
Jerri Nielsen

I still hoped that the media would lose interest in me, but I had misjudged the appeal of a "mystery woman" in distress, as well as the doggedness of the international media when it smelled a "story." The Associated Press had known for weeks that I was the woman with the lump but had not run the story, apparently because no one would confirm my identity. Then we heard that CBS News had my name and was planning to disclose it.

From: Jerri Nielsen
To: Family and friends
Date: 12 Jul. 1999 21:24:27 +1200
Subject: My identity released

Dear Folks,

Looks like they are compelled to release my identity and try to ruin my life. I can't understand it. It should not be such a public matter. I didn't commit a crime. It is a private medical matter. I don't need this. I am overwhelmed by the amount of work that I have to do here, especially now. And now I am starting the drugs that could make me sick and moody. We are all so very, very tired. My office is filled with stuff to inventory and put away. Then another biopsy and a lot of work.

Love, Duff

From: Scott Cahill
To: Jerri Nielsen
Date: Thu, 15 Jul. 1999 19:40:27 -0400
Subject: Re: My identity released

Dear Duffy:

Your life is not ruined. You just started living it. Don't worry about who spilled the beans. It may have been intentional or it may have been an accident. Either way it was inevitable. I am very proud of the way that you have handled this. Don't worry about anyone else's opinion. It is what you think that matters: "This above all else—to thine own self be true and it must follow as the night the day thou canst not then be false to any man." Be above the moment, keep your cool, and be Duffy. You have earned my respect and my unconditional love and it is yours forever—always—no matter what. I will always be on your side. You make us all proud.

I love you,
Scotty

I had many reasons for asking to not be identified. Being a medical person, I felt that the sick have a right to privacy. I also did not want to bring attention to myself when so many people had worked so hard and others had risked their lives to help me. And I didn't want to be seen as a victim when my life was devoted to being strong and giving strength to others.

The part that I could not and would not explain to anyone was my fear of my ex-husband's anger. He had always been irrationally jealous of my accomplishments, or any public recognition I achieved. One of my old friends in Ohio had recently written me that my ex had remarried. Some hoped this would temper his resentment, but I doubted it. I knew from past experience that seeing my name in the paper would enrage him. And since he could no longer control me, I knew he would try to destroy and humiliate me.

I also feared for the children, since his pattern was to use them to hurt me, which was why I'd gotten a restraining order against him. I couldn't predict what he would do if I suddenly became a public figure. I didn't know how he would strike back, or when. Just that it was only a matter of time.

As it turned out, the *New York Times* decided to break the story first, despite all my pleas for privacy. Its headline read: TRAPPED AT SOUTH POLE, DOCTOR BECOMES A PATIENT. Although the *Times* never used my name, it wouldn't take a rocket scientist to look up the station's physician. I could easily believe that a reporter would betray my privacy, but I was truly shocked to discover who had leaked my identity to the press: "The woman herself is the only medical doctor at the station, said a cancer expert who was consulted in her case and who spoke on the condition of anonymity. The consultant on the case said that the woman would be performing her own biopsy, or perhaps already had . . ." The "consultant" went on to discuss all the options for my medical treatment. I felt violated and humiliated. Worse, I was now afraid that I couldn't trust anyone, not even my own doctors.

From: Jerri Nielsen
To: Gerry Katz
Date: Tue, 13 Jul. 1999 08:42:32 +1200
Subject: Dr. tells all

Dear Gerry,

I read the *New York Times* story in horror to find out that my identity had been revealed by "a consultant on the case." This person was also identified as a "cancer expert." As you are aware, it was important to me that I not be identified if at all possible. This was made very clear by both ASA and NSF in all of their communications. I am now in the very uncomfortable position of not trusting those people who are in charge of my medical care. If my doctor is the one who is leaking personal, confidential medical information to the press, then how can I continue to provide the needed information to my own physicians, knowing that one of them is a direct conduit to the *New York Times*?

I am no longer comfortable with sending any information regarding my case.

Please advise.

Fondly, Jerri Lin

Gerry Katz, consulting physician of the Antarctic Program, wrote back assuring me that none of my primary physicians could have been the source of the leak. My case had been presented to "tumor boards" and various "curbside" consultants—these were likely to be the ones who talked. This information did not make me feel much better, but I didn't have time to dwell on it. Now that the *New York Times* had opened the door and revealed my identity, the foreign press pounced on the story and felt no compunction about using my name. Before long, the international media was in a full-blown feeding frenzy. My parents, brothers, even childhood friends were deluged with phone calls from reporters. Every new report made me sicker inside.

From: Mom
To: Jerri Nielsen
Date: 15 Jul. 1999 10:14:21 EDT
Subject: RED ALERT

Expect an email from the *Sunday Mail,* a newspaper in London. A woman named Annette just called and interviewed me on the phone. Wanted to know what you are like and asked about all sorts of things. I told her you are divorced but said nothing about any kids. Shut her up on the personal stuff. "I don't want to get into her personal life," I said, when she asked me if you had an amicable relationship with your ex-husband. Asked the boys' names, i.e., Scott and Eric, and what they do for a living. Asked if you have a steady, I reminded her that I didn't want to get into your personal life. I described you as an adventure-some woman. She was quite specific. Don't think I made any mistakes. I had a hard time with her accent. She seemed nice but it's a good thing that I was alert 'cause she was prying.

LOOK OUT. She is going to email you.
Love MOMMA

It got worse. I soon found out that the *Mail* reporter and a photographer had showed up at my parents' house in Ohio. Mom and Dad let them in and made them cocktails and gave them something to eat and talked to them all evening. They were conned, but I couldn't blame them. They still trusted people then and had no reason to believe that reporters and photographers did not have our best interests in mind.

My parents were mortified when the article finally appeared. It was full of false information about my family and my job, and it ended with a quote from my daughter, Julia, indicating that she didn't care what happened to me. I could only hope that the tabloid reporter had misquoted her, but each word felt like a stab in the heart. Until this moment I had held out hope that my children would finally try to contact me now that they knew I might be dying. I actually thought it would all be worth it if my illness brought us together again. But now I realized my children were beyond my reach, maybe forever.

From: Jerri Nielsen
To: Mom
Date: 20 Jul. 1999 03:32:10 +1200
Subject: my scandalous life
Dear Mom,

Can you believe this whole thing? Just when it looks like it can't get worse! I just can't believe it. Seems like no matter how hard I try, nothing works. Now, I am getting letters from the NSF and ASA and everyone, about the scandal. God, all I was doing was trying to turn my life around.

Sometimes it seems so incredible, my life, that is. I don't understand it. I have become numb. I can't feel pain anymore. I truly feel nothing now. I used to think how bad it could get so that when it got worse, I could take it. Now I am out of horrible things to imagine. I am starting to simply not care about myself anymore

I love you both. You were had by those people. It is not your fault.

I have brought on so much grief to you all. My life has not been perfect, and that is what they want to write.

Love, Duffy

Sure enough, my ex-husband had surfaced, giving interviews to scandal sheets, newspapers, and anyone who would listen to him. He had contacted my employers, ASA and NSF, by phone and by email. In one letter to NSF, he asked that all communication regarding Dr. Nielsen go directly through him, as the ex-husband. He also wrote another letter to the NSF saying that they should look at my résumé, I was not always what I appeared to be. This suggestion was strange, since he had helped me write my résumé, but it didn't surprise me. I heard through my family that he was telling reporters I really didn't have cancer, that I was making it up to attract attention. He was trying to convince those who were deciding whether or not to save me that I was deceiving them. I hate to think what might have happened if they had taken him seriously.

Although reporters apparently didn't find him sufficiently credible to quote directly, they used his statements as a way to coerce information out of my family and friends. Journalists and producers would call or show up and say, "We just interviewed her ex-husband, and if you won't set the record straight then we'll have to use what he said."

Most of my friends and family members wanted to break their silence to protect my good name. I told them not to. I wanted to avoid a nasty "he said, she said" marital fight in the papers that would just expose my kids to more humiliation. Every time I had tried to fight him in the past, he'd managed to come out ahead. Nobody could fight him and win; he simply never gave up until he wore you down. I knew the situation would only escalate if I spoke out and started to defend myself, even though everyone said that I was making a mistake.

Meanwhile, my parents were literally under siege in Ohio. Reporters lurked in the woods, people knocked on the door bearing requests for interviews, flowers, letters from celebrity journalists. They sat at home with all the lights out, afraid to answer the door because once someone just walked in the house and started taking pictures. My father was accosted by a news crew in the driveway. The phone rang so often that my parents had to get a private phone number. I enlisted the help of public relations people from ASA and NSF to help take the pressure off my family.

These were the most miserable weeks of my life. The likelihood of having cancer and dying did not trouble me as much as the way the media were hounding my parents, my brothers, and my friends at Pole. It was as though a virus had invaded my last sanctuary on earth, infecting everything that was dear to me.

At the same time all this media madness was going on, pathologists back in the States were still trying to interpret my biopsy slides, now restained with fresh dye and retransmitted to them. Lisa had rigged up a new video microscope system with equipment from the airdrop. But despite all the new information we were now able to give them, the doctors still weren't satisfied with the images. Without fanfare, a week after the airdrop Walt and I performed a second biopsy, and Ken Lobe worked up a new set of slides for transmission.

By now I was anxious to learn what the diagnosis would be, but for days there was no word from my doctors.

On Thursday, July 22, while Lisa and I were looking through her email to see if there was any more news on the quality of the slide images, we spotted a message from a pathologist at the National Cancer Institute in Washington, D.C. While I stood over her shoulder, Lisa clicked it open and we eagerly began to read. Only a few sentences into the message, a technical discussion of staining and slides, the doctor wrote in passing, "these slides show carcinoma of the breast . . ."

For a moment I couldn't breathe. I felt like someone had kicked me in the stomach, and ice water was flushing through my veins. I held on to Lisa's shoulders, as a phrase kept running though my head: *This is the way the world ends. . . this is the way the world ends . . .* All of my mental exercises had not prepared me for this awful news, not when it was delivered like this, tossed casually into a correspondence between strangers. I felt like an eavesdropper at my own execution.

This is the way the world ends . . . not with a bang, but a whimper . . .

Lisa put an arm around me.

"What a way to be told," she said.

I couldn't even speak to her. At that moment I was almost as upset about the way I had learned about my cancer as the cancer itself. Why didn't they write to *me,* the station physician? Why not have Kathy tell me? Lisa tried to console me, but I had a patient waiting to see me and excused myself.

The next thing I remember from that morning was seeing one of the carpenters lying on the cart in Biomed. While examining him I realized from the expression on his face that he could tell that something wasn't right with me. For once I couldn't summon up the impassive mask that I always wore when I saw my patients. There was no way I could hide my feelings from him, or any friend at the Pole. We were too connected by now, like cells in a simple organism. He deserved to know what was wrong.

"I just found out that I have cancer."

The patient got up from the bed and held the doctor.

CHAPTER 12:

Club Med

This is the Hour of Lead—
Remembered, if outlived,
As Freezing persons, recollect the Snow—
First—Chill—then Stupor—then the
letting go—

—Emily Dickinson

To: Jerri Nielsen
From: Kathy D. Miller
Date: 23 Jul. 1999
Subject: chemotherapy

Hi Jerri,

The other pathologists have reviewed the slides and they agree—you definitely have breast cancer. We will connect again at 9:30 tonight and will begin chemotherapy. The dose of Taxol is 140 mg—infused over 1 hour. Plan on doing this weekly for 3 weeks, then having a one-week break (overall 4-week cycle). This regimen should cause very little myelo-suppression, virtually no nausea, and minimal hair thinning. You may notice some muscle aches the day after treatment but this is usually mild and something like Tylenol or ibuprofen will make it go away. The liver tests only need to be done once a month—you don't have to repeat them now.

Talk to you tonight,
Kathy

Kathy Miller was appalled to learn that I'd received my diagnosis in a secondhand email from a doctor I didn't know. She had planned to tell me herself during a videoconference scheduled for that evening. However it came to me, the news cut like a knife. There was no more room for denial. I was a dead woman walking.

From: Jerri Nielsen
To: Scott Cahill
Date: July 23, 1999
Subject: diagnosis

Dear Scott,

I found out tonight that I have cancer. It is aggressive and fast growing. That is all I know. They can't tell me if I will die in the next year or in 20 years, until I get off the Ice. Even then I won't know unless it is really bad and has spread a lot. It seems that it is in my lymph nodes already. Please call the family as I don't know how they are going to be tomorrow with the bad news.

Love you so much.
Duffy

*   *   *

From: Scott Cahill
To: Jerri Nielsen
Date: Jul. 23 1999 09:18:59 -0400
Subject: Re: diagnosis

Hi Duff,

I am being bad this morning. I am late for work already and still on the computer.

I am powerless to be of any help at all—what a horrible feeling it is. I had felt that you were sick, I knew it just like Dad knows when a building is falling down. I know it must be driving you crazy. Stay upbeat. You are stuck with us Cahills as your support group—halfway around the world—but we will be with you through this and you will not be going through your treatments alone.

I will be there to hold your hand when you hurt and to give you cups of ice. That is all I know how to do, but you will get better and we will be old farts together and we will sail and sit on the swing at the beach and reflect on all of the hell—that is life—that we have endured. I promise you that. I have no right to—but I just know.

Today the windlass goes on the boat. It is big & shiny & she is very happy—she has been pushing hard to get it on early—but I was firm. I worked most of the day yesterday. I'd better get to work. I love you, sister. I am very proud of you. I know that this is hard. Keep your chin up. Brother boy is here & the boat & I are waiting for you to get home so we can get you straightened up so we can fly & sail. I love you.

Scotty

From: Dad
To: Jerri Nielsen
Date: July 25, 1999 8:05 PM
Subject: From Daddy

Dear Duffy,

As you know, writing letters is not my bag and this one is really tough. I would like to tell you how much we love you, but I think you already know that. One thing you may not know is how often I think about the times we had when you were growing up. Bricker Farm, Duckcreek, the country club, SCUBA diving in the quarry, acrobatics, cheerleading, but most of all the times we spent talking and being together. Mom and I love you more than life itself and when we get you home we will take good care of you. Thank your friends for me for all the help they have given you, and I hope someday to be able to meet them.

Love you, Duff,
DAD

Although I doubted chemotherapy would save my life, I agreed to start immediately. It was better than doing nothing. The plan was to begin weekly infusions of Taxol, a relatively new drug that had shown good results in shrinking large, fast-growing tumors like mine. Lisa and Comms Tom had figured out a way to set up a live videoconference with Kathy in Indianapolis so she could monitor the chemotherapy and be on hand in case anything went wrong.

Taxol's effect on the human body depends on the size of the dose and how long it is infused into the bloodstream. Kathy Miller prescribed an hour-long drip. Any shorter time would increase the risk of a dangerous allergic reaction. Longer infusions could cause serious myelosuppression—shutting down blood cell production in the bone marrow.

Unlike big-time American hospitals, Biomed didn't have special pumps to administer drugs at the prescribed rates, so I chose the next best thing: Big John. Kathy and her assistant, an amazing oncology nurse named LaTrice Haney, calculated the rate of drips per minute based on the type of IV lines we were going to use. Big practiced regulating the flow to complete the infusion on time. He also helped me measure the size of the mass right before chemo so that we could gauge any changes. We accomplished this in true polar fashion: I defined the edges with my fingers and Big traced them with a felt-tip marker. Then we took a green plastic ruler and measured the thing. It had grown since June, and was now 5.5 cm. by 4 cm., roughly the size of a hen's egg. In the arena of breast tumors, this was a heavyweight.

To administer the infusions, I had already assembled essentially the same group as the biopsy crew with the addition of Heidi Schernthanner, the heavy-equipment operator whom I trained to help with IVs and to keep track of medical materials. We called ourselves Club Med.

Welder Walt and Ken Lobe started the IVs, Big mixed the drugs and monitored the flows, Mike kept up communications with Comms Tom and Indianapolis, and Lisa and Liza operated the videocameras. We even had a mascot named Rover.

Rover was one of the little black Sony auto-tracking videocameras we had received in the airdrop. It could be programmed to follow movements without human guidance during the chemo sessions, and it sat on a pedestal in my bedroom, zooming and pivoting like a menacing little robot guard. Lisa, finding the camera too intimidating, gave it the cute nickname. Other members of Club Med added canine features, such as a red felt tongue and pointy ears made out of green silk leaves. It was hard to look at Rover without bursting into laughter, which was just what we needed as the conference drew closer. We all knew that if something went wrong—if, for instance, I had a bad reaction or went into shock—then it would be up to my friends to save my life. It was quite a responsibility for people without medical backgrounds.

My friends took care of my spirit as well as my body. Soon everyone at Pole learned about my diagnosis, and a postcard arrived in Biomed from Bai Xinhua, the Chinese physicist. There was a poem, written in Chinese, with an English translation printed below it:

> *In this icy world friendship, like the sunlight in the*
> *spring*
> *Cherish you with warmth love, like the flowers*
> *blooming in the spring*
> *Hope it can bring you, our Jerri the best wishes from*
> *my heart*
>
> *July, 1999 Bai, South Pole*

On Friday, July 24, we set up the cameras and laid out the equipment and medications we would need. At 9:30 p.m. a video image from a clinic in steamy, summertime Indianapolis traveled across the Internet, bounced off a satellite skittering along the polar horizon, and appeared on the computer monitor on my desk. Kathy and LaTrice were easy to recognize from the pictures Kathy had attached in her email. Still, our first videoconference was disorienting. Mostly we saw them in profile as they peered into their own monitor, watching us watch them. The sound was delayed, like a badly dubbed foreign film, and our colleagues in America seemed to jump around the screen, like dancers caught in a disco strobe. I hate to think how we looked to them.

After introducing ourselves we got right to work. The chemotherapy began with a dose of Kytril, taken orally, to prevent nausea, followed by infusions of Decadron, a steroid, and Benadryl, an antihistamine, to minimize any allergic reaction to the Taxol. The drugs made me woozy, and I watched the rest of the procedure through one eye or the other—they wouldn't focus together. We were instructed to start the Taxol slowly for the first ten minutes and watch carefully for a reaction. When none came, Big cranked up the flow.

At about this point in the procedure, we lost our audio link to Indianapolis. Losing Comms was a familiar event in polar communications, but this time it put a scare in all of us. My team was standing by with epinephrine and other emergency medications in case I reacted adversely to the chemo, but they needed directions on administering them. I wouldn't be available.

Luckily, audio and video links come through on separate channels. We were able to maintain visual contact, but for the remainder of the session we had to scribble notes on pieces of paper and hold them up to the camera.

From my bed I dictated questions and Lisa would write them out for me: "What do we give after the Taxol?"

We could see Kathy and LaTrice squinting at their monitor, conferring, and then writing a reply. Lisa would read it back to me:

"Flush the IV tubing with saline for fifteen minutes."

We'd pause for a few moments, then I'd have another question.

"Why is the Taxol running so slowly?"

"We don't know!"

Big and I noted that we had opened the line a half hour ago but the bag was still almost full of fluid. We did what we could to speed the drip, but nothing worked. It was troubling because the longer infusion carried a greater risk of side effects. We scrambled, trying to figure out the problem, but after an hour, we lost the "bird" and the screen went dead. The liquid Taxol went on dripping into my arm for another two hours. We learned later that although the correct dosages and equipment had been sent with the airdrop, the drip chambers we had at Pole were smaller than those in Indiana. The calculations had been inaccurate.

From: Kathy D. Miller
To: Jerri Nielsen
Date: 24 Jul. 1999 10:01:26 -0500
Subject: whew

Okay, we made it. I assume everything went all right after we lost the satellite connection for the final time? I have to tell you how much respect LaTrice and I have for you and all your assistants. It was difficult, stressful, frustrating, frightening for us last night—we kept trying to reach through the monitor to help but couldn't get there. The group's ability to hang together was most impressive.

You should feel well this week. Only blood test you need to do is a CBC [complete blood count] on Friday. The Taxol in this dose and schedule has very little myelosuppression but I don't want to take any chances.

Congratulations,
Kathy

From: Jerri Nielsen
To: Kathy D. Miller
Date: July 24, 1999 4:27 AM
Subject: Re: whew

Dear Kathy,

Welcome to the Marx Brothers do chemotherapy at home!

It was a little rough there finding the "right stuff" but we got it. Now you see what the practice of medicine is like here. Usually, though, I don't have the "right stuff." I often have to make it or make do.

The chemo went well. It took 3-1/2 hours to run it in due to the IV. I had a little dysphoria. A feeling that I couldn't get comfortable but that could have been the tricky positional IV. My bed is in the hospital so I was able to be in my own nest for it. My best friend refused to leave and stayed up all night listening to me sleep, sure that I would stop breathing any minute. Such are friends at the Pole.

He said that he spent the night talking to me about adventure, sailing to South America in my brother's boat, traveling to Mongolia to see my friend in the Peace Corps, and things that would give me good dreams. Things that now, I guess, I will never do.

I woke up at peace. I think that I was relieved to finally have treatment but I feel such a sense of overwhelming loss. Is that normal? I have been through such hell in my life (you can imagine being a woman in medicine in the early '70s, a bad marriage with a horrible divorce, and more). I have always had such a positive and resilient nature that kept me fighting and coming back. But dying now is not what I had in mind.

I must confess that I have lost all hope. I even see treatment as a useless and stupid way to end a life. I have often felt that for my patients. Why bother, after a point? To me breast cancer is repeated pleural effusions, bone metastases, brain mets, radiation pulmonitis, and disfigurement. I had not considered the loss of sexuality, the obesity, and the rest. Is that my lot? Is that what everyone with this faces? My books paint a horrible picture. Why does anyone even try? Do they believe the support groups with people who have lived 7 years, 3 months and 4 days? I am now at a confused point where I can't even think. But I am not depressed. I just can't see why I should try.

So, I got up early this morning, with little sleep, to decorate for the party tonight. It was my idea (the party) so I had prior commitments. We are having "Christmas in July" and also celebrating the birthdays of two Polies. It will be a toga party. That's easy for us, as all you have to do is strip your bed, and you are dressed. I made Jell-O shots, strawberry and lime. And I made my special recipe from my Indiana friend (Sue Lehman) who sent you to me. So I was a busy girl this morning. This is pretty and tasty and great to have in the freezer for guests at Christmas. She made it for my first baby's shower.

Sue's Pink Drink

Limeade 1 can, add 1/2 the water called for

Pink lemonade 2 cans, add 1/2 the water

White rum, in the amount of water that you should have added above, but didn't.

Freeze solid (easy here), scoop out into stemmed glasses still frozen. Strawberries are very nice on the side of the glass.

Don't ever trust my manual CBCs, sorry but true.

Fondly, Jerri

From: Kathy D. Miller
To: Jerri Nielsen
Date: 24 Jul. 1999 18:56:47 -0500
Subject: RE: whew

Dear Jerri,

I'm not sure how to respond but let me try.

I would love to say that I know and fully understand all the emotions and the depth of your loss—but that would be a lie and you know it. I am truly privileged to share these feelings with my patients on a daily basis. It's one of the gifts they share with me—I am constantly reminded that life is a tenuous gift with no guarantees. You now have that fact pushed in your face whether you want it or not. Whenever my priorities get out of line, I am humbled by one of my patients.

The sense of loss is quite real. How can I put it best—this SUCKS! Breast cancer is a lousy, rotten disease that you did nothing to deserve—regardless of any ill-fated choices in your past. In many respects the treatment is just as bad.

Your medical training doesn't help us here. Especially in the ER you see the worst of my field. My long-term survivors just don't end up there. The "counting the years, months, days" has always seemed a little strange to me. One of my favorite long-term survivors put it best—"My breast cancer doesn't deserve that much power in my life anymore. To keep track in such a detailed way would be like admitting that the disease still controls me."

I don't know how to convince you of this since we have never met. One thing I can promise you is honesty. No matter what I will always be honest with you. Unfortunately I can't always give you the answers you want. Averages and statistics don't tell me a damn thing about you. I don't have a crystal ball and I don't get to decide how long you live (neither do you). I haven't seen or heard anything (repeat: ANYTHING) that tells me your disease is not curable. That's the goal and the chemo is the best way to get you there.

If I thought your disease wasn't curable I'd say so and we would have a much more difficult decision to make about your treatment—I agree that spending your last days with chemo doesn't sound good. In fact one of my goals has been to never treat someone with chemo during their last 3 months of life.

One thing my job has taught me is to never underestimate the power and strength of a woman. All my patients struggle with these same thoughts but when it really comes down to it, they do what needs to be done.

I'm glad to hear that you have such wonderful friends at the Pole. Let them do their job and help you! You would do exactly the same thing if it was one of them.

Kathy

I was reading Kathy's words, but I was not hearing the message. A voice in me drowned her out, and it kept saying, *You're a dead woman. Why bother?* I was daring her to give me hope, and making it as difficult as possible for her to do so. That was something that I had observed so often from the other side of the desk but never really understood until now. Hope was something that had to be won, not given. At first, like so many patients, I regarded any offer of hope as a possible deception. It had to be challenged.

From: Jerri Nielsen
To: Kathy D. Miller
Date: July 26, 1999 4:50 AM
Subject: Re: triumph, wisdom and questions

I read that Taxol causes total hair loss. Is this true? When do I get sick from the chemo? I felt okay Saturday a.m., but threw up two times Saturday evening. I also got one episode of abdominal cramps on Sunday. Was that something I ate or was it chemo? Sunday, I think I was a little nauseated. Today I am tired.

I just want to know what will happen so I can plan. All of my plans and dreams are gone, now. I need new ones. Ones that won't be fun, but perhaps functional. I am going to lose my insurance in a year. I worry about things like that.

Should I even worry about insurance in a year? I don't think that it is abnormal to grieve and want answers when you are handed a death sentence.

Fondly,
Jerri

From: Kathy D. Miller
To: Jerri Nielsen
Date: 25 Jul. 1999 17:05:43 -0500
Subject: triumph, wisdom and questions

Hi Jerri,

I am sweating in my living room after watching the final stage of Le Tour de France while spending the hour on my NordicTrack. I have been fascinated by the Tour for years but this year was even more special. Lance Armstrong just completed the most amazing comeback—it was just two and a half years ago that I admitted Lance for his second and (3 weeks later) third cycles of chemotherapy for his advanced testicular cancer. I was the fellow on service that month—I can take no credit for his treatment or recovery. I can marvel at the man and his strength.

Your comments yesterday remind me very much of those days with Lance. He came to IU after starting treatment in Texas. He came to IU demoralized and beaten, having watched his whole life change in an instant. Even if he survived (chances were not great) there was little chance he could ever return to competitive cycling. It was the only life he had ever known or wanted. I witnessed an amazing change in the time between cycles. He came back calm and resolved—still frightened but no longer a beaten, hopeless man. He could only explain the change as a conscious decision not to focus on death but to speak of life. I have been honored to witness that transition many times—I still don't have a clue how it comes about or how to point you the way. It is a very personal journey that only you control.

I wish you peace along the way.

Kathy

I would always remember those words. If someone could give me peace, or show me the road to peace, then I could heal. But I was impatient to get there.

I had witnessed the progress of fatal illnesses so many times that I knew what was coming: When I finally understood that my disease could kill me, I had to go through the process of watching myself die, of seeing my life for what it was, and setting aside my dreams. Only after I had buried myself could I take stock of what was left, put the sadness aside, and go forward. But I could not do this alone.

For someone trained and accustomed to saving others, it was strangely liberating to feel a great need for people. Eventually I handed my heart, and my life, to my family, my dear friends, and to a gifted and compassionate doctor in whom I saw my younger self. But for all my experience, I could not predict that this journey to the point of surrender would be such a turbulent, white-knuckle flight.

Meanwhile, the email *pas de deux* continued:

From: Kathy D. Miller
To: Jerri Nielsen
Date: 26 Jul. 1999 18:39:56 -0500
Subject: RE: triumph, wisdom and questions

Okay—let me try again.

I don't think all of your hair will fall out because the dose was less than half what we would generally use for the 3-hour infusion. IF it does you wouldn't notice that at all until about 2–2.5 weeks after the treatment.

I doubt if the nausea was from the chemo. The dysphoria was both from the Decadron and the Benadryl. Good news—since you didn't have a reaction we can decrease the dose of Decadron this Friday to 10 mg, that will help. I think it is worth taking Kytril with each treatment to avoid any nausea. Kytril doesn't cause weight gain or hair loss but in a few people can cause a headache. If that's a problem we sent other anti-emetics.

You need new short-term goals—simple ones that you can control. You should continue making long-term goals because I expect you to be around to fulfill them.

I am not trying to dodge your question about expected survival—we are just not that good. The best I can tell you is that about half the women in your situation at some point will have a recurrence of their breast cancer somewhere else in the body. That recurrence is almost always obvious in the first 5 years after diagnosis and will eventually take their lives (on average about 2 years after the recurrence is diagnosed). That also means that half the women like you never have a recurrence—they have an expected survival that is the same as other women their age. You never see these women because they have no reason to frequent an emergency room. I see them in my clinic all the time—they really do exist. The problem is I don't know which half you are in and no one does. I wouldn't know that even if you were here.

Bottom line—you'll need and want to get back to work when we are finished with treatment.

Duration of treatment—plan on about three months of chemo (should be just about the time you get out) followed by surgery, probably followed by more chemo with a combination it wouldn't have been safe to use at the Pole, and radiation.

We'll be more organized this Friday—on both ends of the satellite. I assume we have a date for 9:30 again?

Kathy

From: Jerri Nielsen
To: Kathy D. Miller
Date: 27 July 1999 2:33 am
Subject: details

I am so glad that I might not lose my hair. That seems so stupid, but I need something of myself intact. Will it come out anyway with the next round of chemo once I get home? If so, I am worrying about nothing and might as well mourn the loss of one more part while I'm at it.

I was glad to get the letter with the details of what is really going to happen to me. I forwarded it to my mother. She believes that knowledge is everything, a true scientist. Both of us are very reality-oriented. We are better off knowing what is happening so that we can make the best decisions.

Fondly,
Jerri

This intellectual sparring was difficult for both of us. Kathy took the heavy load for me because she was the only one who could do it. I was in touch with many doctor friends, but they didn't want to roll in the dirt with me. Instead, as many people do when confronted with a person with a fatal disease, they tried to give me false hope, statements like "You can beat this thing." Most of them were as well meaning but unhelpful as my friends outside the profession, who said the same thing. They were just trying to be kind, but they only made me feel even more alone.

I couldn't act out this internal drama in front of the people who depended on me. Almost all of my Polie friends thought I was handling my illness with great good humor. To make things worse, I was feeling the effects of chemical menopause, caused by the drugs that were blocking my estrogen production. The hot flashes were terrible. I would suddenly be pouring sweat until I had to take off my hat and a layer of clothing. Then I'd be cold as my sopping wet hair froze to my skin. I'd put the clothes back on and start to overheat again. I would repeat the process until I wore myself out.

The sharp drop in estrogen can also produce mood swings. I could no longer tell if what I was feeling was real, or caused by hormonal changes. My only emotional outlet became email letters to Kathy, my mother, and my brother Scott.

From: Scott Cahill
To: Jerri Nielsen
Date: 26 Jul. 1999 15:24:54 -0400
Subject: holding up
Hi Duffy:

How are you holding up??? I went to the folks over the weekend. They can't wait to get you home—me either. Mom is doing okay—sad & worried about her dear little girl. Dad is not able to sleep. They are so dear. They love you so much. I do too.

I am sneaking away to work on the little boat this afternoon. I will finally finish the last bit of the teak deck. I still have not started on the interior—I am working on the deck and the painting and addition of the hardware and ports. It is pretty much on track for the great launch. You will be there—next spring just south of Annapolis.

We all love you and miss you—your little brother,
Scotty

From: Jerri Nielsen
To: Scott Cahill
Date: July 27, 1999 5:08 PM
Subject: Re: holding up

Dear Scotty,

Not holding up. Sad about already being dead. No hope from my doctor. Even wrote to her begging for something to hold on to. Nothing good came back. She says that I am basically a dead person waiting to be buried. I could die now while taking the treatments here or I could become an old lady. But probably somewhere close to five years or something. No one will even chance at giving me an idea. I won't be able to make plans or have any hopes or dreams. That is the worst part, as I could always muster up hopes and dreams no matter how bad things were.

I thought about the boat all weekend. Big brought me a sailing magazine from the upper galley (four years old) and we looked at the pictures and dreamed of sailing to South America. It was the first time I was excited since all this happened. I really want to live on the boat for a few months so that I have lived on a boat once. It sounds so wonderful. And such a beautiful boat.

The chemo made me sicker than they said I would be. Threw up twice at the party. My breast really hurts. Please write. I love and miss you so much.

Duffy

From: Scott Cahill
To: Jerri Nielsen
Date: 27 Jul. 1999 07:40:15 -0400
Subject: Re: holding up

Dear Duffy:

The boat will be ready!! You need to keep a positive attitude. I can't even pretend to know what hell you must feel now. I am so sorry that I can't hold you in my arms and rock you. You are a fine sister and my best friend and I should be caring for you now. Soon I will be.

Cancer sucks and it is scary as anything gets—but it can be beaten and is being beaten. You are the strongest person I know. We will beat this thing so that one day you will not even think about it. I love you. I wish I was the doctor now. We all think of you all of the time and we can't wait to get you home. You are a Cahill and we have the luck of the Irish and we will beat this!

Love always,
Scotty

The second round of chemotherapy, one week after the first fiasco, went much more smoothly. Club Med was developing beautifully as a group. One of the reasons I love being an ER doc is the element of teamwork. The more you work together, the more everyone knows their job, and the better the group performs.

It was exciting to watch this happen with my team at Pole. I trained Big John to administer my chemo, then John trained Heidi and Liza to do it, and they trained each other. Ken and Welder Walt started IV's and drew blood, Lisa and Comms Tom, our unseen Club Med member in the Comms shack, kept vigilant watch on the computer systems and satellite links that were our lifelines. In the end, the team was so together and knew everything so well that the chemo went perfectly. They were fast, they were good. Kathy and LaTrice were impressed with how quickly we got it down. In fact, once we figured out the right calibrations, Big John did such a good job regulating the drip that Kathy offered to hire him.

"Big, when you get out of there you come work for me," she told him with a chuckle. "You do a better job than my thousand-dollar pumps!"

Meanwhile, I was anxious to hear the results of more recent tests. Walt and I had taken another tissue sample from the mass during the first chemo session. We had placed some of the samples in Navy pathology jars for me to take back to the States. That way I would have tissue obtained before chemotherapy altered the cancer cells. Kathy told me I didn't to have to do this, but I had insisted. I was beginning to regain control of my life, just as I was starting to imagine a future. Ken processed the new cell samples with the fresh stains from the airdrop, and Lisa transmitted the slides to Kathy's pathologists for analysis.

My doctors needed to learn as much as possible about the tumor. One important test was to determine if the cancer cells were fueled by estrogen. If they were, then another test revealed whether or not the estrogen receptors were positive (ER+) or negative (ER-). My limited supply of medical books and papers all said that negative receptors decrease survival chances, because cell growth won't be slowed merely by cutting off estrogen.

During the second round of chemo, Kathy broke the news that my estrogen receptors were negative. She tried to temper the impact by saying it really didn't matter with the course of treatment we had chosen. But I took it as a terrible sign, the latest item in the chain of bad news I'd received about the tumor: Instead of two masses, as we first thought, it was one, big irregular mass. Its size was greater than 5 cm., it grew quickly, and because my lymph nodes were swollen and painful, it might have metastasized, or spread through my body. All of these conditions decreased my chances of survival.

After learning that my cancer was ER-, Big and I sat down with a sheet of paper and a calculator and tried to figure out my odds. As an emergency room physician, I was trained to live off percentages. Kathy didn't think that way and was reluctant to quantify her thinking. When I figured my own chances, my worst fears seemed to be confirmed: According to the somewhat dated statistics I had before me, my chances of surviving more than two years were around ten to fifteen percent.

I wrote Kathy Miller asking her for the whole truth, now. No more sunshine.

From: Jerri Nielsen
To: Kathy D. Miller
Date: July 30, 1999 12:02 PM
Subject: Details
Dear Kathy,

I am better off to know everything from the outset so that I can collect all my losses, grieve, and start over with what I have. I am able to always start over, but it is harder when the losses keep popping up each time that I think that I now know the score.

I am confused on an important point. All of my reference materials, and I admit I don't have many, state absolutely that the absence of estrogen receptors greatly decreases the chance of survival. Tonight, I think that you said that the negative receptors didn't really make that much difference. I really need to know the truth so that I know how to think about my chances and therefore make decisions about my future. It greatly affects my feelings about undergoing therapy, leaving the Ice early, and how I should look at my chances for curative therapy.

I know that there are statistics for all of this. From what I can tell by looking at the statistics that I can understand, I have a very poor chance.

I need to know how to look at my disease in terms of whether or not I have any future. It could greatly affect how I live now, what decisions I make about working toward my general health, and many other important factors. For example, if I have a good chance, I will start to exercise, if I have a 10% chance I won't waste my precious time on a treadmill. There are so many things like that.

Thank you, Jerri

From: Kathy D. Miller
To: Jerri Nielsen
Date: 31 Jul. 1999 20:21:05 -0500
Subject: RE: details

Hi Jerri—

Let me try to unconfuse you. If this missive doesn't give you the information you need, ask again and I'll keep trying.

First—I would bet that your tumor is ER- because it is behaving like an ER- tumor. The likelihood of any tumor being ER+ increases as the age of the patient increases. You are young for breast cancer so with your age alone the chances of your tumor being ER+ start at about 35%. The rapid growth you described also fits with an ER- tumor.

Now, that being said—I don't think we really know the ER status of your tumor since you didn't have any positive controls. The ER stain on your tumor looked negative BUT the stain is very fickle and in the "non-Pole world" would never be done without positive controls. Without the controls there is no way to know if your tumor is really ER- or if the stain just didn't work. We'll know for sure when we can repeat the test on the cells you saved in the Navy bottles.

In general ER- tumors are more aggressive (more dangerous, more likely to recur, etc.) than ER+ tumors. If you made everything else about 2 tumors the same except the ER status, the ER- tumor is about 5%-10% more likely to recur. This isn't a perfect science—sorry.

You are a young woman with a large aggressive tumor. Nothing I learned in the last week helps me be more specific than about half the women with your tumor (with the little we really know about it) will eventually develop metastatic disease that will claim their lives. Half will not. Even if I could make this a better split, 10% survival isn't zero and 90% isn't 100. That's what you really want to know—I can't tell you that and they don't let me decide.

I think what that means for planning is that none of us have guarantees in this life—you just know that more clearly than the rest of us have to face. My patients are a wonderful reminder of that in my own life.

Hope that helps—now get on that treadmill.

Kathy

From: Jerri Nielsen
To: Kathy D. Miller
Date: July 31, 1999 7:43 AM
Subject: Medical stuff

Dear Kathy,

I need to know how to think about my disease so that I can determine if I am even going to try to recover. As I said in the letter regarding this, my prognosis looks very grim from my books. I am all alone at the damn South Pole with no resources, trying to make life-and-death decisions. I need percentages. I am able to gamble the odds if I have information in percents.

I am not like many people whom you have treated (that is why you are treating me at the South Pole). I don't believe that life can be counted by years or days, but by experience and how you leave the world by the way you live. I do not want chronic disease. I understand it much better than most people, having been immersed in it for 25 years. I have always believed that I would kill myself before going on dialysis. If my chance of survival is good, I will come home, have surgery and chemo and radiation, be sick as a dog, disfigured, ugly, and fight with all I have to survive. I will try to get off the Ice and to you as quickly as possible. If I don't have good odds, I will not return to the USA. I will stop all therapy. I will finish training the new doctor here. I will instead travel the world until I am too sick to do so, and sail to South America with my brother, as planned. So I need to know the truth.

Waiting for important answers,
Jerri Lin

From: Eric Cahill
To: Jerri Nielsen
Date: 31 July 1999 14:55:17 +0400
Subject: <no subject>

Jerri,

I just talked to Momma—she says that she reads the receptor
thing is bad. But I'd think this doctor would know better
than mother's books. No matter—take your medicine—
which I'm sure is awful. I'm sure you feel extremely upset—
anyone would, but please don't give up. Momma doesn't
believe that fighting is any use, but I don't agree—son of a
bitch—fight like hell.

I'm really proud of you and what you're doing. My little girls
are proud too.

I wish there was something I could do—but I feel helpless
and sad. You might as well cry, cry and cry like hell, and
then go back to living life the best you can—that's all you
get—that's all anyone gets.

Love,
Mr. Baby

From: Kathy D. Miller
To: Jerri Nielsen
Date: 31 Jul. 1999 21:12:41 -0500
Subject: RE: medical stuff

Jerri,

I do understand that you are not like most of my patients.
We are very much alike and I enjoy our relationship very

much. Please believe that I am not trying to dodge your questions or paint a rosier picture than I truly believe or think possible.

I am at a distinct disadvantage in answering your questions. The statistics I can give any patient are estimates at best. I have much less information about you at this point than I usually do.

The 50-50 numbers I gave you originally were based on the assumption that your tumor would be ER-. That's why I didn't change the figures. I would adjust that up slightly if the cells were ER+.

If I knew you had metastatic disease with no possibility for cure I would say so—you have not told me anything that tells me that is the situation. I plan a thorough evaluation with CAT scans of your chest and abdomen and a bone scan as soon as we can get you out to make sure there is no obvious evidence of metastatic disease. I would generally do that before starting treatment for someone with your presentation but the situation with you at the Pole caused a necessary deviation from that plan. I think delaying treatment for an additional 3-4 months would significantly alter your chances.

Certainly IF those tests find metastatic disease we have a much more difficult situation. In that case I never argue with patients who decide not to pursue treatment. I know of no law that says one must have chemo before death.

The response to the chemo is a dramatic and powerful prognostic factor. Patients with a complete pathologic response have a 10-year survival of around 90%, patients with a small amount of residual disease have a 10-year survival of about 50%, patients with no response have a 10-year survival of only about 20%. Those numbers are regardless of the original size of the tumor. It is too early to know your response but it certainly doesn't look like you are in the last group.

This is your breast cancer and we will do it your way. I honestly believe my role is to provide the best information for you to base your decisions. Ultimately the decisions are yours alone. I only ask that you not make long-term decisions until I can give you that information—unfortunately I don't think I can do that better until we can get you out and take a full look at where we are, what really is the status of your disease, what are our options, and what is best for you. I'll keep trying.

Kathy

From: Jerri Nielsen
To: Scott Cahill
Date: 2 Aug. 1999 01:44:35 +1200
Subject: Re: Live to sail

Dear Scott,

I feel a lot better today as my doctor finally gave me definite percentages of chance to survive. That's what I needed. Also, I am happy as I have decided that I really want to live so that I can circumnavigate the globe in a sailboat. I can't wait to live on your boat for a summer to see if I can stand it, then I may get my own to live on.

As soon as the satellite comes up I am going to talk to the NSF PR person about going public with the media. I am tired of being hunted, so I must come out of the closet. Mom and Dad have been through hell with these people. I wasn't strong enough earlier in the week as I was trying to deal with the realities of the cancer. It is all happening to me so quickly and with no way out.

I love you.
Duff

The media barrage had trickled off for a while after the airdrop when the world's attention fixed on the tragic plane crash that killed JFK Jr. We all hoped the press would forget my story, but it was not to be. The NSF had received boxes of requests from reporters who wanted to interview me. Photographers and TV crews were staking out my parents' house again. And a newspaper in Ohio had tracked down my ex-husband, who was now openly disparaging me and telling anyone who would listen that I was inventing my disease to get attention.

I realized that my silent strategy was not working. The story would not die of neglect, as I had hoped. I now felt I needed to set the record straight about who I was and what had happened to me. I decided to write to Julia Moore, who handled public relations for the NSF, to tell her that I had changed my mind about the press blackout.

From: Jerri Nielsen
To: Julia Moore
Date: 2 Aug. 1999 6:41 AM
Subject: Media

Dear Julia,

I am now in the mood to talk to the media. I don't really want to, but they keep attacking my parents. The Columbus newspaper even went to see my divorce lawyer. I don't want them to just get my story from my angry ex-husband, as they threaten. Otherwise I would do nothing. I thought that this would go away, but it hasn't. I am also afraid that it will affect my ability to get treatment for my cancer. I don't want to feel like a hunted animal while I am trying to fight this thing and deal with the illness and losses while undergoing surgery and serious chemotherapy.

Can you set up the interview with one newsmagazine and one TV network as we discussed?

Please advise. I am now comfortable with my diagnosis and feel that I can do a positive interview. I have my second chemotherapy tonight. I think that the ugly thing has already gotten smaller! Maybe I am just hoping.

Fondly, Jerri Lin

From: Jerri Nielsen
To: Kathy D. Miller
Date: Sunday, August 1, 1999 8:17 AM
Subject: boat

Dear Kathy,

It really helped to have the statistics. It made me much more at ease with the lump. Thank you for taking the time to compile them. I am one who really needs to know.

I have decided, after the statistics, that I am going to live so that I can circumnavigate the globe in a sailboat, as soon as I have recovered from therapy. It will really be a gas. I think that I will just live on the boat and go. I want to call my friends and have them visit me at different ports. First, I am going to South America, then who knows?

My friend from summer, Dorianne, has been to Japan twice, the Philippines once, New Mexico three times, and Oregon twice since she left the Ice in January! I am hoping to get done with my treatment in time to visit her in Japan before she leaves in December and then meet her in Belize for a big New Year's party she is throwing there in January. Then, I want to go see another girlfriend who is now living in Mongolia in the Peace Corps. Maybe I will go with Lisa. I was so very sad that I wasn't going to see the world like the rest of the Polies when I get off. Instead I am just going to go when I can, what the Hell?

So that is what I decided I want to live for.

I really think the "lump thing" is even smaller.

Fondly, Jerri

From: Jerri Nielsen
To: Mom and Dad
Date: 2 Aug. 1999 01:47:35 +1200
Subject: Live to Sail

Dear Mom,

I am happier today as I have decided to live so that I can circumnavigate the globe in a sailboat. That is what I will do if I live, what do you think? I find it an exciting idea that, what the Hell, I might as well.

Talking to Julia Moore about going public today so that we won't have to keep worrying about it.

Love,
Duff

* * *

From: Mom and Dad
To: Jerri Nielsen
Date: Aug. 2, 99
Subject: Good morning Dear,

I have to get Dee and the kids up to go to SeaWorld today. Dad and I will hide out in the beautiful woods. It's to be in the 70s and sunny. Maybe I will get my hair cut. That might make me feel better. We are all relieved that you are getting ready to go public.

I like to think of you sailing around the world. That can be another great adventure for you. Duffy, my dear kid, I want nothing more than for you to have a wonderful life. If there is a chance, whether it be 10% or 90%, take any chance on life. Now I go to get Dee up. I will write later. Although Dad accuses me of making my whole life around this emailing and reading. He doesn't understand that I very much need to write to you because I feel as if you are here and we are talking. When I am on this thing you are not so far away.

Love,
MOMMA

From: Jerri Nielsen
To: Kathy D. Miller
Date: 5 Aug. 1999 21:41:39 +1200
Subject: checking in

Dear Kathy,

My tumor was originally 5 cm across and 4 cm down. Now it is 3 (down) X 3.5 (across) X 1.5 (deep). It is really hard to measure, though. The borders are very indistinct. Originally, I couldn't measure depth due to inability to find the bottom of it.

Fondly,
Jerri

From: Kathy D. Miller
To: Jerri Nielsen
Date: 05 Aug. 1999 17:53:44 -0500
Subject: RE: checking in

Jerri—

That is an excellent response. I can now "fess-up" my one remaining omission. I always tell patients that it takes at least two cycles of therapy to really know how well a regimen is working. That is true but when it's working really well I can tell much sooner. This difference with only two weeks of therapy is outstanding! The change in measurements will slow down over the next several weeks—this is normal and does not mean the chemo isn't working as well. See you Friday.
Kathy

From: Jerri Nielsen
To: Family and friends
Date: 10 Aug. 1999 08:36:04 +1200
Subject: Toastino's

Dears,

Saturday night we had such a treat. Donna, Power Plant Thom, Tim, Pakman, and Liza set up Toastino's Italian Restaurant, a restaurant to take us out of the daily *Groundhog Day* existence that we face here in the dark polar winter. There was a lot of covert activity in the station, for a week, while plans were being made. We all got invitations in our (never used) mailboxes. Reservations had to be made in advance. No one was allowed in the galley after breakfast. It was exciting. You had to enter the galley from the upstairs bar. There, our server, Pakman, offered us wine while we waited for our table. When I showed up in the bar, Big and Lisa were already there. Andy and Loree came a bit later. You were only permitted to have up to four people at a table, but I couldn't bump any of my close friends, so we got a special consideration for five.

When our table was ready, Pak took us down the stairs. What a surprise! The galley was completely transformed. It did look like a very nice restaurant. They had dimmed the lights and hung flags and large sheets of red material to hide the kitchen and to break up the galley into intimate areas. There was nice music, and plastic plants from who knows where. Tim was our server in the actual restaurant. He really acted the part. (Tim is an actor, as well as a contractor and fisherman.)

Everyone had such a wonderful time. It was so special to us all. Things like this are what makes life at Pole. You find so quickly what makes life sweet. It is all the small things in life. Good friends and family are the most important. Then, a community working toward a common goal. In our case the goal is survival in the most hostile, remote place on earth. Intellectual stimulation, for me, is next. For others, it is food. Food for the soul first, then food for the tummy. It reminds me of Aunt Eva's favorite poem, with the line "buy hyacinths to feed thy soul."

I can't imagine the Pole, the isolation, the darkness, the cancer, without my two best friends, Lisa and Big. They are such special and magical people. But without them, there would have probably been someone else to fill the void of life. Lives that are joined here are forever joined.

We are all starting to think of travel or to think of home. Our time here is soon to end. The horizon glows a faint blue, with promise of the coming sun. While those I am close to think of great adventure, I think of prognosis. Am I at the very end of my life, or at a new beginning? I can only guess. It weighs heavy on me now.

From the wonderful Ice,
Jerri Lin

CHAPTER 13:

The Longest Month

Counting flowers on the wall,
That don't bother me at all,
Playing solitaire till dawn,
With a deck of fifty-one,
Smoking cigarettes and watching Captain Kangaroo,
Now don't tell me,
I've nothing to do.

—*"Flowers on the Wall"*
by the Statler Brothers,
a favorite among Polies

Early in August one of the meteorologists got on the All-Call and gleefully announced that there was a glow on the horizon: First light! I was feeling stronger than usual that day, so I decided to take a walk outside the Dome to see for myself. I added twenty pounds of clothing and chemical hand warmers to my indoor ensemble and slipped through the small wooden door that now served as the front entrance to the Dome. A steep corridor carved in the drifted snow led to the outer buildings. I looked up through the ice canyon and saw, directly overhead, the Milky Way looking like an explosion of diamonds, incredibly bright and close. A green aurora rolled and shimmered in the black sky beyond. I wanted to get up to the skiway and lie on my back to watch the stars and listen to the singing ice, but after two weeks of storms a tremendous snowdrift was blocking the way to the flight line. I started pulling myself up the drift in the dark until I reached a ten-foot ice cliff. My mittened hands, stuffed with the hand warmers, had no grip in them, and I toppled back down from the edge. Figuring that I really didn't need a fractured leg, I gave up.

As I trudged back home, I thought about things that I hadn't considered since childhood. Why, if I am at the very bottom of the earth, do I not fall off? (Some might argue that I did.) Why do I seem to be at the top of the earth? Where does the universe end? These were all "deep thoughts," elemental questions beyond understanding that had been buried since I learned to "reason." The Pole did this to people. We lived in a realm outside of reason.

Back home, I ran into Big who said that he had "seen the light." He said it took two people to get over the cliff and offered to help me. We went back outside and got to the top, where I saw the first whisper of sunlight. It was a happy moment, but at the same time, sad. I was about to lose the polar night, my comfort and my cloak. Strangely it seemed like the only certainty left in my precarious world.

As the days passed, I began to rely on the escape fantasies my brother Scott created for me. In my mind, I could already be sailing around the globe, out on the fresh blue ocean. Just like when we were children sharing a bedroom in Ohio, Scott spun detailed stories of how we would travel together and where we would go:

From: Scott Cahill
To: Jerri Nielsen
Date: 04 Aug. 1999 08:53:04 -0400

Subject: Re: hello
Dear Duffy:

You are absolutely welcome to the boat when you get back. I will have her done & I think that it would be an excellent place to recoup. If you work at it, you can learn to sail in a couple of months. It will take longer before you can feel it. People have left for circumnavigations without ever having sailed before, but I think it is crazy. There are all kinds of books on the subject and I will teach you all that I know.

I think that you should live on & sail mine for a while before you buy a boat. Your ideas of what you want will change as you sail for a while. I hope that after you are settled we could go on a moderate cruise—maybe Bermuda—it is a good blue—water shakeout cruise. It is a wide open passage—best sailed in the fall outside of Atlantic hurricane season. You could continue your treatments on the way over & we could fly back. We—or you—could then sail the boat back at a future date when we are ready. I have set her up to be sailed by a crew of two. In moderate weather, you could handle her alone. In heavy weather, it would be nice to have two on board.

I love you very much.
Scotty

After I began chemotherapy I tried to settle back into a normal routine. I saw patients and even tried to scrub down my little hospital. I could easily have justified devoting all my time to a cancer patient if she were someone else, but since I was the patient, whenever I attended to my own illness I felt guilty for neglecting my other work.

And then there was Pic. He first came to me with pain in his head and jaw which had begun during his travels in Africa, after his mishap with a Ugandan dentist. We both worked on his chronic sinus infections and his temporomandibular joint pain: I did massage and myofacial-release therapy and tried multiple medications, while he practiced yoga and relaxation techniques. Meanwhile his neck was hurting him. Next, he started having stomach and back pain. It was amusing to watch him try to cover up his legendary dietary indiscretions. Did he really think he could hide his jalapeño pepper pizza from me?

Soon after the airdrop, he developed severe pain in his hip. Although he could not remember an injury, he was clearly miserable and found it more difficult to work.

Pic being Pic, he would not let his duty slide to care for his health. He was compelled to make sure that this last piece of clean Earth was clear of hazardous material, and he would drag himself across the ice to do it. The day I took him off work for his disability, I found him riding the tractor outside the Dome in terrible temperatures.

Mike offered to do his job until he recovered, but we couldn't get him to stop. We tried hiding the keys of the front-loader. We offered to move him to the hospital, but he refused. Mike wanted to build a walker, but our ex-Marine Eagle-Scout tyrant of trash wouldn't go for it. We finally had to order him to rest when he could barely stand. He claimed that he read seventy-two books during that time.

Pic and his problems were always on my mind, and I felt terrible that I couldn't figure out how to fix him. He later developed restless leg syndrome and severe insomnia. We set up a regular schedule of appointments, at least once a week. The x-ray machine was too unpredictable to be much use in diagnosing Pic. The lab analyzer showed blood abnormalities but we could not be sure what they meant, since it, too, was unreliable.

To escape the hardships of this life, Pic and I created an elaborate world of our own. Scotty and I had gone to sea, and now Pic came along too. Pic and I decided we would all get boats and float in an armada. We could have a Polie boat neighborhood outside New Orleans, a city he liked, and help each other until we could find work in Africa. Then we could sail our boats to Mombasa. I imagined Pic and me, singing all the words to all the John Prine songs we knew— and we knew them all—as we anchored our boats side by side in a perfumed harbor on the other side of winter.

In the last days of July, shortly after I began chemotherapy, I wrote to Karl Erb, director of the U.S. Antarctic Program, thanking him for his efforts on my behalf and informing him that my treatment had begun. He quickly responded with a friendly email that contained some surprising news: he had requested the Air National Guard to study the possibility of sending a special flight to take me out of the Pole "in September or October in case the tumor doesn't respond adequately to the treatment." This was the first I had heard that an early "extraction" was being considered. I wasn't sure how to react. I was grateful for the government's concern, but I didn't want another air crew to risk their lives for me, especially if I didn't need to be rescued. I emailed Karl with my thoughts.

> From: Jerri Nielsen
> To: Karl Erb
> Date: Wed., 28 Jul. 1999 18:25:59 +1200
> Subject: no subject
>
> Dear Karl,
>
> I guess that an early extraction will depend on my response to chemo and what Kathy Miller thinks as far as when I should leave here. I would rather stay out my tour, but not at the price of risking my life. I still don't know how to think about all this (cancer, that is), the diagnosis is so new. I am such an optimist that I didn't permit myself to think about it until it was certain. Now I must put my life in perspective with this. I'll ask Kathy what she thinks.

Kathy says that I will have surgery immediately, or maybe the big gun chemo, as soon as I get home, then radiation and more chemo. It all depends on my response.

I'll keep you informed. Thank you for thinking about me,
Jerri

From: Jerri Nielsen
To: Kathy D. Miller
Date: Wednesday, July 28, 1999 12:28 A.M.
Subject: regarding getting me out

Dear Kathy,

The National Science Foundation is making plans to get me out of here early if need be. I didn't know what to tell them. Does it depend on my response to treatment?

Jerri

To: Jerri Nielsen
From: Kathy D. Miller
Date: Wed., 28 Jul. 1999 18:17:05 -0500
Subject: RE: regarding getting me out

Jerri,

Karl Erb and Gerry Katz have asked me directly about this but I'm not sure my answer helped them very much. What I could tell them:

1. If your tumor shrinks with the Taxol we can continue that until it is safe to get you out with the

rest of the winterover crew. Even if you were here we would plan about 3 months of chemo before surgery so that wouldn't be a major departure from standard care.

2. If your tumor doesn't respond to the Taxol we can certainly try the other regimen (that's why I sent it), but the other regimen we would switch to if you were here could not be safely given at the Pole. If your tumor doesn't respond I want you out of there as soon as possible.

We will have some idea about the response in 4 weeks—I think they want to know sooner than that but it's the best I can do.

Kathy

I began to look forward to the weekly chemo sessions (three weeks in a row, and one week's rest) and the meeting of Club Med. Even though the IVs were painful and the drugs wiped me out for a few days after, I felt like it was helping me kill the beast.

The tumor had responded very quickly to Taxol, and it was wonderful watching it shrink in size for the first couple of weeks. But I was still worried that the cancer had metastasized, spread into my lymph nodes, bones, and other organs. I had terrible pain in my breast, under my right arm and beneath my shoulder blade. Kathy had told me that detectable "mets"—metastatic disease, or spread—in breast cancer had a horrible prognosis; only about 1.6 percent of these patients were disease-free after two years. The grim statistic reinforced my belief—if it's spread, you're dead. I worried that my pain signaled metastatic disease, and that I was going through needless treatment. I wrote Kathy about my concerns just before my third scheduled chemo session.

From: Kathy D. Miller
To: Jerri Nielsen
Date: 6 Aug. 1999 17:07:29 -0500
Subject: RE: checking in

Hi Jerri,

Metastasis to lymph nodes does not mean the same thing as metastasis to anywhere else. That is regional disease only. When I talk about mets I mean to lungs, bone, liver, or anywhere outside the breast and axilla. Disease in the axillary lymph nodes does not mean you are going to die. I think the pain you are having is from inflammation of the axillary lymph nodes. This is common with large tumors and does sometimes get worse with shrinkage of the tumor. All the dead tumor stuff has to get out somewhere, somehow.

From what I know of your disease you do not have obvious metastatic disease. I plan more sophisticated tests when we get you out—if we find metastatic disease I would make different recommendations and you would make different decisions. There is nothing you have told me that makes me more worried that I will find metastatic disease in you than in any other of my young patients with large tumors (large in breast cancer is over 5cm). Part of my job is knowing when to worry and breast cancer in young women always worries me.

Giving the chemotherapy first has at least two advantages. First if I can shrink the tumor more women can avoid mastectomy. More important it lets us all know if the treatment is working and how well. Overall prognosis is more determined by the response to chemo than to any of the initial factors (size, lymph nodes, etc.). By response I mean how much residual tumor is left at the time of surgery after "good" chemotherapy. So—to answer one of your questions directly—yes, if the tumor is shrinking the chemo is doing the same thing to any other areas of disease. You are definitely responding to this treatment—it's just too early to know how well and we really won't know that until surgery.

What I would suggest: Continue this treatment as long as your tumor is responding and as long as you are stuck at the Pole. When we get you out the first thing we do is tests to make sure you don't have metastatic disease (I don't think so but you'll have to prove it). Once those tests are normal I have more chemo planned with drugs I can't safely give you there followed by surgery and radiation.

The fatigue will slowly get worse. It tends to be a bit worse after each treatment but then recovers almost entirely during the week off. The easiest times for you to get work done will be the week off and the first week of each cycle. The third week (next week) will be the toughest. I know they are investigating ways to get you out as soon as possible. If I hear anything I'll let you know. The NSF does periodically ask me about the medical risk of keeping you there.

See you in a few hours,
Kathy

From: Jerri Nielsen
To: Mom and Dad
Date: 7 Aug. 99 12:14:16 +1200
Subject: hi

Dear Mom,

It is 5 a.m. Saturday. I can't sleep. I had my third chemotherapy last night. It made me pretty strange feeling. For the first time, I have hope that just maybe I don't have mets all over the place. I am looking forward to the early "extraction" of me. I just want to get this over with.

Kathy said that the fatigue will be worse this week. Now I am wired. The fatigue will probably be in a couple of days.

I wish that I could get this media thing out of the way. They haven't told me anything. Everything is secondhand about the media and about the extraction. There is a funny idea about winterover Polies that everyone has in the Polar Program. They believe that we are better off with as little information as possible, that we are "edgy" or something. This is true of all information, not just pertaining to me. I have not seen any evidence that Polies can't deal with info, but this is the "historical concept" of us.

I am tired of being here, only because of the cancer. It (my little adventure) has lost its glow and fun. I have started to think of going home. The rest of the Polies are looking at maps every day and planning their trips around the world. The stupid cancer has taken over my life and mind.

Love, Duff

Just as Kathy had predicted, the fatigue hit me like an anvil after the third chemo session. Everywhere I went, I felt like I was walking through neck-deep Jell-O. I still saw the sick folks, but I was behind on my paperwork and other projects.

It was getting hard to tell the difference between fatigue caused by the chemo and what was normal for the Pole at this time of year. It was the season of maximum toast, and everyone was feeling it. Along with the effects of sensory deprivation, we were experiencing physiologic altitudes of more than eleven thousand feet for days at a time. Studies had shown that we were expected to lose some of our capacity for memory by the time we got off the Ice. We were all noticing it already. Big, who normally used a large and varied vocabulary in his conversation, was having trouble putting sentences together. He said he could visualize the words he wanted and knew what they meant, but he just couldn't bring them up. Donna told me that she now needed to write everything down in order to remember. The sensory deprivation and chronic hypoxia were also affecting our vision, and our tempers.

By now I was too tired to stay up for both movies of our Saturday night action double feature, but I heard that one night, between viewings of *Mission: Impossible* and *Clear and Present Danger*, an inane scuffle erupted over a seat on the couch. The combatants will forever go unnamed (all fighting is illegal in Antarctica) but before it was over, a woman had kicked a man in the chest, the man had thrown the woman back down on the couch, popcorn was tossed in someone else's face, and, as one witness remembered, "Language was exchanged that called into question the ancestry, sexual preference, and physical prowess of all involved." The fight broke up as quickly as it began, and afterward everybody was shocked and horrified—particularly the perpetrators, who were among the nicest people on station. We chalked it up to a bad case of toasting.

As our winterover crew dealt with each crisis in turn—the power failures, the mysterious hacker invasion that was still not solved, the airdrop, my cancer—it was abundantly clear that each of us played an important role that was necessary for the survival of the group. Like half of Noah's Ark, there was only one of each. No spares. Not only were our job skills all equally needed and diverse, strengths of personality and character were also different and vital to the survival of the group. I came to see how in order to build a society, you need people of diverse temperament, social and intellectual skills. But as the darkness and sameness of endless winter continued with fewer and fewer resources, I watched the group undergo previously unimagined challenges. Each person's strengths became more obvious, as did their weaknesses. Weaknesses became strengths and vice versa. A seemingly weak person may have a wonderful gift of patience and empathy, insight and organization; while a seemingly strong person might be disguising insecurities and fears with bluster. The movers and shakers might easily succumb to boredom. Like energetic animals in a cage, those individuals could drive the others crazy. Fortunately, in every emergency the petty squabbles tended to disappear, and the tribe pulled together to survive.

Meanwhile NSF had still said nothing about when or how I should speak to the media. I was beginning to worry that I would soon be too sick to handle the interviews. Even more horrifying, I was losing my hair. Every time I brushed it, long yellow strands would clog the bristles. Soon big clumps came out in my hand every time I touched my head. This was unbelievably depressing. It had taken me six years to grow out long, thick blond hair. It was my best physical feature, and an important part of my self-esteem was attached to it. Losing my hair was like losing a vital piece of my identity. I looked in the mirror and saw a stranger, a sick, ugly thing that bore no relation to who I was. I did not want the world to think of me as a partial person. Inside I was still very strong and professional, and if I had to step in front of the cameras, that was how I wanted to appear. I was even more concerned about my short-term memory loss and disintegrating verbal skills. I would need all my faculties to meet the press. But time was running out.

I shared my fears with Kathy, who agreed that I should get the media ordeal over with as soon as possible.

From: Kathy D. Miller
To: Jerri Nielsen
Date: 16 Aug. 1999 17:07:29 -0500
Subject: Hair

Sorry about the hair. It does sound like all your hair will come out before you are off the Ice. The pattern you are describing is much more like what happens with the higher doses of Taxol given over 3 or 24 hours than the weekly regimen. I can't tell how much of that is from the longer infusion

time or if the altitude might also have played a role. I
checked with the company that makes Taxol after your first
treatment and asked them to go back to some of their early
data. They didn't see dramatic hair loss at the doses you got,
but there definitely was some. Once the hair loss starts there
really is no way to reverse the process.

Kathy

Soon after we started pressuring NSF to speed up its media strategy, I received word that the organization's officials had changed their
minds. Even though my parents were still barraged with interview
requests, the NSF people were convinced that media interest had
tapered off. Although there had still been no decision on an early rescue flight for me, I was told that talking to the press now would only
set off another feeding frenzy, which might complicate and even jeop-
ardize their efforts to extract me from the Pole.

Even more confusing to me, I then found out that NSF had been
fielding requests from TV networks to allow a news crew on board the
plane whenever I was extracted from the Pole. They even wanted to
follow me to the hospital in Indianapolis to record my reaction to my
test results and document my treatment! I explained to NSF that I
would be much too sick to deal with the media by then, and that
being followed by a TV crew would be a terrible invasion of privacy.
Luckily, we were able to jettison that plan.

Perhaps to soothe my feelings, the NSF and ASA decided to allow
both of my brothers to take part in the extraction plan. The "Bro
Squad," as Scott and Eric came to be known, would meet me as soon as
I got to Christchurch and take me home.

From: Jerri Nielsen
To: All

Date: 20 Aug. 1999 22:54:34 +1200
Subject: A Go on Bro Squad

Dear Family,

NSF has given a go on the Bro Squad! (That is what it is now referred to at the Pole.) I am so delighted I can hardly stand it! Happy happy happy day!

Love,
Duffy

I decided that since I wasn't going to be interviewed on television, and I was going to lose my hair anyway, I might as well get it over with. In true polar fashion, we turned my ultimate haircut into an event. Loree and Lisa and I threw a "make Jerri totally bald party." We played Bob Dylan music and got out the electric razor. It took only minutes to destroy six years of growth. As I watched my old life fall away and drop to the icy floor, I grieved quietly, trying not to show it on my face. Mourn it, bury it, move on.

Word of my new look traveled fast. The minute I left the hospital, Heidi and Wendy came up to me and took off my hat to have a look, then insisted that I follow them into the galley. I told them that Big John was waiting in the Heavy Shop to take me for a snowmobile ride. Heidi dragged me in. Inside, the women giggled with delight as they pulled hats out of their blouses. Wendy had knit me a brown light-weight "indoor hat" that would soon have a matching afghan with squares made by a bunch of Polies. Heidi had knit me a warm blue-and-pink wool, bopping-around-the-Dome hat. On my way home with the hats, I was intercepted by Liza, who added a fleece jester hat to my collection.

I was so moved by the generosity of this little community of women and their surprise hat shower. The women at Pole were not particularly close. We ranged in age from twenty-two to forty-seven—I was the oldest—and we were different in so many ways. But when one of us had a problem or need, it was amazing how we banded together. I cherished their compassion and support, but I needed to grieve alone. After my snowmobile ride, I went back to my room, curled up in Dorianne's wonderful comforter, and opened my book of Yeats. I turned to "For Anne Gregory," and read the lines over and over:

> 'Never shall a young man,
> Thrown into despair
> By those great honey-coloured
> Ramparts at your ear,
> Love you for yourself alone
> And not your yellow hair.'

> 'But I can get a hair-dye
> And set such colour there,
> Brown, or black, or carrot,
> That young men in despair
> May love me for myself alone
> And not my yellow hair.'

> 'I heard an old religious man
> But yesternight declare
> That he had found a text to prove
> That only God, my dear,
> Could love you for yourself alone
> And not your yellow hair.'

From: John W. Penney
To: Jerri Nielsen
Date: 20 Aug. 1999 18:20:46 +1200
Subject: copy of letter

Hello Scott & Eric:

Just wanted to drop you guys a line and let you know the latest.

I am sure by now you know that Doc shaved her head yesterday. She said that when she saw Manager Mike picking long blond hair off his black pants in the galley, it was time for some maintenance.

The girls threw her a "Hat Party" yesterday. She got some very nice handmade knit hats, and a hat with a big set of ears on it that she can wrap around her neck. She likes the hats, but she really misses her beautiful long blond hair. I think this has been the most traumatic event for her. More so than finding out she has cancer.

She is very concerned with "body image." Us boys don't really seem to give a damn about things like that, but she sure does. She says that she is now ugly enough to "scare small children on the subway."

I told her to stay off the subway.

I took her for a snowmobile ride yesterday. We went a mile or so out onto her beloved polar plateau. She REALLY enjoys getting away from the station. We couldn't go very fast, because of the sastrugi, but we went steadily. She gets very concerned about crashing and getting injured. I don't know where she got that idea. I have only crashed with her once. After our ride yesterday, I asked her if I had frightened her at all. She said the only time she was concerned was when it took me a minute or so to tug our recalcitrant machine back to life for the trip home. I told her she shouldn't have been worried, that snow machine likes me and would never strand me away from the station like that. We stood on the plateau for about seven minutes or so. We looked at the promise of the coming sunrise; a blue hint on the horizon, the Southern Cross, the wide expanse of the Milky Way, a small but pretty aurora, Mars, twinkling red just above the horizon, and the bright white quarter moon. All too soon we had to return to the Heavy Shop to warm up. Even though it was only minus 76 F., the wind was blowing at fifteen knots, and that can cool you off in a hurry.

Yesterday was the first time that I have seen her really truly happy since this whole mess started. She always maintains a positive front when she is out in public. Shucking and jiving, smiling and glad-handing. Yesterday she was giggling and laughing, truly happy.

The event that precipitated this show of giddiness was the thought of her BROTHERS coming down to get her. She has been inordinately concerned with the coming attack of the media when she gets off the Ice. It was truly frightening to her to contemplate traveling halfway around the world fending off the attacks of the rabid media dogs.

She dug through her pictures and showed me the shots of her brothers. The ones she showed me (I have seen them many times before, but asked to see them again) were of you guys at the Cleveland Clinic, when your Pop was there, and a great shot of you three standing on the beach. She said, "Would you mess with a woman escorted by these guys?" I told her of course not, and that I imagined a trail of camera-men with camera enemas, and reporters with microphone enemas, wherever you guys choose to travel.

I just wanted you guys to know that even though you are a world away from your beautiful sister, you gave her the best mental boost imaginable. As I tucked her in last night I told her what to think about as she was going to sleep. Usually I tell her to think about some of the things that we see in the auroras. The auroras are like the clouds were when we were kids. You look at them and see animals and people's faces. I told her to think about a bunny rabbit with long ears, a chameleon with a long tongue, and a dinosaur, like the one Alley Oop rides in the comics. I make her promise to think about those things so she will not lie there and worry about the NSF, the media, mets, etc. Last night I told her to think about her brothers as she was going to sleep. She looked up at me and said, "We're going to have a gas."

Regards,
Big John

Big John was now in frequent contact with my family. When they wanted to know how I "really" was doing, they wrote to Big. Big John always sent me copies of what he wrote about me. I could rarely do the same. My feelings for Big were better left unsaid. We had a painful understanding. Our relationship was one of the most profound that either of us would experience, although I knew it could never be a conventional love relationship. But I would gladly take the compromise of great friendship and understanding. As I wrote to Scotty:

The other person who loves the winter as much as I do is Big John. You would really like Big. He has ruined my relationships with guys forever. I will always be looking for someone like him. I will miss him, but I am so used to losing people I care about. He has been such a wonderful friend. I can't imagine being here facing my illness without someone who cares about me, who deeply cares. It has made so much difference. I can't do much for myself at times. Most people tire of caring for the sick, but he misses great parties to sit up and watch me breathe after my chemo. I could go on and on. He says that it makes him sad that he is so poor and has

nothing to give to me, but he gives and gives all the time. I
didn't come here to find a guy. That is why it seemed okay to
have a married best friend—we could just like and respect
each other and provide company. Now, I must say that it
hurts, a bit.

Soon after my head-shaving party, Big took a picture of my new
look. No wigs, no scarves. I decided that "what you see is what you
get" was the best policy. I posed standing in a corner of Big's office in
the Heavy Shop, bald as a cue ball and wearing the most radiant smile
I could muster. It was a "showtime" moment worthy of an Academy
Award. And it worked.

From: Jerri Nielsen
To: Family and friends
Date: August 21, 1999 2:06 P.M.
Subject: The new me

Hot off the press, a picture of the new me.

Love, Duff

From: Scott Cahill
To: Jerri Nielsen
Date: 21 Aug. 1999 11:46:55 -0400
Subject: Re: The new me

OH MY GOD!

Mom had told me that you were beautiful with your head
shaven. I honestly thought that she was overreacting. YOU
ARE AWESOME!! You REALLY look good! I am so proud
of you to have the balls to do it. You never stop surprising
me—pleasantly—I am so proud of you. Mom is right. I pre-

fer it. I hope that you will maintain it at least for a while. A lot of sailors shave their heads on the first day out on a long crossing. I think I have ugly bumps & points on mine! Perhaps we will see when we first leave sight of land on our first long crossing!

I want very much to come to Christchurch and meet you & take you home. I have checked on tickets & they are not too bad. Eric really wants to go, too. He says that he will keep me from being like Sean Penn & beating up on reporters.

Real beauty cannot be hidden—it lives within the beautiful and will surface in the hearts of those close. It is like the warmth of the sun. It cannot be camouflaged, it is felt by the heart. I love you.

Scotty

From: Eric Cahill
To: Jerri Nielsen
Date: August 21, 1999
Subject: The new me

Dear Jerri,

You look like an intelligent alien.

Love,
Mr. Baby

From: John W. Penney
To: NIELSEJE@spole.gov

Date: 23 Aug. 1999 18:13:21 +1200
Subject: copy of letter

Hey Doc:

Thought I would let you read the latest to your Mom, before I sent it.

Big

> Hello Mrs. Cahill:
>
> It was nice of you to write. Please feel free to write me anytime. I am not leaving town until November.
>
> Doc is doing surprisingly well, considering the circumstances. She is still taking care of her patients, as well as her other many duties as medical officer and second in command. She is still shucking and jiving when she is in the public eye. If you didn't know of her illness, you would never guess it from her actions.
>
> She thinks she is going to make it. She has some things to live for, and some things she wants to do before she checks out of the big game. She says she doesn't think she has mets. I told her that was good, because she has been right about everything so far.
>
> After I get off the Ice, I am going to spend a month in N.Z. touring with my family. When I do get back to the world, sometime in early December, the first thing that I will do is come to visit the Cahills in Ohio.
>
> I don't want to get a bunch of grief from the larger members of the family when I show up, so I will explain "Big." After I had been on station awhile in the summer, some of the crew began calling me "Big John." The Doc began call-

ing me "Big" late in the summer, and the name has stuck for the duration. This nickname has nothing to do with physical size. I am quite diminutive by Cahill standards. I am 5'10" 250 lbs. Big is a measurement of what is inside.

That is probably a lot more than you wanted to know, but you asked for it.

Time to go pick up the Doc for lunch.

Best Regards,
Big John

From: Jerri Nielsen
To: Family and friends
Date: 31 Aug. 1999 00:36:03 +1200
Subject: August, the Longest Month at the Bottom
    of the Earth

Dear Folks,

This is my latest attempt at explaining what life is like here:

They say that August is the longest month at Pole. It is the end of the dark winter with promise of light but light is yet so far away. It reminds me of February in Ohio. You have had enough winter, but you still must face March, before the crocus and daffodils come. For me, it has gone by all too quickly. Time here is so contorted, and now at the end, it is greatly contracted. The coming of light on the horizon makes me sad, while for so many it is a cause of celebration.

Living here is like being in a sensory deprivation tank for nine months. It is like being suspended on strings in dark water. Nothing changes. You become bored in a strange way, a way that I have not previously experienced. All that changes, that causes human sensation, comes from the mind. Then, the brain dulls and you have the stimulation of trying to contain and expand your own mind. This is a test of how successfully one can control one's own perceptions.

For me, this has not been at all difficult. I have always chosen my own reality, to greater or lesser degrees, depending on the strength of onslaught from external sources. One of my great interests in life, since childhood, has been the human's ability to affect his own perceptions. I began very young to try and control my own. Here, I have had the greatest laboratory.

The difficulty of August is the fatigue. Fatigue of internal creation. The hypoxia, the decrease in barometric pressure with resultant increase in physiological altitude, lack of anything new, slowly diminishing supplies—it all makes the mind less acute. We have so many physiological changes that are not understood. As the winter lingers, the mind becomes duller. With this dullness, for some, comes decreased internal coping strategy. For others, it permits a deepening of understanding, charity, and a new clarity of thought. It is the difference between a POW who goes permanently insane, and a monk who finally finds the God that he has been searching for. They are in the same environment of lack, pain, discomfort, humiliation, deprivation of the senses. One chooses to be there, one does not. And yet, there are monks who go mad and POWs who find the true meaning of life.

Many of us at Pole are searchers, many are travelers, and many have come, as I did, to destroy demons and to find answers. We also came to see how much we could count on ourselves and our abilities, alone. More often, we have found and conquered demons, thoughts, weaknesses, questioning of the self, that we did not before know existed. And in doing so, we have learned

that those things that plagued us in the world were not important, or had gone to rest years ago. For some reason, we had
chosen to keep them alive. Here, you can let go of these
thoughts, and embrace the newly discovered strengths that
only this place can illuminate. This is something that I have
witnessed in myself and in a number of my friends. I came here
with a list of things that I wished to accomplish. I did none of
them. Instead, those things lost meaning. New goals and ideas
took their place, goals that I would not have imagined in my
former life. I was too busy to think and to see. There was way
too much background noise in my existence.

For me, the last months have seemed surreal. It has been
challenging to experience all of this while knowing that I
have a potentially fatal disease. I wonder how differently I
will feel and perceive my experience as I go through chemi-
cally induced menopause and suffer the mental and physical
effects of chemotherapy. The changes in my perspective, of
the life that I have had and of the life that I aspire to, must
be affected deeply by facing death, here, in this sensory
deprivation tank. I will therefore never know what changes
were from living at Pole and what changes came from my
close look at mortality.

I am only so grateful that I had the chance to wonder.

From the Ice,
Duffy

CHAPTER 14:

Endurance

Out of whose womb came the ice?
And the hoary frost of Heaven,
who hath gendered it?
The waters are hid as with a stone,
and the face of the deep is frozen.

Job 38:29
—from a page Ernest Shackleton
tore from his Bible to keep with him
on the Ice

Ten months after landing in Antarctica, I got my first case of frost-bite. Earned it, I should say, because frostbite is a rite of passage at the South Pole. Without being able to talk about frozen body parts and peeling dead skin, a Polie has no bragging rights at Bailie's Pub. I got mine during another tradition: the winterover photograph at the Pole.

By early September a predawn twilight bathed the plateau. The sky was tinged blue and burnt orange; its reflection spread a false sense of warmth over the wind-carved sastrugi. In fact, on the day the whole station marched out to the Geographical Pole for our group picture it was minus 95 F. with a wind-chill that made it feel like 150 below. I

317

was disgusted by how hard it was for me to climb the hill outside the Dome. The energy that I had depended upon all my life was now gone, and I wondered if I would ever get it back. I missed the young woman who could scale these drifts without pausing for breath.

As I got closer to the Pole, I started getting sick to my stomach. With that well-known feeling came some peculiar thoughts: Would I vomit on ice thousands of years old, polluting the cleanest snow in the world? Would it be classified a toxic spill? Would I have to clean it up, since that was usually my job?

I made it to the photo op without having to find out. We set four cameras on auto and arranged ourselves around the bronze Geographic Pole Marker, with the glowing horizon as our backdrop. Large emergency flashlights provided extra lighting. At the count of ten, we tore away our goggles and gaiters to reveal smiling faces around our nation's flag, just like the old-time explorers. Walls of the public areas at Pole are lined with photos and paintings of those who came before us: Scott and Amundsen; foreign expeditions that made it to 90 degrees south by wind, by dog, by ski, or on foot; and photos like these: "Winterover party 1975," "South Pole Night Shift." Soon we would add "The Fun 41," the largest party to winter in the most remote place on earth. The last party of the century.

On the way back, I felt it coming on but could not prevent it. The frostbite began as a terrible sting and then turned into intense pain. When I became aware that my face was freezing, I tried to protect myself by pulling another gaiter over the area and securing it under my goggles. The pain continued, then faded.

By now I was feeling weak and was partially blinded by the gaiter. I almost had to be carried down the ice cliff in front of the Dome. I remember staring down the hole, wondering if I could make it down the wall, and being so glad to recognize Floyd's silhouette, and then his mittened hand reaching out for me.

Once I was back in my relatively warm nest, I stripped off the wads of extra clothing and found the left side of my face was hard as a rock and cold to the touch. For a Dome Slug, there was some honor to it. I had survived nearly a year at the coldest place on earth only to lose my "virginity" in the final weeks. As it turned out, five of us had gotten a significant 'bite for the sake of tradition. Two women developed bad external ear injuries and looked like the losers on a wrestling team. After thawing, my face was red for a while and rather blistered (the hangnail of frostbite cases). It was a good experience for me. Now I understood how people could get frostbite when they "knew better."

By now Club Med was running like an Olympic relay team; we had the Taxol infusion timed down to within three minutes of an hour. Except for the occasional satellite glitch, our video chemo sessions had become almost routine. During the down times, when the drugs were dripping, there was little to do but wait and make small talk across thousands of miles of microwaves. Sometimes we were introduced to new people. Kathy's mentor, Dr. George Sledge, one of the country's foremost breast cancer specialists, stopped by to meet us. He wanted to learn the routine so that he could fill in for Kathy if she had to miss a session. One night when Kathy was asking us about our lives at Pole, we told her about the Friday night poetry slams.

"Hey, that sounds fun," she said. "Let's have an international poetry slam next time!"

The following week everyone brought poems to read—except me, since I couldn't read well during the chemo. Lisa chose a funny one by Shel Silverstein about a melting ice cream cone. Then George Sledge poked his head into the camera frame and said, "Can I contribute? I've got some poetry here . . ." He proceeded to recite "The Cremation of Sam McGee," by Robert Service. I could see Big grinning ear to ear underneath his beard. When George was done he said, "So Big, what do you have tonight?"

"Well knock me down with a feather, Doc," said Big John. "I planned to read 'The Men Who Don't Fit In,' also by that fine poet Robert Service . . ."

After the manly poems were read, Kathy introduced her submission as a "womanly poem": Veronica Shoffstall's "After a While," sent to her by a friend from her student days in Africa. Between the Benadryl buzz and the jumpy audio connection, I couldn't make out all the lines, so she sent me the words the next day:

After a while you learn
the subtle difference between
holding a hand and chaining a soul
and you learn
that love doesn't mean leaning
and company doesn't always mean security.
And you begin to learn
that kisses aren't contracts
and presents aren't promises
and you begin to accept your defeats
with your head up and your eyes ahead
with the grace of a woman, not the grief of a child
and you learn
to build all your roads on today
because tomorrow's ground is
too uncertain for plans
and futures have a way of falling down
in mid-flight.
After awhile you learn
that even sunshine burns
if you get too much
so you plant your own garden
and decorate your own soul
instead of waiting for someone
to bring you flowers.
And you learn that you really can endure,
you really are strong
and you really do have worth
and you learn

and you learn
with every goodbye, you learn . . .

Meanwhile, the routine of the Pole remained unchanging, except for whatever stimulation we could bring to it. There were, for instance, birthdays to celebrate. As a special birthday gift for Wendy, Big and I volunteered to cook a turkey dinner for forty-one. Lisa made the birthday cake, and she was our "house mouse" who did the cleanup.

The preparations took a full day and night, but it was so much fun to do something involving nothing medical—except for the 20cc syringe and number-14-gauge IV catheter that Big used to inject a mixture of butter, garlic, and hot sauce into the birds. (He said it was nice to stick a needle in something other than me for a change.) We used Big's Texas auntie's recipe for deep-fried turkey, which took an hour and a half to cook each of three birds, twice the time it would take at sea level. We improvised the rest: I boiled down canned mandarin orange sections with butter and OJ to make orange glaze for the carrots, while Big created sour cream out of cream cheese, vinegar, and powdered milk. I needed it for Mom's "Green Mashed Potato" recipe, made from pureed spinach, potatoes, and sour cream (delicious, but Floyd wouldn't touch it). We also made white mashed potatoes, gravy, scalloped tomatoes, creamed corn, and olives. And we made deviled eggs out of hard-boiled eggs frozen in brine. The whites were like rubber, and the filling didn't taste quite right, but the crew devoured five plates of them. At least they looked like eggs. We finished off the meal with Jell-O with black cherries and a birthday cake. Everyone enjoyed the feast and gave us an ovation, which was a huge relief.

The troops had been touchy about food lately, and we'd suffered major performance anxiety. Food becomes a major issue as people get toasted. I found myself constantly thinking about cooking and food in general. One weekend, my friends and I talked about nothing else for two days. I leafed through cookbooks, reading the recipes aloud in public. I couldn't stop thinking about lettuce and fresh fish, crisp green peppers and creamy cottage cheese. Like some guys look at *Playboy,* I loved to gaze at pictures of whole fish garnished and ready to cook—and I'm usually not fond of seafood!

The last of the freshies from the airdrop were long gone and the greenhouse production was sporadic. At one supper, we were each presented with two small leaves of lettuce and one cherry tomato from the hothouse garden. You have no idea how long a person can chew on one leaf of lettuce until you have gone without for months. I was so touched when Reza walked over to me and placed his portion on my plate. Then Wendy and Big did the same. It was one of the greatest gifts that I have ever received.

At the beginning of September, Kathy Miller wrote Gerry Katz at ASA and Karl Erb at NSF to tell them that while I was responding well to the chemotherapy, my veins were not. I had always had strong, ropelike veins, but now they were collapsing from constantly being jabbed. For a couple of weeks in a row, the Taxol infiltrated my arm—a painful experience—and the IV had to be restarted several times. "I am becoming increasingly concerned about our ability to continue to manage [Dr. Nielsen's] treatment at the Pole," she wrote. "A late October evacuation would require us to be able to administer another seven weeks of therapy. I honestly don't see how that is possible. I think it is time to re-address the question of early evacuation . . ."

An early rescue flight had always depended on the progress of my treatment, with Kathy calling the shots. Now I was relieved that she felt it was time to pull me out. I was tired of being tired all the time, tired of being sick. I now started to imagine myself returning to the U.S., and I asked Kathy precisely what kind of treatment schedule I could expect when I got home. As my doctor and advocate she had by now completely immersed herself in government bureaucracy in order to help me—right down to negotiating for satellite access. In mid-September we were having communications problems because President Clinton was paying a state visit to New Zealand. The satellites belonged to him while he was around. Luckily Air Force One was expected to leave the area before our scheduled chemo videoconference that Friday.

From: Kathy D. Miller
To: Jerri Nielsen
Date: 14 Sep 1999 08:05:04 -0500
Subject: Friday

Hi Jerri,

I hope this gets through before they yank your satellites. I haven't heard from Lisa about a time for Friday yet. If there's a problem I'll check with NSF and see if there is any way they can at least temporarily redirect the satellites back in our direction for at least two hours Friday.

As to what you might expect when you begin treatment back in the States: Most patients are only in the hospital for one night after breast surgery (lumpectomy or mastectomy without reconstruction), usually 2 nights with immediate tissue reconstruction. The surgery has improved dramatically over the last several years—I think you'll be surprised at the speed of recovery.

Radiation is daily Monday through Friday for about 6 weeks. We'll arrange that as close to home as possible.

Hair starts to come back about 6-8 weeks after the last chemotherapy, typically darker and curlier than before (at least initially).

As for your other question: I don't think I can explain the groin pain you're experiencing—that is not a typical place for breast cancer to move. In fact I don't think I have ever seen mets to the inguinal [groin] nodes.

Hope to see you Friday!
Kathy

From: Jerri Nielsen
To: Kathy D. Miller
Date: September 15, 1999 11:27 AM
Subject: medical

Dear Kathy,

I am doing better this week. My mind is clearer but not normal. I had enough energy to wash the floor in the hospital. It would be good to sleep all of the time. Tired of being tired. Too sick to practice medicine but must. Hot flashes and cold sweats continue. Already saw seventeen patients this week by Tuesday. People think that I look better and are coming in for small things again. Of that I am glad, but at times it is hard to manage. Had to fill a tooth yesterday. Today I am doing some elective surgery. The world is light all the time now. No darkness, ever, even in the middle of the night.

Here are the latest measurements as of 9-14-99: Tumor size: 3 cm wide, 2.5 cm across, 1 cm deep. Margins indistinct.

Fondly, Jerri

For my first few weeks on Taxol, the tumor continued to shrink with each session. Then, for a while there was no change. But recently the mass area seemed different, and I wondered if it was starting to grow again. I took a few new measurements, and sure enough, the tumor appeared to be getting larger. Kathy didn't seem worried, however, explaining it might be just a function of our primitive measuring devices. We agreed to check it again before the next round of chemo.

* * *

It had been six months since the onset of darkness. For weeks the sky had been getting brighter, and although we could not see the sun yet, the long night was finally over. On September 20, the equinox, the first rays of sunlight blazed upward from the horizon and touched off Antarctica's one and only annual dawn. If there ever was an excuse to party, this was it.

The bacchanal was held in Skylab, the only structure attached to the Dome that had windows. We draped a banner over one reading 99 NIGHT SHIFT HAS ENDED. In the brilliant light pouring in off the plateau everyone's skin looked translucent and unearthly pale, like albino salamanders brought up blind and squirming from deep in the earth on the end of a shovel. As if to accentuate our pallor, we dressed in a tropical theme. The guys wore shorts and plastic leis; the girls wrapped up in bright sarongs and sundresses. Everybody autographed the main window with washable paint. Fun in the Sun!—Thom. Goodbye dark, Hello light—what a long night—Yubecca. Mine was: Here comes the sun! Little darlin', it's been a long, dark, not so lonely winter—Jerri.

It was amazing how intimate all of us had become over the winter. People who hardly spoke to each other six months ago were now playing party games, such as passing a LifeSaver from mouth to mouth down a line of people on a couch! I knew we had all caught each other's germs by now, but still I worried, because it was my job. Middle John, our elder statesman, watched from a safe distance and marveled, "Is this a wild party, or what?"

The music was loud and fast and the dancing was furious until three in the morning. Big John, who had hardly had a drink since the end of summer, put down a few belts of his favorite beverage and started leaping around with utter abandon. The whole building shook like a California earthquake as Big thrashed up and down, clearing the floor and dancing by himself, yelling, "Dance, like nobody's watching!" As Heidi and Wendy joined him. I added, "Live like there's no tomorrow!"

We all let off steam at the Sunrise Party. It was fun, but it was also crucial, because the whole station seemed to be toasted. People were spacey and irritable, and everyone felt the strain.

From: Lisa Beal (South Pole Station)
To: Winterovers (South Pole Station)
Date: 21 Sept. 1999 21:07:21 -0000
Subject: Door slamming

Dear Neighbors—

ONE (or more) of you is being insensitive to people who live and work in the Science/Upper Berthing building. For almost as long as we have been here, one or more people have been slamming doors in this building. The door-slamming occurs at all hours.

I do not care if you slam doors because you are the victim of shoddy upbringing, a deprived (or is that depraved?) culture, or just slam doors to take out your frustrations. I would like it to stop NOW.

This morning at 8:45 I was rudely awakened with a shower of various items (toothpaste tubes, tins of tea bags, and a handful of mercury-filled vacuum tubes among them) because somebody slammed a door in this building SO HARD that these items were knocked off the shelf and fell on my face as I slept. This made me PLENTY angry, and filled my mind with thoughts of retaliation toward the yet-unidentified door-slammer.

PLEASE show a little courtesy for your neighbors—I was NOT the only one you woke, by the way!—and use the round plunger knob (or spring-loaded handle) to *ease* the door shut. Even if you lean on the door hard (vs. flinging it shut with all your might), it will not make a loud noise or send a vibration measuring 6.0 on the Richter Scale through the building.

If I catch the responsible individual(s) slamming the doors again, my anger may not stop with only words. Please: don't risk this!

Lisa

If Lisa could get toasted, nobody was immune. She had months and months of Ice time behind her and was normally the class clown, trying to make everybody laugh to keep up our spirits.

I had been told by my friends that I was one of the least likely to toast in the crew, and I don't think I ever went fully over the edge. Now, I was experiencing odd neurological changes, and I was getting clumsier and more forgetful all the time. I dropped my tableware and stumbled in the hallways.

On the night of the Sunrise Party I caused a major flood in Biomed. Doing the dishes, I accidentally left the sink water running when I turned away to look after a patient. This was not like me at all. Then I went to the party, still forgetting the running faucet. My brain was gone! Luckily Mike came home early and found water on the floor. He stopped the flow, but two rooms were already flooded and turning into skating rinks. Then he plugged in space heaters to dry everything out and they caught on fire. One of the guys who responded to the alarm said that between me and Mike, we had most of the biblical calamities covered.

For several weeks I had been receiving oxygen every day after lunch and sleeping with it at night. At first I didn't want it: we had limited resources and I felt I shouldn't get special treatment when everyone could benefit from extra oxygen. But Kathy thought oxygen was a great way to combat my nausea and mental fuzziness, and to help heal my veins. So Big chained a 144-cubic-foot oxygen tank to the wall next to my bed so I could use it every day. I admit it made me feel much better, and I wonder if it didn't help me start to regain my memory.

From: Jerri Nielsen
To: Family and Friends
Date: 24 Sept. 1999
Subject: owl memories

The memories that had gone away are all coming back to me like a fire hydrant opened on a hot summer day.

Until recently, when I would try to remember things that happened before the Ice, I could only recall short, ordinary snippets of my life. It was as if I were a cyborg and my circuitry was programmed with only enough past to convince me that, perhaps, I had had one. I could, with difficulty, remember my childhood home, the forest, my place at the beach, my family, and not much else. When I thought of my adult life, or of being with my children, it was always the same bits and pieces, not the rich repository that had previously been available to me with any small associated memory, song, smell, or thought from a similar time.

Now the pieces are coming together. Lately I've been thinking about the great horned owls that lived in the woods close to my mother's house. They would perch on the porch with a hungry eye for Digger, my white Chihuahua. The best thing they did was to use my dad's car windshield for a sliding board! We watched from the porch as they would fly to the top of the car, then slide down the windshield with their feet, then fly to the top and start again.

This sudden return of memory after so long is quite puzzling. I wonder if other people who are trapped in a prison, or in a place with no escape, quit remembering the past or planning for the future as a type of adaptation. Here on the Ice, it has only been the Ice for me. I have noticed that the people who have done well in this circumstance are the ones who have made a life here, fully in the present. Those who don't do as well pine for sweethearts at home, write to their wives every day, or live on the Internet. They are never really here—it is only what they do to have something to write home about.

For me, the memories of the past have only returned in the past three weeks, when the light has come on the horizon and we are all having thoughts of leaving. Did I suppress all of this in order to live well here? Or am I dying and my life is passing quickly before me? I wonder if I had suppressed my past to forget my horrible marriage and what happened to my children, and now, with the growth that I have experienced here, my mind has the strength to deal with it. Or is it just that my soul now knows that with the coming of light is the coming of a plane, and that I can now dare to remember?

I'll go to sleep now and think about when my children were small.

From the Ice,
Duff

The videoconference transmissions from the Pole were usually sent through one of two satellites hovering on the horizon, which relayed the digital transmission to a satellite ground station in the States, where it was then connected to Indianapolis via the Internet. As our satellites rose and set, satellite "windows" would overlap. At these times the communication link would bounce from one satellite to another, causing great difficulty in maintaining a dependable transmission path. Comms Tom always babysat our satellite links during the chemo sessions to make sure this didn't happen, since it confused the routers and broke the Internet connection.

Recent chemo sessions had gone off without a hitch, but during our next round, on September 24, there was a problem. Halfway through the Taxol drip we suddenly lost video and audio links to the States. While we were now much more relaxed about chemo than we had been, there was always the possibility—however remote—that I would develop a sudden allergic reaction to the Taxol, or that my vital signs would unexpectedly drop. Kathy always wanted to be in contact with us throughout the drip, and when we lost communications, we knew they would be frantic back in Indianapolis.

Lisa grabbed my bedroom phone and called Comms.

"Hey, what happened? We've lost all channels here!"

She listened for a moment, then said, "Tom says his satellite link is live, but no data's getting through. There's a problem with the routers and he's trying to fix it." She hung up and headed for the door.

"I'm going to get the Iridium phone and see if I can't raise Kathy . . ."

The Iridium phone, which connected directly with its own commercial satellite system with links around the globe, had been included in the airdrop for emergencies like this. The main problem was that the aluminum Dome blocked the signal. Plus it was 70 below zero outside. But Lisa was gone before I could remind her to take her coat.

Big John kept his eye on the Taxol drip, and Heidi climbed into bed next to me to keep me warm and keep a close watch. A few minutes later the phone rang and Mike Masterman snatched it up.

"Okay, I got you," he said. "Lisa's on the line with Kathy, Doc. She wants to know if everything is all right."

"Tell her everything's fine, Mike. . ."

And so it went, back and forth for the rest of the session. Lisa had run through the bitter cold inside the Dome to get the phone and its access codes from Comms, then hustled over to Skylab, plopped down in a couch by a window to catch her breath, and called Kathy on the Iridium phone. Using the hardwired phone in Skylab with her other hand, she connected with us in Club Med and relayed messages.

Luckily, everything else went smoothly that night.

I was increasingly worried that my tumor was growing again and that the cancer might be spreading. When Comms was able to reestablish our Internet link, Kathy and I got on the computer to talk it over.

From: Kathy D. Miller
To: Jerri Nielsen
Date: 27 Sept. 1999
Subject: RE: congratulations

Please send my congratulations to the entire polar team. As usual they did a great job!!! What time is best to meet this Friday (when I will once again try to be seen and heard simultaneously)?

Kathy

From: Jerri Nielsen
To: Kathy D. Miller
Date: September 27, 1999 2:43 P.M.
Subject: Re: congratulations

Dear Kathy,

My tumor hurts today. It seems to be getting larger. Measurements this weekend: 3 cm wide, 2.7 cm tall, and 1 cm deep. The measurements concur with my feeling that it is growing. Sort of scaring me. Is it okay? Is it going to grow and spread while I am on the Taxol?

Jerri

From: Kathy D. Miller
To: Jerri Nielsen
Date: September 27, 1999
Subject: RE: congratulations

Jerri,

I am concerned about those measurements as well. The measurements you had sent me last time were slightly larger than previously but stable (essentially within the slight variation of doing the measurements). Stable I can live with, growing is a problem.

Should the tumor grow on Taxol? NO. But tumors don't always cooperate. In any cancer the cells are not homogeneous—there are many populations of cells with often dramatic differences in their rate of growth and sensitivity to different chemotherapies. Eventually the cells will become resistant to the Taxol and the tumor starts to grow.

What I would like to have you do is the repeat the measurements Thursday—if it really is growing on the Taxol we will have no choice but to switch your chemotherapy regimen to CMF (Cytoxan/Methotrexate/5-FU). Your instincts and judgment have always been on target.

Side effects of CMF are in many ways similar to Taxol—not much nausea, fatigue still a problem, less hard on hair, much more likely to cause myelosuppression. (Do you have oral antibiotics available?)

Sending good thoughts your way,
Kathy

From: Jerri Nielsen
To: Kathy D. Miller
Date: September 30, 1999 9:18 P.M.
Subject: new measurements

Dear Kathy,

THE THING IS A MONSTER!
4 cm tall
4 cm wide
1.5 cm deep

Does this mean that it is spreading through my body?

I am so afraid. Things have not seemed as good this week. I note that I am again thinking about death. It is probably because I am having a lot more pain again in my breast. It is like in April when it was growing very fast and the breast felt like it was expanding. The back and arm pain is more prominent. I am very sick to the stomach and feel like my liver hurts.

Fondly, Jerri

From: Kathy D. Miller
To: Jerri Nielsen
Date: 30 Sept. 1999
Subject: RE: new measurements

Local growth does not necessarily mean it is spreading elsewhere but I can't (and wouldn't) deny that concern. If the
chemotherapy (CMF) is successful we can prevent both further growth and the potential for spread elsewhere.

See you soon.

Armed with this new information about the rapid growth of the
tumor and my physical deterioration, Kathy Miller made two decisions. She told me it was time to stop the Taxol infusions and proceed
with a different combination of chemotherapy drugs—the CMF cock-
tail. The new drugs, which had been included in the air drop as a
backup in case the Taxol didn't work, might arrest the cancer until I
could get to a surgeon. And she was now urging NSF/ASA to evacuate
me from the South Pole as soon as possible. NSF concurred, and Harry
Mahar, the NSF official coordinating the rescue effort, emailed me
with the news that my extraction would likely take place two and a
half to three weeks from now, depending on the weather in McMurdo
and the Pole. Since the first flight of the season usually arrived on
October 25, I wondered if it was worth the risk just to get me home a
week or so early, but my doctors and employers seemed to think my
time was running out.

It is hard to describe how discouraging these new developments were
to me and all the members of Club Med. We had all worked so hard and
had been through so much together—the airdrop, the biopsies, the gru-
eling hours of chemotherapy. For a while, when the tumor was shrinking, we felt like we were winning, that we were beating the enemy into
submission, that we were in control. Now that the monster had come
back bigger than ever, we wondered if it had all been for nothing. By
going through it all I had probably bought myself time, but would it be
enough? The pain in my back, my chronic cough, my lack of coordina-
tion and mental cloudiness were all symptoms that could mean the cancer had metastasized and spread throughout my body.

Big John, Lisa, and my closest friends tried to put a positive spin on the news: I'd be out of here soon. But if I turned quickly and caught them off-guard, I could catch the flicker of anguish in their eyes. It was sad to think that this great adventure might end badly, but by now I had moved beyond fear. As my father always said, "What will be, will be."

When I was feeling my worst, Big would sit up next to me at night reading me passages from *Endurance.* The only illumination in my bedroom came from a desk lamp that Big had fixed for me months ago, a lifetime ago. In these times my whole world consisted of the deep, even sound of his voice and the yellow pool of light that lit his hands and the book in his hands, but not his face.

The story of Shackleton's struggle in 1915 to survive and keep his crew alive touched me deeply and comforted me. He was the explorer who best understood the wild, seductive lure of Antarctica: "I have ideals," he said, "and far away, in my own white South, I open my arms to the romance of it all." It was Shackleton who led the craziest of expeditions—to walk across the continent from shore to shore—and Shackleton who pushed himself and his men to the limits of endurance. Even though he failed to reach his goal, he kept his promise to bring everyone back alive.

Forty years later, a writer named Alfred Lansing put Shackleton's diaries together with those of his men and produced a classic account of the expedition. Big read to me from the chapters that seemed to reflect my own predicament, clinging to hope and waiting for rescue: Shackleton and his crew were stranded in Antarctica when the pack ice crushed their vessel. Lost for months and presumed dead, they camped on the floe, waiting patiently for the ice to break up in the austral summer and drift north on the current. Then, as winter neared, they set out on open water in two small boats salvaged from the wreck. They sailed through stormy seas for days and nights, drenched in icy seawater, hungry, seasick, and half-mad with thirst. They were heading to Elephant Island, an uninhabited speck of rock and ice, where the crew thought they might survive the winter.

Big read to me: "Toward three a.m. the wind began to fall, and by five o'clock it had dropped to a gentle breeze. Gradually the sea grew calmer. The sky was clear, and finally the sun rose in unforgettable brilliance through a pink mist along the horizon, which soon melted into flaming gold. It was more than just a sunrise. It seemed to flood into their souls, rekindling the life within them. They watched the growing light quenching the wild, dark misery of the night that now, at last, was over."

In the new light, they could see the jagged outline of Elephant Island. But Shackleton's trials were far from ended. They had come so far, and suffered so much, only to find more obstacles in their path. There still were treacherous waters to cross and mountains to scale before they could all be safe. Big read to me until I drifted off to sleep. Shackleton's courage, dispensed so long ago, reached across the years and piloted me through another night.

CHAPTER 15

Deliverance

Statement by

DR. KARL A. ERB, DIRECTOR,
OFFICE OF POLAR PROGRAMS
NATIONAL SCIENCE FOUNDATION

Status of South Pole Medical Situation

October 5, 1999. The National Science Foundation (NSF) has requested that the 109th Airlift Wing of the New York Air National Guard deploy to Antarctica and conduct a flight to the South Pole to bring out the physician at Amundsen-Scott South Pole Station. The physician, Dr. Jerri Nielsen, has been carrying out her normal responsibilities since the U.S. Air Force airdrop of medical supplies in July. Her stateside physicians are now recommending to us that she be returned to the United States at the earliest safe opportunity. The onset of summer in Antarctica, with its gradual increase in sunlight and temperature, makes it feasible to evacuate Dr. Nielsen and to replace her with another physician. Two aircraft and three aircrews will depart from Stratton Air National Guard Base in Schenectady, N.Y., on Wednesday, Oct. 6, 1999. They are expected to arrive at NSF's McMurdo Station in Antarctica on or around Oct. 12, where they will await favorable conditions to fly the roughly 800 miles to the Pole.

Club Med met again on the first Friday in October to begin the new round of chemotherapy. Since I had never been exposed to this drug combination before, everyone watched carefully to make sure I didn't have a bad reaction.

This time when we lost our audio line due to satellite problems, Lisa was prepared: We had an Internet phone to call Indianapolis on another channel. She had also added another layer of communication by using AOL Instant Messenger during the chemo sessions. It was good to have the drug dosages spelled out, to make sure they were accurate. Now, instead of scribbling notes and holding them up to the camera, I was telling Lisa what to type to Kathy, who was simultaneously typing instructions and answers into her computer, all the while watching us on the monitor and listening to the telephone. Lisa's handle was "Polarpal," and Kathy was "Spoledoc."

> **Polarpal:** Hi Kathy! Brrr, my keyboard is cold.
>
> **Spoledoc:** LaTrice is tired!
>
> **Polarpal:** Me, too! :-)
>
> **Spoledoc:** Methotrexate is a total of 70 mg . . .
>
> **Polarpal:** I start with 400 cc normal saline solution;
>   run until empty during entire chemo treatment . . .
>
> **Spoledoc:** Lisa—the phone went dead.
>
> **Polarpal:** Oh @#$! . . . calling back!
>
> **Spoledoc:** Lisa, Lisa . . . where are you??
>
> **Polarpal:** :-) Here . . .
>
> **Spoledoc:** The yellow stuff is dripping nicely . . .
>
> **Polarpal:** Boredom is relative!
>
> **Spoledoc:** Heidi has nice earrings.

And on it went into the night. We all did our best to stay upbeat, making idle conversation and joking in our strange multi-tech forum. The IV was painful at first. Most of my accessible veins had been used several times, and my hands and arms were bruised from previous attempts to find a site. Once, during an earlier Taxol infusion, we had to dig out a 1970s edition of *Gray's Anatomy* to direct my needle squad to a new vein. This time the procedure went well, but we were forcing a show of good humor. Everyone felt edgy and distracted, our attention fixed on the defiant, growing tumor that seemed like another presence in the room, like a stalker in the shadows.

I had so many questions to ask Kathy about the tumor, and whether its sudden growth might indicate a spread of disease. It was, however, too frustrating to hold a technical medical Q&A through a translator over the Internet. I would have to wait to "talk" to Kathy in private. Once again, I needed to get the plain facts from my doctor in order to process the news, good or bad, and make a plan of action.

I sent her an email later that night, and she returned my letter with her answers typed in after my questions.

From: Kathy D. Miller
To: Jerri Nielsen
Date: October 1, 1999 10:52 P.M.
Subject: Re: Hard truth

JN: I would like to know what is really going on. What does the fact that this tumor has a doubling rate of about two weeks mean to me and my hope for survival? Does this usually mean spread or not? Does the fact that my tumor did this mean that I have less chance of living?

KM: This is the most important question and the most difficult to answer. Let me give you some background first. In any cancer the cells are not homogeneous—there are many populations of cells with often dramatic differences in their rate of growth and sensitivity to different chemotherapies. . . In your case, the cells that were sensitive to the Taxol are gone but the cells that are left are growing very quickly . . .

JN: I am sure that I am not making myself clear, but is this going to affect my chance of living? I don't know how to put these new developments into my perception of the rest of my life, if there IS a chance for the rest of my life. To me, I heard NO GOOD NEWS tonight. Maybe I am wrong and I am just getting a bit scared.

KM: Let me be bluntly honest—I didn't have any good news to give you last night. I know you want the truth but our videoconferences are also a somewhat public forum. I sometimes don't know how much personal (and difficult) information to share. I also sense the fear and frustration of the chemotherapy team—they have done a truly amazing job. I have at times consciously tried to remain calm and optimistic for their benefit. They seem to need me to tell them that we (you) are doing fine here. I don't always know how to juggle your needs and the needs of the group. You are more important but I need to keep them focused and with me as well. The honest answer is that I don't know how to calculate the effects of the last two weeks' events on your chance for overall survival. It certainly didn't help. BUT I still have no proof that you have metastatic disease. I am worried about the back pain but that is so nonspecific that I won't know if it is related to your breast cancer until we can do a bone scan. Bottom line—I think you still have a real chance for long-term survival. My best estimate today: 35-40% probability of being alive, well, and without breast cancer 10 years from now (there is very little fall-off past 5 years).

JN: It has not been the best of times. Thanks for trying to get me "extracted."
Jerri

KM: It's not been the best of times here either. I have rarely felt so helpless. Looking forward to being able to talk to you in person and finally getting some answers to your questions.

Kathy

I reread Kathy's words and took what hope I could from them. No proof that I had mets. But a better than sixty percent chance I'd be dead in a decade. Well, I could try to make that decade last a lifetime.

People always use the word *fight* when discussing cancer treatment. By now I was starting to see the process more as an acceptance, followed by a leap of faith. Now that my memories were returning, I was reminded of a time years ago when I almost drowned while white-water rafting. The raft hit a huge set of waves and I was catapulted high into the air. I landed in a hydraulic and felt my body sucked into the depths of the whirlpool. Even though I was a strong swimmer and was wearing a life vest, I was no match for the river. I was shocked and horrified that I couldn't keep myself from being pulled underwater. At first I struggled, then realized there was nothing to do but wait for an opportunity. I relaxed completely and thought very calmly, "This time I might die." I let the water spit me to the surface, just long enough to take a deep breath, then pull me back under. The next time I surfaced, a man in a raft held out his hand and I took it, letting him pull me into the boat. I surrendered, and I was rescued.

Months ago, when I first realized I had cancer, I didn't want to read about it or talk to others who had had it. I suppose I was in a state of denial. It was as if I was afraid to associate myself with the disease, that to do so would cast me into the world of the dying. This was a barrier I had built to protect myself during the past twenty-five years, when as a doctor, I often cared for people in the last days or minutes of their lives. I needed to construct a difference between them and me: "I'm not sick, I just work here."

I think it was easier to have cancer here, at the South Pole, than back in the world of high-tech medicine. Here, I had no option but to accept my fate. It was easier, in some ways, to accept having "no chance" of a cure than to have "some chance," especially while you are learning to accept your diagnosis. "Some chance" can cause you to claw frantically for survival, before the peace that comes with knowing, as my dad said when he got cancer, "What will be, will be."

If I did not have much time left in my life, I wanted to make the most of it. Since a cancer patient would never be allowed to live in Antarctica, I set my sights on the open ocean. Pic, still suffering from crippling hip pain, spent days and nights with me, fantasizing about our maritime adventures. Sometimes we would sail to Madagascar, sometimes Marseilles. Scotty still wrote to me often, firing up my dreams of the sea with stories of his own:

From: Scott Cahill
To: Jerri Nielsen
Date: 2 Oct. 1999
Subject: Hold on

Dear Duffy:

Relax & hold up as well as possible. I will be there waiting & I will take up whatever battles need to be fought. You can relax & get home & get better. Eric & I will be there to whisk you away back to Ohio & Indiana & good medical help.

You needn't worry about sailing. You will love it, all right. Here is a story about my old boat:

It was midsummer and very hot. I lived in Wrightsville Beach and kept my 27' North American docked there. At about noon it was unbearable everywhere—so I decided to go sailing. Nobody wanted to go along (goody) so I cast off at noon and headed out to sea. I didn't have a destination—just the horizon. My original goal was to sail out of sight of land. I kept her sailing east all afternoon. When twilight came the wind died. It was not so hot now in the quiet water. There was only a little chop. I fell asleep with the sails hanging like laundry.

When I awoke it was midnight. I was out of sight of land. I crawled up on the stern and realized that my boat had been transported into outer space. There were stars everywhere. Up, to the sides, down, everywhere! I held the back stay to keep from falling and looked carefully. It was incredible. My movement on the stern made a ripple and it rolled out to the horizon, shutting off the stars one at a time and then back on they came. The ocean had died completely and had turned into a mirror. It was incredible!

Another day I was sailing off shore and I saw what I thought was a shark fin to the right, then the left of the Hobie Cat that my friend and I were sailing. They glided along undulating up and down—not like a shark swimming—as we sailed. The sea turned from green-blue beneath us to deep black as the back of the huge ray very nearly lifted us off of the face of the sea. He turned and dived, never to be seen again.

There are so many stories. I have stories that I don't even remember. If you hate sailing—and no one can—you will love the places and beautiful animals who you get to know enough that it will make up for the sailing. You will love to sail. I am a pretty good teacher and if you will put up with a little Capt. Bligh in me, I will show you how to make her dance. I will feel very safe with my beloved sister in my boat. I have built her well & strong & she will keep you safe while you learn.

I love you, sis.
Scotty

Ordinarily, everyone at the Pole mobilized at the beginning of October to prepare for the station opening, traditionally scheduled for October 25. This year we knew the first flight would come sooner, and everyone stepped up the pace to get ready. Floyd and Ken started firing up furnaces and electric heaters out at Summer Camp and getting the Jamesways ready for summer residents. Big John coaxed the tractors and 'dozer into cold-weather service. Power Plant Thom, Tool Man Tim, and Ken Lobe worked twelve-hour shifts grooming the three-mile-long airplane skiway in minus 90 F. temperatures. They had to carve through the sastrugi and wind-hardened snowdrifts, pulling snow planes and drag lines behind the tractors. We also had to bulldoze a ramp down to the main Dome entrance and remove the snow canyon that was now twenty-five feet deep.

Everybody was working to swab out the station for the arrival of the next crew—cleaning their quarters, the upper galley, the pool hall and TV room, everything. I was determined to scrub down the walls and floor in Biomed, wash the linen, clean the drawers. Yubecca volunteered to help me, and we eventually got it done. But balance had become a problem for me. I would be sitting at my computer and, without warning, the world would start to spin. The vertigo would be over in a second, but it was the most alarming symptom yet—I was concerned it meant that the cancer was attacking my cerebellum, which controls balance. It was getting hard for me to get out of bed, or to simply walk down the hallway—I never knew when I would suddenly pitch over and slam into a wall. But I hid these episodes, along with the chills and leg pains I was getting, from everyone except my doctor and my closest friends at Pole.

From: Jerri Nielsen
To: #winter
Date: October 02, 1999 10:13 P.M.
Subject: Brunch

Dear Friends,

Please come to Brunch this Sunday.

There will be ham and egg casserole, egg and pepper casserole, fried potato cakes, fruit, and toast.

As a special festive touch, we will be making Bloody Marys to your order. Virgin and High Octane. (Sorry, no celery stalks.)

Please attend. We are hoping to see you there.

Jerri

From: Jerri Nielsen
To: Kathy D. Miller
Date: October 5, 1999 11:22 P.M.
Subject: Medical

Hello Kathy:

This is Big John. I am writing this for the Doc, she is lying in bed talking, and I am typing.

The fatigue is profound today. Doc thinks you ought to know this. She doesn't believe that anyone could feel like this and continue on, driving, working, functioning. It feels like there is something wrong. She can only perform very small tasks, then it is back to bed. She called me this afternoon to get her medication for her, she didn't feel as if she could get out of bed. She loves to go eat and socialize, but when she got out of bed she was so shaky, VERY cold, and unsteady on her feet. I brought her lunch today, we ate in her room. I worked late this evening (preparing the machines for grooming the skiway) and Wendy brought dinner to her room. VERY unlike her to miss an opportunity to go to the galley and socialize.

Kathy, I keep a real close eye on the Doc. The first day after the new chemo, she looked okay. We did the preparation for our brunch (you know you have to shop early and get everything defrosted before you can even THINK about cooking) Saturday. It took us about three hours. Doc got a little fatigued, but nothing I was worried about.

On Sunday, she got out of bed, after a full night's rest, and we began to cook. About three hours into our cooking, she began to look very fatigued. I watched her very closely. She dropped her spatula a couple of times, but anyone could do that. Then she became very unsteady and fell against the front of the hot griddle. I told her that was enough. I asked her to sit down. She sat down, ate a couple of bites, then went to bed.

We usually watch a movie together every night. The last few nights she has had trouble staying awake until the end of the movie. This is after spending most of the day in bed. This behavior is very much unlike her. I am quite concerned about her lassitude.

Regards,
Big

From: Kathy D. Miller
To: Jerri Nielsen
Date: 6 Oct. 1999 18:43:25 -0500
Subject: RE: Medical

Jerri (and Big),

I can't begin to tell you how frustrated I am—the side effects of this chemo are not unexpected but they are certainly worse than I anticipated. I suspect this is because of the cumulative fatigue from the previous chemo and the long-term effects of the altitude.

Jerri—the CBC before treatment tomorrow is most important. If your white count has dropped too low I need to adjust the doses of the drugs. If you are not up to doing the differential yourself I may be able to do it. I'll ask Lisa if it is possible to connect the camera directly to the scope—I'll review the slide and count.

I am glad to hear that the breast and axillary pain are a little better. I wouldn't expect to see much change in tumor measurements after just one week but decreasing pain is a step in the right direction.

I can't explain the calf pain or the chills. I agree that a vascular response is most likely—this may be related to the hot flashes but I can't find any information on the effects of altitude or chronic hypoxia on menopausal symptoms.

Please use the oxygen whenever possible. The persistent cough worries me a bit but less so since it has continued all winter. I think the shortness of breath is as much related to the fatigue and deconditioning as to the hypoxia.

Look forward to talking to you soon!
Kathy

Big—thanks for the assist. You and Lisa are my eyes and ears there. I value your observations and care tremendously!!!

Packing for my early extraction was another tiresome and painful exercise in loss. I had to ask Big to help me, and he hated to pack even his own things. He was clearly unhappy, but I had to be sure I had everything I needed ready for the rescue flight, and I could no longer trust my memory. My books and personal possessions would have to be shipped back to the States.

Kathy had told me to bring enough chemotherapy drugs for another three sessions, in case my plane got stranded somewhere by bad weather. I also had to bring the Navy pathology jars with my cell samples, the slides, and some other items.

Both ASA and NSF were warning that media interest in my story had exploded again after the announcement of the rescue mission. They were receiving hundreds of requests for interviews and pictures. Even the Air National Guard was asking that an Air Force photographer be aboard the plane with me. All queries were politely but firmly rejected. Still, we worried that a mob of reporters and cameramen would be waiting to ambush me when I arrived in New Zealand.

People did their best to shelter me from this kind of news, because it was so upsetting, but I occasionally got glimpses of the madness back in the world in emails from my family. My father, who rarely wrote, reported that one day in early October they had received forty calls from reporters by midafternoon. A rumor had been going around that the rescue flight was on its way to get me.

Meanwhile, Scott and Eric were preparing for their role in the mission. Scott tried to convince Eric that they should both shave their heads in sibling solidarity before meeting me in Christchurch. Luckily, they both decided I would be better served if they didn't draw attention to themselves while trying to smuggle me past the camera crews. But it was the thought that counted.

The Bro Squad left the States on October 12, following roughly the same route I had taken to Christchurch eleven months earlier, when I stepped through the looking glass. At the Pole, we watched the weather, and waited.

From: Jerri Nielsen
To: Winterovers

Date: Tue., 12 Oct. 1999 20:26:31 +0100
Subject: Party Music Fun!

Dear Polie Friends,

The 15th of October is Big's 44th birthday! Come hear our very own South Pole band, Scott's Revenge, in the comfortable surrounds of our galley. As a special celebration, they have offered to play. More information regarding times will come from Comms Tom, aka Fiddlin' Tom. We can dance, stamp our feet, or sing! Or just groove to the music with friends.

If I am still here, I will be making Margaritas, high octane and virgin, for the revelers. If I am gone . . . well, BYOB.

Hope to see you there.
Jerri

A barrage of springtime storms arrived in Antarctica along with the rescue mission. Two LC-130s were launched from their base in New York state on October 6, arriving in Christchurch four days later. The extra plane, and two extra flight crews, were deployed in the event that another plane was needed for a search and rescue mission, and for backup in case of equipment failure or excessive delays.

High winds grounded the planes in New Zealand until October 14. McMurdo, the next stop, had been open to air traffic for weeks but was suffering from a spell of extreme cold temperatures. The rescue planes were able to land at McMurdo but were immediately grounded again. We had to wait for the temperatures there and at Pole to rise above minus 58 F., normally considered the lowest reading for a safe landing. As soon as conditions improved, one plane would leave for the Pole while the other stood by in MacTown.

We were updated almost hourly on the status of the mission, and I tried to learn what I could about the crew that had come so far to help me. The pilot was Major George McAllister of the New York Air National Guard, who had a great deal of experience flying ski-equipped Hercules planes in the Antarctic. Colonel Graham Pritchard, the airborne-mission commander, was on board, as was Major Kimberly Terpening, a flight nurse and Gulf War veteran. The mission planning team had been led by Col. Edward L. Fleming, an expert in rescue operations and medevac. I was relieved that the crew of volunteers on this risky mission was so experienced. My greatest fear was that someone would get hurt or killed just trying to buy me a week or so of extra time.

I could almost justify the mission to myself because Pic was to be extracted with me. His hip problems had been getting worse, and I still couldn't find the cause of the pain in his limbs, back, and neck. I felt he needed to see a specialist as soon as possible, and this flight would be his ticket out.

Meanwhile I was receiving emails from my mother and sisters-in-law, keeping me current on Scott and Eric's adventures in New Zealand. The Bro Squad had arrived and they were being escorted around Christchurch by Sam Feola, the logistics expert from ASA. Both ASA and NSF had worked tirelessly to coordinate all the arrangements for my extraction and redeployment to the States. They had flown my brothers down, along with Val Carroll, the ASA public relations person, to handle any media nonsense once I got off the Ice. The plan was to sweep me through the hordes of waiting reporters, get me on a flight to the U.S., and take me straight to the hospital in Indianapolis and into the care of Kathy Miller. My parents would be waiting for me there.

The morning and afternoon of October 15 came and went without a break in the freezing temperatures. One LC-130 took off from McMurdo but turned around that same day because of the weather. While the rescue mission cooled its heels in MacTown, I got to go to my best friend's birthday party. I had set everything up so that it would take place even if I was gone. Now I was able to attend it, too.

It was a beautiful night in the galley: The big mess tables were broken up and reconfigured as café tables with linen cloths, candles, and crystal wineglasses. Lisa and Power Plant Thom served Margaritas (virgin and regular, all frozen, of course) while Scott's Revenge provided the music. As a special treat, Comms Tom put on a monkey mask and serenaded Big with an old-time birthday song: ". . . I can tell by your jaw that a monkey was your pa! You're bound to look like a monkey when you grow old!"

The cooks brought out a birthday cake, and we gave Big his gifts. Lisa had hoarded a bottle of Wild Turkey for him, and I gave him my favorite book, *The Selected Poems of W. B. Yeats*. Each moment that ticked by tugged a bit at my heart. I wondered if my life would ever again feel so complete.

For the first time since I was a child I felt at peace. I knew precisely who I was and where I belonged at this moment in time: I was a member of this band of restless hearts. My past was gone, my future impossible to see. If you asked me then, I would have told you this was a good day to die.

I started feeling weak and asked Big John to take me home. He carefully pulled me up by the elbow and walked me back to Biomed, so that no one would see me stumble. Then he put me into bed and turned on my oxygen. He wanted to stay there with me, but I made him go back to the party. I refused to spoil his birthday.

The next morning, the weather was still terrible but expected to be just barely warm enough to land. When we were told the plane had taken off from MacTown, Mike Masterman called us all to the galley to review the procedure for landing. He told us in no uncertain terms that we had only a few minutes to get everyone in and out of the plane. The longer it was on the ground, the greater the risk of a mechanical problem. There was no time for mistakes. I can barely remember what else was said at that meeting. As people stood up to leave, I saw the faces of my dear friends approaching me through a watery haze: Roo, Nick, Loree, Andy, Comms Tom. I couldn't really hear their voices, but I must have said something back to them, to tell them good-bye, to thank them for everything they meant to me. But in my mind I was already gone, suspended in deep water, drifting out to sea.

I went back to my dear little hospital for the last time. My things were all packed and lined up at the door. The orange bags I had dragged through MacTown a lifetime ago were filled with the same items I had arrived with, but now so tattered and worn most of them were unusable. Just as when I arrived, my things were accompanied by a Styrofoam cooler of medicines and cell samples that could not be frozen.

The rooms were clean and emptied of my physical presence. The pictures of the dead doctors remained. I couldn't part with Dorianne's comforter, but I left my replacement (I still wasn't sure who it would be) my electric blanket and warm flannel sheets and the colored Christmas lights that I had strung around my bedroom ceiling to cheer myself up. I hoped he would like the map of the southern night sky that I had painted on the ceiling with my glow-in-the-dark nail polish.

Big waited with me. We thought the plane would get boomeranged again, so both of us jumped when Comms Tom announced on the All-Call that the aircraft had radioed in Papa 3—meaning it was thirty minutes out.

We pulled on the last layers of our ECW gear, and Big went outside to warm up the snowmobile. I had walked from Biomed to the skiway hundreds of times in the past eleven months, but today I was too frail to risk it. As I climbed on board behind Big, Lisa came up to say good-bye and give me a final hug. I had been so careful to keep my emotions under control through all my good-byes, but this was a hard one. She gave me a sweet, soft kiss on the cheek and pressed her face against mine.

"Take care of yourself," she said. "I'll catch up with you back in the world."

As soon as we cleared the entrance tunnel we were engulfed in a swirling ground blizzard, a total whiteout. Neither of us could imagine how a pilot could land in such terrible conditions. The temperature hovered around minus 60 F. Even if the Hercules could thread the needle and land on our skiway in zero visibility, there was always the danger that the aircraft's hydraulic systems would rupture or freeze and lock up the landing gears.

"He'll never make it," said Big. "He'll have to circle and turn back."

Suddenly we heard a noise rising above the howling wind. It was the roar of all four engines of an LC-130 powering in for a landing. We could hardly believe it was happening. Then the noise changed in pitch and grew louder as the pilot reversed the props. The plane was on the ground.

I turned to Big John. Every part of our bodies was layered against the cold, but I wanted to see him one last time. I pulled off my goggles.

"Let me see your eyes," I said. He pushed his goggles up on his forehead. We looked at each other for a moment and nothing more was said.

The plane was on the taxiway, and we knew we had only a few minutes to get everybody on board and disembark the arriving passengers. The engines were still cranking as we made our way up to the forward door. It swung open and down, and Hugh Cowan, the arriving doctor, hustled down the stairs. There was no time for greetings, but I was relieved to know another doctor would be on station and that he was a fellow Polie. Pic hobbled out to the flight line on crutches and Charlie got ready to help him board. First it was my turn. The stairway hung at least a yard above the ice, and there was no way I could climb it on my own. I grabbed a cable and tried to get my knee onto the step. Suddenly I felt Big John's arms around me, picking me up. He literally threw me into the plane, where I landed on my knees on the flight deck. When I turned around to wave good-bye, he was already gone.

From: John W. Penney
To: All

Date: October 16, 1999

Subject: Mission accomplished

Hello All:

Just wanted to let you all know that the Doc got out of here today. It was the earliest and coldest landing ever at the South Pole. We didn't think the plane would land. The wind was blowing at almost 20 knots, and visibility was poor. We expected them to do a couple of circuits and go back to MacTown. I took her up to the flight line on my snowmobile.

She is very short of breath nowadays and gets dizzy easily. We stood around, and everyone said their last good-byes, even though we did not expect the plane to land. Well, land they did. I took the Doc by the arm and marched her out to the door and helped her up the steps.

I then walked back to the safe area to watch the takeoff. I knew it would be a good one when I saw the flight engineer go to the rear of the plane and arm the ATO [auxiliary take-off] bottles. ATO bottles are rockets attached to the rear of the plane. I don't know if they are solid or liquid fuel. There are four on each side. When everyone and their gear were inside, the plane attempted to taxi. They couldn't, the engines were at full throttle and the plane wouldn't budge. They had to retract their skis, which had become frozen to the ice, and rest on the tires. They then put the skis back down on the ice and revved up their engines. This time they moved. The plane taxied out and went to the far end of the skiway. We could not see them, but we could hear them. As soon as we heard them turn around, they put the throttles to the fire wall and lit the ATO bottles. What a show. Fastest-moving LC-130 that I have ever seen. They were off deck by the time they came into view in front of the Dome. We got to see the last five seconds of the ATO burn. A very deep blue pointed flame. The bottles then flamed out, not all at the same time, and sputtered lazy yellow flames. The plane did the normal go around. As they came over the Dome, the pilot waggled his wings, and they were off.

I stood and watched it until it was out of sight. It took about four minutes for them to fly out of view. It was kind of weird, blowing snow and nasty on the ground, but as we watched the plane climb out, the sky above opened up and it was flying in the middle of a huge patch of blue sky and clouds.

Big

Epilogue

Memories are slowly returning to me.

I was sick for a long time after I left the Ice. I dimly remember the rescue flight from the South Pole to McMurdo, and the switch to another plane that took me to Christchurch. Although I was painfully aware of the media interest in my case, I was still not prepared for the mobs of reporters and television crews that were waiting for my arrival in Cheech. I was met at the plane by a white van, nicknamed, of all things, the White Rabbit. The driver sped me to my hotel, where I was driven around to the back entrance and spirited up to my room. Now that I was back at sea level, I felt energized by the oxygen flooding my brain after so many months at altitude. When the door opened, Scott and Eric were waiting for me with hugs and kisses and a huge plate of fruit and vegetables. I was laughing and trying to talk to them but I couldn't stop stuffing lettuce and green peppers into my mouth. It was like a sensory orgy: Suddenly the world was saturated in color and fragrance and flavors. Even though we risked running into a camera crew, I asked my brothers to take me to the gorgeous Botanic Gardens along the Avon River, just to walk around the flowers and trees that I had only seen in my dreams for so many months.

We slipped out of town like thieves, or royalty, depending how you look at it. We flew back to the U.S. without ever walking through an airline gate, or seeing a fellow passenger until we were on the plane. NSF and ASA did a wonderful job of arranging all our travel, and I never had a camera flash go off in my face, or a question shouted at me. I will always be grateful for their thoughtfulness.

I flew directly to Indianapolis, where my parents were waiting for me at Indiana University Hospital. It was a joyous moment, but there was no time for more than a brief reunion. I recognized Kathy and LaTrice immediately from the video conferences. It was so good to see them. I had looked forward to the day that I would meet Kathy. She was warmer and prettier than I had imagined. It was good to feel so much trust in a person to whom you had handed over your life.

Kathy had a multitude of medical tests waiting for me, to see if my cancer had spread. These were the tests that I had feared for eight months. They would tell me my future. If they were negative, I could have surgery and hope. If they showed the spread of cancer, I would only opt for palliative therapy and prepare for an early death.

I was suddenly frightened, because now I would learn the truth. I didn't feel that crossing my fingers or praying could make any difference at this point. So I simply subjected myself to the process. I was truly surprised each time Kathy came to my room after an exam to inform me that I had passed this test and was on to another. One by one, the bone scan, an MRI of the brain and a CAT scan of my body each came back negative. I was so stunned that it was hard to feel relief. My dad listened while Kathy came in to tell us the good news. Asking me what it all meant, I explained that it meant I might live. He was shocked and overcome with emotion.

The next day I had surgery. I chose a lumpectomy, which would be less disfiguring than a mastectomy. Sue Lehman my old friend, and wife of Juergen, the radiologist who had advised me at the Pole, had driven in from her home in Fort Wayne. She and my brother, Scott, went down to the operating room with me. Later Dr. Robert Goulet, my surgeon, called to tell me that he had wonderful news for me: the cancer had not spread to my lymph nodes! It was almost unbelievable. I felt like a death row prisoner, clutching my pardon.

I returned to Ohio the next day to recuperate at my mother's house. Everything seemed fine for a while, until I started to feel severe pain in my breast, arm, and back. Soon I had a raging fever and drifted in and out of delirium. My parents took me to my hometown hospital, where it was determined that I had a massive staph infection. I was near death. With a weakened immune system after nearly a year at the Pole and months of chemotherapy, I had no resistance left. I was sent by Lear jet back to Indianapolis, and to Kathy. There I remained, on antibiotics and pain control for a week. The infection left permanent damage to the tissues in my breast and my lymph system, which still causes swelling and pain in my right arm.

As soon as I was well enough to talk, I called my attorney to try to arrange a visit with my children. I was still sick and weak, but I needed to see them. My attorney informed me that my ex-husband had complained bitterly when he was told I was too ill to get out of bed, and that my parents would be making the long drive to pick up the children. The lawyer warned me that my ex would probably try more of his "games." Still, I looked forward to seeing the kids and I imagined that they wanted to see me, if, for nothing else, to hear about my adventures. Dad warned me not to count on it. He had seen me disappointed too many times. He called before picking the children up and talked with their father and his new wife. They said that the boys would be ready (my daughter was in college), but again pushed for me to make the drive. It nearly broke my heart when my sons called the next day and said that they were too busy that weekend to see me. My father was right. Sadly, nothing had changed. As of this writing, nearly a year after my rescue from the South Pole, I still have not seen my children. I want them to know that my door is always open to them, should they change their minds.

Big John stayed on at the Pole until late November 1999, a month after my rescue flight. He sent me emails, just as before, describing his adventures. Days before he left the Ice, the glycol ghoul returned again and the power generator went down. Even though it was no longer his job, he raced to the power plant and got the generators back on line, just for old times' sake. He rejoined his family in California after redeployment.

We had promised each other that if we ever wrote a book about life at the Pole, we would do it together. John came to help write our story in a way that showed the devotion and the contributions of our friends at the Pole.

After the operation, I still had to undergo four months of intense chemotherapy followed by eight weeks of radiation treatment, which I underwent in North Carolina, near a beach house I had bought long ago.

My hair is slowly growing back, darker and curlier than before, just as Kathy had predicted so many months ago. Although I still tire easily, I can feel my strength returning as each week goes by. My attitude about cancer has changed profoundly since my return to America.

At first, I was still afraid to join the ranks of cancer "victims." Support groups frightened me. I explained to my radiation oncologist, Dr. Charles Neal, that it depressed me to arrive at his waiting room and join those who were receiving radiation. I felt that I was entering the land of the dying. He said, "No, you are entering the place of hope—where the dying may be cured."

Slowly, I felt my tired body and sluggish brain reaching out to those who were sicker than I. The physician in me would rise out of my chair to speak to the sick being transported back to the hospital on stretchers. Then the human in me began to talk with those in my position, those who could still sit and read magazines for hours of waiting. Soon I had friends among the cancer patients, people I wished to know, to meet for breakfast and talk. They were people with real lives, loves, and friends, who were living with cancer as I was learning to do. These friends had been down the same painful road, and were able to offer emotional support as well as practical suggestions, such as using Kotex for dressing the wounds where my flesh was falling off from radiation burns. I joined a cancer support group and enjoyed the friendship of women who had experienced what I was just coming to accept. I was living with an incurable disease. But I was living.

In April 2000, I drove to Indianapolis for a mammogram and bone scan. Kathy Miller gave me the good news that I was, so far, cancer free. Only time will tell my prognosis.

I have now been given a wonderful opportunity, and a responsibility, to help others with cancer. I have joined the world of hope. And I did find "peace along the way": peace with my disease, peace with my life and with my future. This was facilitated by close friends, family, and community—I only wish everyone could have that type of support during a grave illness. How lucky I was that people were willing to risk their lives to rescue me, and that the NSF, ASA, and the U.S. government supported the mission. Although I did not believe that anyone had the responsibility to save me, I am eternally grateful.

This July I was finally strong enough to thank the people who had helped save me: I flew with my parents to McChord Air Force Base in Washington state and met the airdrop crew. In October, I visited the rescue crew from the 109th Airlift Wing of the New York Air National Guard to personally thank them for all they did for me.

I have kept in touch with friends from the Pole. James "Pic" Evans returned to the States and took a job counting birds in Grand Canyon National Park. He is feeling well again, and hopes to return to the Ice this summer. Paul "Pakman" Kindl traveled to California to pick up the 1966 Pontiac Le Mans convertible he had bought on the Internet while at the Pole. He stopped by my parents' home in Ohio on his way home to New York. After she got off the Ice, Lisa Beal came to Ohio to meet my family and accompany me to chemotherapy. She later flew to Florida to spend New Year's Eve with me while I was recovering in Florida at my parents' winter house. She is now working as a computer tech for a large company in Chicago, and still honing plans to build a storm-chasing vehicle to study tornadoes. Dorianne Galarnyk is living in Japan. Comms Tom Carlson is working as a computer network securities engineer, a skill he picked up tracking the South Pole hackers. He began a new tradition of "cyber-slushies" every Friday night, joining other Polies on Instant Messenger for a "virtual party." Floyd Washington is now working in Denver as maintenance coordinator for Amundsen-Scott South Pole Station, but he no longer works for ASA. Antarctic Support Associates lost its bid to renew its government contract and has disbanded. U.S. scientific stations and vessels in Antarctica are now serviced by Raytheon Polar Services. Many ASA staffers and contractors, such as Norman Wolfe and Gerald Katz, were rehired by Raytheon.

Many Polies returned to the Ice: Power Plant Thom Miller wintered in McMurdo as a power plant mechanic, and is now traveling the world. Giant Greg Griffin and Andy Clarke spent the austral winter at the Pole. I have been in contact with them and most fellow winterovers through email and occasional phone calls, and I know the bonds of friendship I made at the Pole will last a lifetime.

While Big John Penney was helping me put this book together, his mother became seriously ill. He has returned to California to help care for her. He is not sure what his next adventure will be.

I live by the ocean now. I would give anything to return to the Pole, but I doubt I will ever be allowed to work there again. It is too risky; my cancer could return at any time. For now my memories will have to sustain me. I still dream of getting out on a boat and sailing around the world. There are times when the ocean is calm and flat as glass, and the horizon is empty for miles in every direction. Those are the times I can feel at home again, and remember Antarctica.